INSTANT POT COOKBOOK

550 Recipes For Every Day

By

Michelle Sanders

W9-CPL-695

- Ω Omega Press -

© Copyright 2017 by Michelle Sanders

All rights Reserved. No part of this publication or the information in it may be quoted from or reproduced in any form by means such as printing, scanning, photocopying or otherwise without prior written permission of the copyright holder.

Disclaimer and Terms of Use: Effort has been made to ensure that the information in this book is accurate and complete, however, the author and the publisher do not warrant the accuracy of the information, text and graphics contained within the book due to the rapidly changing nature of science, research, known and unknown facts and internet. The Author and the publisher do not hold any responsibility for errors, omissions or contrary interpretation of the subject matter herein. This book is presented solely for motivational and informational purposes only.

Table of contents

13

Stocks and Sauces 337

Introduction

We are living in a fast-paced world. As much as we'd love to cook and prepare healthy and delicious meals for our family, we often don't have the time.

Nutritious and scrumptious dishes often take effort, time, energy, careful preparation, and attention.

Various dishes also need different appliances to make – pots for soups and stews, oven and microwave for baked recipes, frying pan for sautéing, and slow cooker for slow cooked meals.

- Have you ever tried cooking a dish that came out overcooked when you can swear that just a few minutes ago it was undercooked?
- Have you tried cooking cheaper meats and waited for hours until they are tender?
- Have you ever boiled potatoes and they came out too soft and mushy on the outside, but still hard and undercooked in the center?
- Have you ever prepared a slow cooked recipe that called for sautéing the spices and browning the meat in a frying pan?
- Have you ever wished there was one kitchen appliance that you can use for all your cooking?

The **Instant Pot** Pressure Cooker is the answer to your kitchen needs.

About The Instant Pot

Instant Pot is a single piece of equipment that does the work of *seven special kitchen tools/appliances* and is indeed: a multi-cooker that performs the job of an **electric pressure cooker, rice cooker, steamer, browning/sauté pan, slow cooker, yogurt maker** & **warming the pot**.

The **Instant Pot** has an entirely stainless-steel interior and not like the majority of the electric pressure cookers.

Since the cooking bowl is made up of stainless steel, it's very easy to clean it using your hands or you can even place it in a dishwasher.

The cooking process is entirely automatic, you can actually throw in the ingredients, set it to your preference & walk away. You don't need to watch the timer, adjust the heat, stick on the stove top, or remove the food at the right time to prevent overcooking or undercooking of the food.

The pressure & temperature is closely monitored by the built-in microprocessor monitors, it also adjusts the duration & heating intensity according to the quantity of food & liquid you have.

With the help of an **Instant Pot**, you can reduce the cooking time by 70%. You can plan your meal in advance & let it cook later on (for up to 24 hours).

You will love the cooking experience with all the multi functions that the Instant Pot pressure cookers have got.

The Benefits of The Instant Pot

Convenient: 16 turn-key function keys for the most common cooking tasks. Planning the meal with delayed cooking up to 24 hours, reducing cooking time by up to 70%.

Cooking healthy, nutritious and tasty meals: smart programming for delicious healthy food, consistent every time.

Clean & Pleasant: absolutely quiet, no steam, no smell, no spills, no excessive heat in the kitchen. 6-in-1 capability reduces clutter in the kitchen.

Energy efficient: saves up to 70% of energy.

Safe and dependable: Instant Pot is UL/ULC certified UL Logo Instant Pot and has 10 fool-proof safety protections.

Measurement conversions

Use it for accurate measuring of the necessary ingredients.

Metric to standard	Fahrenheit to Celsius	Cups to tablespoons	Oz to grams
5 ml = 1 tsp	300 F = 150 C	3 tsp = 1 tbsp	1 oz = 29 g
15 ml = 1 tbsp	350 F = 180 C	1/8 cup = 2 tbsp	2 oz = 57 g
30 ml = 1 fluid oz	375 F = 190 C	1/4 cup = 4 tbsp	3 oz = 85 g
240 ml = 1 cup	400 F = 200 C	1/3 cup = 5 tbsp + 1 tsp	4 oz = 113 g
1 liter = 34 fluid oz	425 F = 220 C		5 oz = 142 g
1 liter = 4.2 cups	450 F = 230 C	1/2 cup = 8 tbsp	6 oz = 170 g
1 gram = .035 oz		3/4 cup = 12 tbsp	7 oz = 198 g
100 grams = 3.5 oz		1 cup = 16 tbsp	8 oz = 227 g
500 grams = 1.10 lb		8 fluid oz = 1 cup	10 oz = 283 g
		1 pint 2 cups = 16 fluid oz	20 oz = 567 g
		1 quart 2 pints = 4 cups	30 oz = 850 g
		1 gallon 4 quarts = 16 cups	40 oz = 1133 g

Abbreviations

(veg) – Recipes that vegans can use too

oz = ounce

fl oz = fluid ounce

tsp = teaspoon

tbsp = tablespoon

ml = milliliter

c = cup

pt = pint

qt = quart

gal = gallon

L = liter

Buckwheat Porridge (veg)
(Prep + Cook Time: 35 minutes | Servings: 4)

Ingredients:
- 1 banana, sliced
- 1 cup raw buckwheat groats
- 1 tsp ground cinnamon
- ½ tsp vanilla
- ¼ cup raisins
- 3 cups rice milk
- Chopped nuts, optional

Directions:
1. Rinse the buckwheat and then put in the Instant Pot container.
2. Add the rice milk, raisins, banana, vanilla, and cinnamon. Close the lid and make sure the valve is closed.
3. Set to MANUAL, the pressure is HIGH, and the timer to 6 minutes. When the timer beeps at the end of the cooking cycle, unplug the pot, and let the pressure release naturally for 20 minutes.
4. With a long handled spoon, stir the porridge.
5. Divide the porridge between 4 bowls.
6. Add more milk into each serving to desired consistency. If desired, sprinkle with chopped nuts.

Nutritional Info (per serving): Calories - 247; Fat – 2.6; Fiber – 4.4; Carbs – 54.3; Protein – 4.7

Banana Bread Steel Cut Oatmeal (veg)
(Prep + Cook Time: 25 minutes | Servings: 4)

Ingredients:
- 2 cups steel cut oatmeal
- 1 tsp cinnamon
- 1 tsp vanilla
- ¼ tsp nutmeg
- 2 ripe bananas, mashed
- 3 1/3 cups water
- ½ cup walnuts, chopped
- ¼ cup honey
- ¼ tsp salt

Directions:
1. With a potato masher or a fork, mash the bananas at the bottom of the Instant Pot container.

2. Add the oats, water, nutmeg, cinnamon, vanilla, and salt; stir to combine. Close the lid and make sure the valve is closed.
3. Set the cooker to PORRIDGE and the timer to 10 minutes.
4. When the timer beeps, let the pressure release for 10 minutes naturally.
5. Stir in the walnuts and honey.
6. Serve immediately.

Nutritional Info (per serving): Calories - 374; Fat – 12.1; Fiber – 7.1; Carbs - 61; Protein – 9.9

Peaches & Cream Oatmeal

(Prep + Cook Time: 20 minutes | Servings: 4)

Ingredients:
- 2 cups rolled oats
- 4 cups water
- 1 tsp vanilla
- 1 chopped peach

Optional:
- ½ cup chopped almonds
- 2 tbsp flax meal
- Splash of cream, milk, or a non-diary milk
- Maple syrup

Directions:
1. Combine the water, peaches, oats, and vanilla in the Instant Pot.
2. Set to HIGH pressure using MANUAL setting. Be sure the valve is sealed. Adjust the time to 3 minutes.
3. Allow the pressure to release naturally for ten minutes; then perform a quick release for the remainder of the pressure.
4. Garnish as desired and enjoy

Nutritional Info (per serving): Calories - 168; Fat – 2.7; Fiber – 4.5; Carbs – 30.2; Protein – 5.6

Cinnamon Roll Oats

(Prep + Cook Time: 30 minutes | Servings: 4)

Ingredients:

- 3 ½ cups water
- 1 cup steel cut oats
- ¾ cup raisins
- ¼ cup light brown sugar
- 1 tbsp butter
- 1 tsp cinnamon
- ¼ tsp salt
- 2-ounces softened cream cheese
- 2 tbsp powdered sugar
- 1 tsp milk

Directions:

1. Turn your cooker to SAUTE and melt the butter.
2. When melted, pour in the oats and stir until they're toasty and nutty.
3. Pour water and salt into the cooker. Close and seal the lid.
4. Choose MANUAL and then adjust time for 10 minutes on HIGH pressure.
5. When time is up, hit CANCEL and wait 5 minutes before quick-releasing the rest of the pressure. Open the lid and stir in raisins. Cover again, but just let it sit for 5-10 minutes to thicken.
6. In the meantime, mix the brown sugar and cinnamon together.
7. Also, for the cream cheese topping, mix milk, cream cheese, and powdered sugar. If the icing is too thick, add a bit more milk.
8. Serve the oats with a healthy sprinkle of brown sugar and cinnamon, with a drizzle of the cream cheese icing.

Nutritional Info (per serving): Calories - 368; Fat - 11; Fiber - 5; Carbs - 65; Protein - 6

Breakfast Quinoa

(Prep + Cook Time: 10 minutes | Servings: 6)

Ingredients:

- 2 ¼ cups water
- 1 ½ cups quinoa, uncooked, well rinsed
- 2 tbsp maple syrup
- ½ tsp vanilla
- Pinch salt
- ¼ tsp ground cinnamon

Optional toppings:
- Fresh berries
- Milk
- Sliced almonds

Directions:

1. Put all of the ingredients into the Instant Pot and close the lid.
2. Set the pressure to HIGH and the timer to 1 minute.
3. When the timer beeps, turn the Instant Pot off, let the pressure release for 10 minutes naturally and then turn the steam valve to release remaining pressure.
4. Carefully open the lid. Fluff the cooked quinoa.
5. Serve with berries, milk, and almonds.

Nutritional Info (per serving): Calories - 175; Fat – 2.6; Fiber - 3; Carbs - 32; Protein - 6

Softly Millet Porridge

(Prep + Cook Time: 20 minutes | Servings: 3)

Ingredients:

- 2 cups of millet flakes
- 1 cup of water
- 2 cups of heavy cream
- 3 tbsp of maple syrup
- 1 tbsp of coconut oil
- 1 tsp of vanilla extract
- 1 cup of almond butter
- 1 tsp of cinnamon

Directions:

1. The first here is to toss in all of your ingredients in your Instant Pot.
2. Select the pressure cooker setting to be HIGH and cook it at high pressure for 2 minutes.
3. Once cooked, wait for 10 minutes and release the pressure naturally to stay safe.
4. Once done, take out your dish and serve it with some walnuts and pour in some maple syrup as a topping.

Nutritional Info (per serving): Calories - 369; Fat – 28; Carbs – 71.8; Protein – 12.8

Coffecake Pumpkin Steel Cut Oatmeal

(Prep + Cook Time: 10 minutes | Servings: 6)

Ingredients:

For the Instant Pot:

- 1 ½ cups pumpkin puree (or 1 can 15 ounces)
- 1 ½ cups steel cut oats
- 1 tsp allspice
- 1 tsp vanilla
- 2 tsp cinnamon
- 4 ½ cups water

For the coffee cake topping:

- ½ cup coconut sugar or brown sugar (or your choice of sweetener, to taste)
- ¼ cup pecans or walnuts, chopped
- 1 tbsp cinnamon

Directions:

1. Put all the ingredients for the Instant Pot into the pot container. Close the lid and make sure the valve is closed.
2. Set to MANUAL and set the timer to 3 minutes.
3. Meanwhile, mix all the ingredients for the topping and store in an airtight container.
4. When the timer beeps, let the pressure release naturally.
5. When the pressure indicator goes down, carefully open the lid. Divide between 6-8 bowls.
6. Sprinkle with the topping and/ or your preferred non-dairy milk.

Notes: Don't worry if you have leftovers. You can store then in the fridge for a grab-and-go breakfast all week long or freeze them in individual servings for months.

Nutritional Info (per serving): Calories - 184; Fat – 4.6; Fiber – 5.3; Carbs - 33; Protein – 4.7

Lentil Tacos (veg)

(Prep + Cook Time: 25 minutes | Servings: 8)

Ingredients:

- 2 cups dry brown lentils
- 4 cups water
- 4 oz tomato sauce
- ½ tsp cumin
- 1 tsp salt
- 1 tsp onion powder
- 1 tsp garlic powder
- 1 tsp chili powder

Directions:

1. Put all of the ingredients in the Instant Pot. Stir to mix.
2. Close and lock the lid. Press MANUAL and set the time to 15 minutes.
3. When the timer beeps, turn off the pot. Let the pressure release naturally. Carefully open the lid.
4. Let sit for a few minutes before serving.
5. This dish is great as part of a taco or burrito salad. It's great with soft or crunchy tacos.

Nutritional Info (per serving): Calories - 177; Fat – 0.6; Fiber - 15; Carbs – 30.3; Protein – 12.7

Lentil Sloppy Joe's (veg)

(Prep + Cook Time: 55 minutes | Servings: 6)

Ingredients:

- 3 cups veggie broth
- 2 cups green lentils
- 1 chopped yellow onion
- 1 stemmed and chopped red bell pepper
- One, 14-ounce can of crushed tomatoes
- 2 tbsp soy sauce
- 1 tbsp Dijon mustard
- 1 tbsp olive oil
- 1 tbsp dark brown sugar
- 1 tsp black pepper

Directions:

1. Turn your Instant Pot to SAUTE and add oil. Cook the pepper and onion until they've turned softened.
2. Pour in broth before adding soy sauce, lentils, mustard, brown sugar, tomatoes, and pepper. Stir until the sugar has dissolved. Close and seal the lid.
3. Select MANUAL and cook on HIGH pressure for 27 minutes.

4. When time is up, hit CANCEL and wait for 15 minutes the pressure to come down on its own.
5. Stir before serving on hamburger buns.

Nutritional Info (per serving): Calories - 164; Fat – 3; Fiber - 3; Carbs – 38; Protein – 9

Apple and Spiced Lentils (veg)
(Prep + Cook Time: 30 minutes | Servings: 4)

Ingredients:
- 1 cup red lentils, soaked for 30 minutes
- 2 medium-sized apples, cored
- 1 tbsp ground cinnamon
- 1 tsp turmeric powder
- ¼ tsp ground cinnamon
- 1 tsp ground cloves
- 1 tbsp maple syrup
- 1 cup coconut milk, divided
- 3 cups red rooibos tea, brewed

Directions:
1. Drain lentils and place in a 6-quarts Instant Pot along with remaining ingredients except for maple syrup and milk.
2. Stir until combine, then plug in and switch on the Instant Pot.
3. Secure pot with lid, then position PRESSURE indicator and adjust cooking time on timer pad to 2 minutes and let cook. Instant Pot will take 10 minutes to build pressure before cooking timer starts.
4. When the timer beeps, switch off the Instant Pot and let pressure release naturally for 10 minutes and then do quick pressure release.
5. Then uncover the pot, stir until well mixed and then divide equally among serving bowl.
6. Serve with a generous amount of milk and maple syrup.

Nutritional Info (per serving): Calories - 168; Fat - 1; Fiber - 11; Carbs - 34; Protein - 9

Perfect Quinoa (veg)

(Prep + Cook Time: 15 minutes | Servings: 4)

Ingredients:

- 2 cups quinoa (any color)
- 3 cups vegetable broth or water
- 2 pinches salt
- Juice of one lemon
- Handful your choice of fresh herbs, minced

Directions:

1. Rinse the quinoa well.
2. Preferably, you should soak it overnight in filtered water mixed with 1 tablespoon apple cider vinegar or lemon juice.
3. Strain and put into the Instant Pot. Add the broth, lemon juice, salt, and, if using, herbs.
4. Close and lock the lid. Press MANUAL and set the time to 1 minute.
5. When the timer beeps, let the pressure release naturally for 10 minutes.
6. Turn the steam valve to VENTING. Carefully open the lid and serve the quinoa.

Nutritional Info (per serving): Calories - 344; Fat – 6.2; Fiber - 6; Carbs – 55.4; Protein – 15.7

Cranberry-Almond Quinoa (veg)

(Prep + Cook Time: 10 minutes | Servings: 4)

Ingredients:

- 2 cups water
- 1 cup quinoa
- 1 cup dried cranberries
- ½ cup slivered almonds
- ¼ cup salted sunflower seeds

Directions:

1. Rinse quinoa before putting in the pot with water.
2. Seal the lid. Hit MANUAL and adjust time to 10 minutes.
3. When time is up, press STOP and quick-release the pressure.
4. Mix in sunflower seeds, almonds, and dried cranberries.
5. Serve.

Nutritional Info (per serving): Calories - 383; Fat – 9; Fiber – 7.5; Carbs – 66; Protein – 8

Quinoa & Barley Porridge (veg)

(Prep + Cook Time: 45 minutes | Servings: 4)

Ingredients:

- ½ cup barley, raw
- ½ cup quinoa, raw
- 1/8 tsp salt
- ¼ cup dried cranberries
- ¼ tsp ground cinnamon
- ¼ tsp ground cardamom
- Honey to taste
- 4 cups water

Directions:

1. In the Instant Pot place barley, quinoa, salt and water and stir until combined.
2. Plug in and switch on the pot, select PORRIGE option and secure pot with lid. Then position pressure indicator and let cook on default time.
3. When the timer beeps, switch off the Instant Pot and let pressure release naturally for 10 minutes and then do quick pressure release.
4. Uncover the pot, fluff mixture with a fork, then stir in remaining ingredients and transfer to a serving dish.
5. Serve immediately.

Nutritional Info (per serving): Calories - 173; Fat – 3; Fiber – 6.5; Carbs – 45; Protein – 7.6

Apple Spice Oats

(Prep + Cook Time: 10 minutes | Servings: 2)

Ingredients:

- 1 ½ cups almond milk
- 1 peeled and chopped apple
- ½ cup steel-cut oats
- 1 tsp ground cinnamon
- Dash of nutmeg

Directions:

1. Put everything in your Instant Pot and seal the lid.
2. Hit MANUAL and cook for just 4 minutes.
3. When time is up, hit CANCEL and wait for a natural pressure release.
4. Stir and serve!

Nutritional Info (per serving): Calories - 198; Fat – 4; Fiber - 5; Carbs – 39; Protein – 5

Classic Hummus (veg)

(Prep + Cook Time: 35 minutes | Servings: 6)

Ingredients:

- 6 cups water
- 1 cup soaked chickpeas
- 3-4 crushed garlic cloves
- 1 bay leaf
- ¼ cup chopped parsley
- 2 tbsp tahini
- 1 juiced lemon
- ½ tsp salt
- ¼ tsp cumin
- Dash of paprika

Directions:

1. Soak your chickpeas overnight in water.
2. When you're ready to make the hummus, rinse them and put them in the Instant Pot.
3. Pour in 6 cups of water. Toss in the bay leaf and garlic cloves.
4. Close and seal the lid. Select Manual and cook for 18 minutes on HIGH pressure.
5. When the beeper goes off, hit CANCEL and wait for the pressure to come down on its own.
6. When the cooker is safe to open, drain the chickpeas, but save all the cooking liquid.
7. Remove the bay leaf before pureeing the chickpeas.
8. Add tahini, lemon juice, cumin, and ½ cup of cooking liquid to start.
9. Keep pureeing, and if the mixture isn't creamy enough, keep adding ½ cup of liquid at a time.
10. When it's the right level of creaminess, salt, and puree once more.
11. Serve with a sprinkle of paprika and fresh chopped parsley!

Nutritional Info (per serving): Calories - 109; Fat – 3.8; Fiber – 4.1; Carbs – 3.5; Protein – 3.3

Delicious Dhal (veg)

(Prep + Cook Time: 25 minutes | Servings: 10)

Ingredients:

- 1 cup green lentils
- 6 cups hot water
- 1 ½ cup channa dal
- 2 tbsp ginger, minced
- Salt and black pepper to the taste
- 8 medium yellow onions, minced
- 1 ½ tsp turmeric
- 10 garlic cloves, minced
- 3 tsp cumin
- 2 tsp chili powder
- 2 tsp garam masala
- 1 tbsp sultana
- 1 tbsp extra virgin olive oil
- 15 oz potatoes, cut in small chunks
- 15 oz sweet potatoes, chopped

Directions:

1. Heat up a pan with the oil over medium HIGH heat, add all garlic and onions, stir, cook for 3-4 minutes and then transfer to your Instant Pot.
2. Add water, channa dal, lentils, ginger, turmeric, cumin, potatoes and sweet potatoes, stir and cook on HIGH pressure for 10 minutes.
3. Release pressure naturally, leave aside for 10 minutes, add salt and pepper to the taste, garam masala, chili powder and sultana, stir well and divide amongst plates.
4. Serve right away and enjoy.

Nutritional Info (per serving): Calories - 277; Fat – 3.2; Fiber - 13; Carbs – 52; Protein – 11.8

Special Vegan Polenta (veg)
(Prep + Cook Time: 30 minutes | Servings: 2)

Ingredients:

- 2 cups very hot water
- 1 bunch green onion, thinly sliced
- 2 cups veggie stock
- 2 tsp garlic, minced
- 1 tbsp chili powder
- 1 cup corn meal
- ¼ cup cilantro, finely chopped
- Salt, black pepper to taste
- 1 tsp cumin
- 1 tsp oregano
- A pinch of cayenne pepper
- ½ tsp smoked paprika

Directions:

1. Heat up a pan over medium heat. Add a splash of water, the green onion and garlic, stir and sauté for 2 minutes.
2. Transfer this to your Instant Pot, add stock, hot water, corn meal, cilantro, salt, pepper, chili powder, cumin, oregano, paprika and a pinch of cayenne pepper.
3. Close the pot and cook on HIGH pressure for 10 minutes.
4. Release pressure naturally for 10 minutes.
5. Divide amongst plates and serve. Enjoy!

Nutritional Info (per serving): Calories - 200; Fat – 4.5; Fiber – 7.8; Carbs – 13; Protein – 14

Creamy Peaches Steel Cut Oats (veg)
(Prep + Cook Time: 10 minutes | Servings: 4)

Ingredients:

- 2 peaches, diced
- 1 cup steel cut oats
- 1 cup coconut milk, full fat
- 2 cups water
- ½ of a vanilla bean, scraped, seeds and pod

Directions:

1. Put all of the ingredients into the bowl of the Instant Pot.
2. Close the lid and the vent. Set the pressure to HIGH and the timer for 3 minutes.
3. When the timer beeps, let the pressure release naturally for 10 minutes.
4. Turn the steam valve to release remaining pressure.
5. Sweeten the oats, if desired.

Nutritional Info (per serving): Calories - 236; Fat – 15.8; Fiber – 4.1; Carbs – 21.9; Protein – 4.5

Creamy Strawberry Rolled Oats

(Prep + Cook Time: 20 minutes | Servings: 2)

Ingredients:

- 2/3 cup whole milk
- 2 tbsp strawberries, freeze-dried (or your favorite dried or frozen fruit)
- 1/3 cup rolled oats
- ½ tsp white sugar
- 1 pinch salt

Directions:

1. Pour 2 cups of water into the Instant Pot container and then put a steamer basket or a rack with a handle in the pot.
2. In a small-sized, heat-safe mug or bowl, add the oats, strawberries, milk, and salt.
3. Close and lock the pot lid. Set the pressure to high and the timer to 10 minutes.
4. When the timer beeps, unplug the pot. Let the pressure release for about 7-10 minutes naturally or until the pressure indicator is down and then open the lid. You can turn the steam valve to release remaining pressure before opening. Carefully remove the mug/ bowl from the pot.
5. Mix the contents vigorously and then sprinkle with sugar to taste. Serve.

Nutritional Info (per serving): Calories - 214; Fat – 7.1; Fiber – 3.1; Carbs – 29.2; Protein – 8.9

Coconut and Creamy Steel Cut Oats (veg)

(Prep + Cook Time: 20 minutes | Servings: 4)

Ingredients:

- ½ cup unsweetened coconut flakes
- 1 cup coconut milk, plus additional for topping (full-fat canned or lighter varieties)
- 1 cup steel cut oats
- 1 pinch salt
- 1 cinnamon stick or
- ½ tsp ground cinnamon, optional
- 2 cups water
- 2 tbsp brown sugar

Directions:

1. Put the coconut into the Instant Pot container.
2. Press SAUTE and cook the coconut flakes, frequently stirring and closely watching to avoid burning.
3. When the flakes starts to lightly brown, remove 1/ 2 and reserve for topping.
4. Add the oats and cook for a couple of minutes until both the coconut flakes and the oats are fragrant.
5. Add 1 cup of milk and the remaining ingredients; stir to combine. Press CANCEL to stop sauté mode.
6. Close the lid, press MANUAL, set the pressure to HIGH and the timer to 2 minutes.
7. When the timer beeps, let the pressure release for 10 minutes naturally and then turn the valve to release remaining pressure. Carefully open the lid.
8. Divide the oatmeal between 4 bowls.
9. Drizzle each serving with coconut milk, 1 tablespoon of toasted coconut, and your desired toppings.

Nutritional Info (per serving): Calories - 268; Fat – 19; Fiber – 4.3; Carbs – 23.1; Protein – 4.4

Coffeecake Pumpkin Steel Cut Oatmeal (veg)

(Prep + Cook Time: 10 minutes | Servings: 6)

Ingredients:

For the Instant Pot:

- 1 ½ cups pumpkin puree (or 1 can 15 ounces)
- 1 ½ cups steel cut oats
- 1 tsp allspice
- 1 tsp vanilla
- 2 tsp cinnamon
- 4 ½ cups water

For the coffee cake topping:

- ½ cup coconut sugar or brown sugar (or your choice of sweetener, to taste)
- ¼ cup pecans or walnuts, chopped
- 1 tbsp cinnamon

Directions:

1. Put all the ingredients for the Instant Pot into the pot container. Close the lid and make sure the valve is closed. Set to MANUAL and set the timer to 3 minutes.
2. Meanwhile, mix all the ingredients for the topping and store in an airtight container.
3. When the timer beeps, let the pressure release naturally. When the pressure indicator goes down, carefully open the lid.
4. Divide between 6-8 bowls.
5. Sprinkle with the topping and/ or your preferred non-dairy milk.

Nutritional Info (per serving): Calories - 184; Fat – 4.6; Fiber – 5.3; Carbs – 33; Protein – 4.7

Steel-Cut Oats
(Prep + Cook Time: 10 minutes | Servings: 4)

Ingredients:
- 2 cups of water
- 1 cup steel-cut oats
- Pinch of salt
- Milk
- Sugar

Directions:
1. Pour 1 cup of water into the Instant Pot and lower in the trivet.
2. In a heatproof bowl, mix 2 cups of water, oats, and salt.
3. Set on top of the trivet and lock the pressure cooker lid.
4. Select the MANUAL setting and cook for at least 6 minutes, but no more than 7.
5. Heat a cup or so of milk (depending on how much you want) in the microwave.
6. When the oats are done, scoop into individual serving bowls.
7. Pour milk on top and add sugar before serving.

Nutritional Info (per serving): Calories - 155; Fat – 3; Fiber - 2; Carbs – 28; Protein – 4

Pear Oats with Walnuts (veg)
(Prep + Cook Time: 10 minutes | Servings: 4)

Ingredients:
- 2 cups almond milk
- 2 cups peeled and cut pears
- 1 cup rolled oats
- ½ cup chopped walnuts
- ¼ cup sugar
- 1 tbsp melted coconut oil
- ¼ tsp salt
- Dash of cinnamon

Directions:
1. Mix everything except the walnuts and cinnamon in an oven-safe bowl that you know fits in the Instant Pot.
2. Pour 1 cup of water into the pressure cooker and lower in steamer rack.
3. Put the bowl on top and lock the lid. Select MANUAL and then HIGH pressure for 6 minutes.
4. When time is up, quick-release the pressure.
5. Carefully remove the bowl, divide into 4 servings, and season with salt and cinnamon.

Nutritional Info (per serving): Calories - 288; Fat – 13; Fiber – 4.5; Carbs – 39; Protein – 5

Three Lentil Chili (veg)

(Prep + Cook Time: 35 minutes | Servings: 6)

Ingredients:

- 1 cup split red lentils, rinsed
- 2/3 cup brown lentils, rinsed
- 1 cup French green lentils, rinsed
- 1 medium-sized white onion, peeled and chopped
- 2 tsp minced garlic
- 2 medium-sized green bell peppers, seeded and chopped
- 28 ounce diced tomatoes
- 2 tbsp olive oil
- 1 tbsp salt
- ½ tsp ground black pepper
- 1 tsp red chili powder
- 1 tbsp ground cumin
- 7 cups vegetable stock

Directions:

1. Plug in and switch on a 6-quarts Instant Pot, select SAUTE option and add oil.
2. When the oil is heated, add onion and pepper and cook for 3-5 minutes or until onion is tender.
3. Then add garlic and sauté for 1 minute or until fragrant.
4. Add remaining ingredients into the pot, press cancel, select multigrain option, secure pot with lid and then position pressure indicator.
5. When the timer beeps, switch off the Instant Pot and let pressure release naturally for 10 minutes and then do quick pressure release.
6. Then uncover the pot, stir and serve immediately.

Nutritional Info (per serving): Calories -320 ; Fat – 3; Fiber - 20; Carbs – 58; Protein – 20

Black-Eyed Pea Cakes (veg)

(Prep + Cook Time: 1 hour 40 minutes | Servings: 4)

Ingredients:

- 1 cup dried black-eyed peas
- 1 chopped onion
- 1 roasted red pepper
- ¼ cup veggie broth

- 1 tbsp tomato paste
- 1 ½ - 2 tsp
- Old Bay seasoning
- 1 tsp salt
- ¼ tsp white pepper

Directions:

1. Rinse and pick over the peas to take out any stones.
2. Soak in a large bowl of hot water, so there's two inches about the peas. Soak for one hour and then drain.
3. Put the peas in a food processor and pulse until they're just broken.
4. Put the peas in the bowl and cover with more water.
5. Rub them, so their skins come off. With the skins gone, the peas are white.
6. Put the peas back into the food processor with the onion, red pepper, tomato paste, and 2 tablespoons of broth. Process until smooth.
7. Pour into bowl and add seasonings. You want the mixture to be thick, but still pourable. Add more broth if necessary.
8. Pour 1 cup of water into your Instant Pot. Grease 8 ramekins and pour ½ of the cake batter into each one. Wrap in foil.
9. Lower the steamer basket (or trivet) into the cooker, and place the ramekins inside. Close and seal lid. Select the STEAM program and adjust time to 30 minutes.
10. When time is up, hit CANCEL and quick-release.
11. With a toothpick, check the cakes - a clean toothpick means they're ready.

Nutritional Info (per serving): Calories - 158; Fat – 1; Fiber - 5; Carbs – 9; Protein – 29

Carrot Cake Breakfast Oatmeal

(Prep + Cook Time: 20 minutes | Servings: 6)

Ingredients:

- 1 cup grated carrots
- 1 cup steel cut oats
- 1 tbsp butter
- 1 tsp pumpkin pie spice
- ¼ cup chia seeds

- ¼ tsp salt
- 2 tsp cinnamon
- 3 tbsp maple syrup
- ¾ cup raisins
- 4 cups water

Directions:

1. Put the butter into the Instant Pot; select SAUTE.
2. When the butter is melted, add the oats; toast, constantly stirring for about 3 minutes or until the oats are nutty.
3. Add the water, carrots, cinnamon, maple syrup, salt, and pumpkin pie spice. Close the lid of the pot.
4. Set the pressure to HIGH and the timer to 10 minutes.
5. When the timer beeps, turn off the pot, let the pressure release naturally for 10 minutes, then turn the steam valve to release remaining pressure.
6. When the valve drops, carefully open the lid. Stir in the oats, chia seeds, and raisins.
7. Close the lid and let sit for about 5-10 minutes or until the oats are cooked in the heat to desired thickness.
8. Serve topped with milk, chopped nuts, and additional raisins and maple syrup.

Notes: You can cook a batch ahead of time; just freeze individual portions. When ready to serve, add a bit of milk and serve cold or microwave until heated.

Nutritional Info (per serving): Calories - 159; Fat – 3; Fiber – 2.9; Carbs – 32.9; Protein – 2.6

Quinoa Salad

(Prep + Cook Time: 30 minutes | Servings: 6)

Ingredients:

- 1 cup quinoa
- 2 cups chicken stock
- 1 can red beans
- 1 tsp salt
- 2 tbsp tomato paste
- 1 tsp olive oil
- 1 yellow onion
- 5 tomatoes
- 2 cucumbers
- 1 tsp sour cream

Directions:

1. Place the quinoa in the Instant Pot.
2. Add chicken stock and red beans. Stir the mixture gently and close the lid.
3. Cook the dish at the Instant Pot mode PRESSURE for 20 minutes.
4. Then remove the quinoa mixture from the Instant Pot and chill it well.
5. Slice the cucumbers and chop the onion and tomatoes.
6. Then place the vegetables together in the mixing bowl.
7. Add the sour cream, tomato paste, and olive oil. Stir the mixture carefully and add the quinoa mixture.
8. Then sprinkle the dish with salt and mix up the salad until you get homogenous mass.
9. Serve the salad. Enjoy!

Nutritional Info (per serving): Calories - 227; Fiber - 6; Carbs – 37; Protein – 11

Ham and Peas

(Prep + Cook Time: 55 minutes | Servings: 10)

Ingredients:

- 5 ounces ham, diced
- 1 pound dried peas, use black-eyed (rinse, but do not pre-soak)
- 6 ½ cups stock (vegetable, chicken, or ham OR 6 1/ 2 cups water mixed with 2 tablespoons chicken bouillon – I used Better Than Bullion)

Directions:

1. Put all of the ingredients into the pot. Cover and lock the lid. Press the MANUAL key, set the pressure to HIGH, and set the timer to 30 minutes.

2. When the Instant Pot timer beeps, press the CANCEL key and unplug the Instant Pot. Let the pressure release naturally for 10-15 minutes or until the valve drops. Using an oven mitt or a long handled spoon, turn the steam valve to release remaining pressure. Unlock and carefully open the lid.
3. Taste and season with salt and pepper as needed.

Notes: The cooking time indicated for this dish cooked the peas well-done and soft, with a couple falling apart. If you want the peas to be more firm, then reduce the cooking time for a couple of minutes.

Nutritional Info (per serving): Calories - 85; Fat – 2.3; Fiber – 2.5; Carbs – 7.7; Protein – 8

Farro and Cherry Salad (veg)
(Prep + Cook Time: 60 minutes | Servings: 6)

Ingredients:
- 1 cup raw whole-grain farro, raw
- 2 cups cherries, pitted and then cut in half
- ½ cup dried cherries, coarsely chopped
- 1 tbsp apple cider vinegar
- 1 tbsp olive oil
- 1 tsp lemon juice, freshly squeezed
- ¼ cup chives or green onions, finely minced
- ¼ tsp sea salt
- 8-10 mint leaves, minced
- 3 cups water

Directions:
1. Rinse the farro and put in the Instant Pot. Pour in 3 cups water. Cover and lock the lid. Cook on HIGH pressure for 40 minutes.
2. When the timer beeps, quick release the pressure. The grain should be plump and tender, but chewy.
3. Drain the farro and put into a bowl.
4. Stir in the vinegar, oil, lemon juice, salt, chives, dried cherries, and mint.
5. Refrigerate until cold. Just before serving, stir in the fresh cherries.

Nutritional Info (per serving): Calories - 196; Fat – 2.9; Fiber – 4.4; Carbs – 40; Protein – 4.4

Israeli Couscous

(Prep + Cook Time: 10 minutes | Servings: 8)

Ingredients:
- 1 package (16-ounce) Israeli Couscous (I used Harvest Grains Blend)
- 2 ½ cups chicken broth
- 2 tbsp butter
- Salt and pepper to taste

Directions:
1. Set the Instant Pot to SAUTE mode. Add the butter and melt.
2. Add the broth and the couscous blend; stir to combine. Close and lock the lid. Cook on HIGH pressure for 5 minutes.
3. If using a different brand, adjust the cooking time to 1/ 2 of the recommended time on the package.
4. When the timer beeps, press OFF and quick release the pressure.
5. With a fork, fluff the couscous and season to taste with salt and pepper.

Nutritional Info (per serving): Calories - 201; Fat – 2.9; Fiber – 2.3; Carbs – 35.4; Protein – 7

Cheesy Grits

(Prep + Cook Time: 35 minutes | Servings: 4)

Ingredients:
- 3 cups water
- 1 ¾ cups cream
- 1 cup stone-ground grits
- 4-ounces cheddar cheese
- 2-3 tbsp butter
- 2 tbsp coconut oil
- 2 tsp salt

Directions:
1. On the SAUTE setting, heat your oil.
2. Add grits and stir to toast for 3 minutes. Turn off your Instant Pot before adding the rest of the ingredients. Close and seal the lid.
3. Select MANUAL and adjust time to 10 minutes.
4. When time is up, hit CANCEL and wait 15 minutes. Quick-release any remaining pressure.
5. Serve hot!

Nutritional Info (per serving): Calories - 694; Fat – 38; Fiber - 2; Carbs – 71; Protein – 17

Falafel

(Prep + Cook Time: 30 minutes | Servings: 6)

Ingredients:

- 1 cup chickpea, cooked
- 1 tsp cumin
- ½ tsp coriander
- 1 tbsp sesame seeds
- 1 tsp salt
- ½ cup parsley
- 1 tsp paprika
- 1 tsp chili flakes
- 3 garlic cloves
- 1 tsp garlic powder
- 4 oz shallots
- 3 tbsp tahini
- ½ cup olive oil
- 2 tsp water
- 1 tbsp lemon juice
- ½ tsp sea salt

Directions:

1. Place the chickpea, cumin, coriander, salt, parsley, paprika, chili flakes, garlic powder, and water in the blender.
2. Blend the mixture carefully until you get smooth mass.
3. Slice the garlic cloves and shallot and add the shallot to the chickpea mixture.
4. Continue to blend it for 1 minute more.
5. Combine the sesame seeds and sea salt together in the mixing bowl and stir the mixture.
6. Make the medium balls from the chickpea mixture and coat them with the sesame mixture.
7. Pour the olive oil in the Instant Pot and SAUTE it until the oil is boiled.
8. Then toss the falafel into the hot oil and cook them for 1 minute or until they get a crust.
9. Then transfer the cooked falafel into the paper towels and remove the excess oil.
10. Combine the tahini, sliced garlic, and lemon juice together.
11. Whisk the mixture carefully until you get homogenous mass.

12. Sprinkle the cooked falafel with the tahini sauce. Enjoy!

Nutritional Info (per serving): Calories - 362; Fat – 25.1; Fiber - 6; Carbs – 28; Protein – 9

Instant Pot White Rice (veg)

(Prep + Cook Time: 15 minutes | Servings: 4)

Ingredients:
- 1 cup white basmati rice
- 1 cup water

Directions:
1. Put the rice in a colander.
2. Rinse until the water is clear.
3. Transfer into the Instant Pot and then add the water.
4. Set the pot to MANUAL, set the pressure to LOW, and the timer to 8 minutes.
5. When the timer beeps, quick release the pressure.
6. Fluff the rice using a fork and serve.

Nutritional Info (per serving): Calories - 225; Fat – 0.4; Fiber – 0.8; Carbs –49.3 ; Protein – 4.4

Instant Pot Brown Rice (veg)

(Prep + Cook Time: 30 minutes | Servings: 6)

Ingredients:
- 2 cups brown rice
- ½ tsp of sea salt
- 2 ½ cups any kind vegetable broth or water

Directions:
1. Put the rice into the Instant Pot.
2. Pour in the broth or water and salt. Close and lock the lid.
3. Press the MANUAL and set the timer to 22 minutes pressure cooking.
4. When the timer beeps, naturally release the pressure for 10 minutes.
5. Carefully open the lid. Serve.

Nutritional Info (per serving): Calories - 245; Fat – 2.3; Fiber – 2.1; Carbs – 48.6; Protein – 6.8

Brown Rice Medley (veg)

(Prep + Cook Time: 35 minutes | Servings: 4)

Ingredients:
- 2-4 tbsp red, wild or black rice
- ¾ cup (or more) short grain brown rice
- 1 ½ cups water
- 1 tbsp water
- 3/8-1/2 tsp sea salt, optional

Directions:
1. Put as much as 2-4 tablespoons of red, wild, or black rice or use all three kinds in 1-cup measuring cup.
2. Add brown rice to make 1 cup total of rice. Put the rice in a strainer and wash. Put the rice in the Instant Pot.
3. Add 1 1/2 cup plus 1 tablespoon water in the pot. If desired, add salt.
4. Stir and then check the sides of the pot to make sure the rice is pushed down into the water. Close and lock the lid. Press MULTIGRAIN and set the time to 23 minutes.
5. When the timer beeps, let the pressure release naturally for 5 minutes, then turn the steam valve and release the pressure slowly.
6. If you have time, let the pressure release naturally for 15 minutes. Stir and serve.

Nutritional Info (per serving): Calories - 165; Fat – 1.1; Fiber – 1.8; Carbs – 34.6; Protein – 4.1

Multi-Grain Rice Millet Blend (veg)

(Prep + Cook Time: 15 minutes | Servings: 8)

Ingredients:
- 2 cups jasmine rice OR long-grain white rice
- ½ cup millet
- 3 ¼ cups water
- ½ tsp sea salt (optional)

Directions:
1. Put all the ingredients in the Instant Pot and stir.
2. Cover and lock the lid.
3. Press the RICE button and let the pot do all the cooking, about 10 minutes.

Nutritional Info (per serving): Calories - 207; Fat – 0.5; Fiber – 3.1; Carbs – 45.1; Protein – 4.4

Rice and Lentils (veg)

(Prep + Cook Time: 55 minutes | Servings: 4)

Ingredients:

For the sauté:

- 1 tbsp oil, OR dry sauté (or add a little water/vegetable broth)
- ½ cup onion, chopped
- 2 cloves garlic, minced

For the porridge:

- 1 ½ cups brown rice
- 1 cup rutabaga, peeled and diced, OR potato OR turnip
- 1 cup brown lentils
- 1 tbsp dried marjoram (or thyme)
- 2-inch sprig fresh rosemary
- 3 ½ cups water
- Salt and pepper, to taste

Directions:

1. Press the SAUTÉ key of the Instant Pot and select the NORMAL option.
2. Put the oil/ broth in the pot and, if using oil, heat. When the oil is hot, add the onion and sauté for 5 minutes or until transparent.
3. Add the garlic and sauté for 1 minute.
4. Add the lentils, brown rice, rutabaga, marjoram, rosemary, and pour in the water into the pot and stir to combine. Press the CANCEL key to stop the sauté function.
5. Press the MANUAL key, set the pressure to HIGH, and set the timer for 23 minutes.
6. When the Instant Pot timer beeps, press the CANCEL key. Let the pressure release naturally for 10-15 minutes or until the valve drops. Release remaining pressure. Unlock and carefully open the lid.
7. Taste and, if needed, season with pepper and salt to taste.
8. If needed, add more ground rosemary and more marjoram.

Nutritional Info (per serving): Calories - 390; Fat – 6.2; Fiber – 19.4; Carbs – 88.8; Protein – 18.5

Rice &Chickpea Stew (veg)

(Prep + Cook Time: 35 minutes | Servings: 6)

Ingredients:

- 3 medium-sized onions, peeled and sliced
- 1 pound sweet potato, peeled and diced
- 6 oz brown basmati rice, rinsed
- 30 oz cooked chickpeas
- ¼ tsp salt
- ¼ tsp ground black pepper
- 2 tsp ground cumin
- 2 tsp ground coriander
- 8 fluid oz orange juice
- 1 tbsp olive oil
- 4 cups vegetable broth
- 4 oz chopped cilantro

Directions:

1. Plug in and switch on a 6-quarts Instant Pot, select SAUTE option, add oil and onion and let cook for 10-12 minutes or until browned.
2. Stir in coriander and cumin and continue cooking for 15 seconds or until fragrant.
3. Add remaining ingredients into the pot except for black pepper and cilantro and stir until just mixed.
4. Press CANCEL and secure pot with lid. Then position pressure indicator, select MANUAL option and adjust cooking time on timer pad to 5 minutes and let cook on HIGH pressure.
5. Instant Pot will take 10 minutes to build pressure before cooking timer starts.
6. When the timer beeps, switch off the Instant Pot and let pressure release naturally for 10 minutes and then do quick pressure release.
7. Then uncover the pot and stir in pepper until mixed.
8. Garnish with cilantro and serve.

Nutritional Info (per serving): Calories - 268; Fat – 7; Fiber - 8; Carbs – 35; Protein – 9

Rice and Black Beans (veg)

(Prep + Cook Time: 35 minutes | Servings: 4)

Ingredients:

- 1 cup onion, diced
- 4 cloves garlic, crushed and then minced
- 2 cups brown rice
- 2 cups dry black beans
- 9 cups water
- 1 tsp salt
- 1-2 limes, optional
- Avocado, optional

Directions:

1. Put the garlic and the onion in the Instant Pot.
2. Add the black beans and the brown rice. Pour in the water and sprinkle the salt. Cover and lock the lid. Press MANUAL and set the time to 28 minutes.
3. When the timer is up, press CANCEL or unplug the pot. Let the pressure release naturally. You can let it sit for 20 minutes.
4. Scoop into a serving bowl and squeeze a lime wedge over the bowl.
5. Serve with a couple of avocado slices for garnishing.

Nutritional Info (per serving): Calories - 691; Fat – 4; Fiber – 18.6; Carbs – 136.5; Protein – 28.6

Butter Rice

(Prep + Cook Time: 30 minutes | Servings: 4)

Ingredients:

- 1 ¼ cups vegetable stock
- 1 ¼ cups French Onion soup
- 1 stick (½ cup) butter
- 2 cups brown rice

Directions:

1. Put all of the ingredients in the Instant Pot. Stir to incorporate.
2. Close and lock the lid. Press MANUAL. Set to HIGH pressure and the time for 22 minutes.
3. When the timer beeps, let the pressure release naturally.
4. Serve warm. If desired, garnish with parsley.

Nutritional Info (per serving): Calories - 590; Fat – 26.3; Fiber – 3.8; Carbs – 78.7; Protein – 9.5

Cauliflower Rice (veg)

(Prep + Cook Time: 25 minutes | Servings: 4)

Ingredients:

- 1 medium-sized cauliflower head
- 2 tbsp olive oil
- ½ tsp salt
- ½ tsp dried parsley
- ¼ tsp ground cumin
- ¼ tsp turmeric powder
- ¼ tsp paprika
- 2 tbsp chopped cilantro
- 8 fluid oz water

Directions:

1. Remove and discard leaves from cauliflower, rinse and then cut into large pieces.
2. In the Instant Pot pour water, then insert a steamer basket and place cauliflower florets in it.
3. Plug in and switch on the Instant Pot, select steam option and secure pot with lid. Then position pressure indicator and adjust cooking time on timer pad to 1 minutes and let cook.
4. When the timer beeps, switch off the Instant Pot and do a quick pressure release.
5. Then uncover the pot and transfer cauliflower florets to a shallow dish.
6. Drain water in the pot, then switch on the Instant Pot and select SAUTE option and let heat.
7. Add oil, return cauliflower florets to the pot and mash using a potato masher.
8. Stir in all the spices until combined and cook until warm through.
9. Serve immediately.

Nutritional Info (per serving): Calories - 25; Fat – 0.1; Fiber – 2.5; Carbs – 5.3; Protein – 2

Mexican Rice (veg)

(Prep + Cook Time: 35 minutes | Servings: 6)

Ingredients:

- 2 cups rice, long-grain, such as Lundberg Farms Brown Basmati
- ½ cup tomato paste
- ½ white onion, chopped
- 2 cups water
- 2 tsp salt
- 3 cloves garlic, minced
- 1 small jalapeño, optional

Directions:

1. Set the Instant Pot to normal SAUTE. Heat the olive oil.
2. Add the garlic, onion, rice, and salt. Sauté for about 3-4 minutes or until fragrant.
3. Mix the tomato paste with the water until well combined. Pour into the pot. Add the whole jalapeno pepper.
4. Press CANCEL. Close and lock the lid. Press PRESSURE, set to HIGH, and the timer for 3 minutes is using white rice or for 22 minutes if using brown rice.
5. When the timer beeps, release the pressure naturally for about 15 minutes. Turn the steam valve to VENTING. Carefully open the lid.
6. Using a fork, fluff the rice and serve hot.

Nutritional Info (per serving): Calories - 253; Fat – 1.8; Fiber – 3.3; Carbs – 54; Protein – 5.9

Delicious Rice and Artichokes (veg)

(Prep + Cook Time: 30 minutes | Servings: 4)

Ingredients:

- 6 ounces graham crackers, crumbled
- 6 ounces arborico rice
- 16 ounces vegan cream cheese, soft
- 14 ounces artichoke hearts, chopped
- 1 ½ tbsp vegan cheese, grated
- 8 ounces veggie stock
- 8 ounces water
- 2 tbsp white wine
- Salt and black pepper to the taste
- 1 tbsp vegetable oil
- 2 garlic cloves, minced
- 1 ½ tbsp thyme, finely chopped

Directions:

1. Heat up a pan with the oil over medium high heat, add rice and garlic, stir and cook for 3 minutes.
2. Transfer everything to your Instant Pot, add stock, wine, water, cover and cook on HIGH pressure for 10 minutes.
3. Release pressure naturally for 5 minutes.
4. Add crackers, add artichokes, vegan cheese, vegan cream cheese, salt, pepper and thyme, stir well, divide into bowls and serve right away.
5. Enjoy!

Nutritional Info (per serving): Calories - 240; Fat – 7.1; Fiber – 5.1; Carbs – 23; Protein – 6

Fried Rice
(Prep + Cook Time: 15 minutes | Servings: 4)

Ingredients:
- 1 tbsp butter (or oil)
- 1 medium onion, diced
- 2 cloves garlic, minced
- 1 egg
- 1 cup basmati rice, uncooked
- ¼ cup soy sauce
- 1 ½ cups chicken stock
- ½ cups peas, frozen OR your preferred vegetable

Directions:
1. Heat the Instant Pot to more SAUTE mode. Put the oil in the pot.
2. Add the garlic and the onion. Sauté for 1 minute.
3. Add the egg, scramble with the garlic mix for about 1-2 minutes.
4. Add the rice, stock, and soy sauce in the pot. Press CANCEL. Close and lock the lid. Press RICE and set the time for 10 minutes.
5. When the timer beeps, quick release the pressure. Carefully open the lid. Stir in the frozen peas or veggies.
6. Let sit until the peas/ veggies are warmed through.

Nutritional Info (per serving): Calories - 250; Fat – 4.6; Fiber – 2.3; Carbs – 44.2; Protein – 7.3

Delicious Risotto

(Prep + Cook Time: 30 minutes | Servings: 6)

Ingredients:

- 1 finely chopped medium onion
- 12 ounces Arborio rice
- 1 ½ tbsp olive oil
- 28 ounces chicken stock
- 3 tbsp Romano or Parmesan cheese
- Salt and pepper to taste

Directions:

1. Heat the oil in the bottom of your cooker.
2. SAUTE the onion until soft and nearly translucent.
3. Add the rice and chicken stock.
4. Close the lid and select the RICE function. Set a timer for 15 minutes.
5. Wait for the cycle to end and for the pressure to naturally drop.
6. Open the lid and stir in a little bit of black pepper.
7. Add the Romano or Parmesan cheese.
8. Serve immediately.

Nutritional Info (per serving): Calories - 266; Fat – 4.8; Fiber – 1.7; Carbs – 46.3; Protein – 7.7

Pineapple Brown Rice

(Prep + Cook Time: 10 minutes | Servings: 4)

Ingredients:

- 1 cup brown rice
- 8-ounces crushed pineapple
- 1 cup water
- ¼ cup pineapple juice
- 1 tbsp butter

Directions:

1. Put everything in your pressure cooker and seal the lid.
2. Hit MANUAL and adjust time to 24 minutes.
3. When time is up, wait 5 minutes before quick-releasing.
4. Stir and serve!

Nutritional Info (per serving): Calories - 229; Fat – 5; Fiber – 1.7; Carbs – 46; Protein – 5

Mushroom Risotto (veg)

(Prep + Cook Time: 25 minutes | Servings: 4)

Ingredients:

- 4 oz mushrooms, chopped or broken into small pieces
- 3 cups vegetable broth, at room temperature
- 3 cloves garlic, minced
- 2 cups fresh spinach
- ¼ cup lemon juice
- ½ cup white onion, minced
- ½ cup dry white wine, at room temperature
- 1 tsp thyme
- 1 tsp salt
- 1 tbsp vegan butter substitute (earth balance)
- 1 tbsp olive oil, optional
- 1 cup Arborio rice
- 1 ½ tbsp nutritional yeast
- Black pepper, to taste

Directions:

1. Press the SAUTE key of the Instant Pot. Put the oil in the pot and heat.
2. When hot, add the garlic and onion; sauté for 3 minutes.
3. Add the rice and stir well to mix. Pour in the veggie broth, add the mushrooms, wine, thyme, and salt.
4. Press the CANCEL key to stop the sauté function. Cover and lock the lid. Press the MANUAL key, set the pressure to HIGH, and set the timer for 5 minutes.
5. When the Instant Pot timer beeps, press the CANCEL key. Using an oven mitt or a long handled spoon, turn the steam valve to quick release the pressure.
6. Unlock and carefully open the lid. Stir in the nutritional yeast, spinach, vegan butter, and black pepper.
7. Stir until very well combined. If the dish is still liquidly, just let it sit for a few minutes – it will thicken as it cools.

Nutritional Info (per serving): Calories - 320; Fat – 8.7; Fiber – 3.4; Carbs – 45; Protein – 10.3

Mexican Casserole (veg)

(Prep + Cook Time: 35 minutes | Servings: 4)

Ingredients:

- 5 cups water
- 2 cups uncooked brown rice
- 1 cup soaked black beans
- 6 oz tomato paste
- 2 tsp chili powder
- 2 tsp onion powder
- 1 tsp garlic
- 1 teaspoon salt

Directions:

1. A few hours before dinner, put your dry beans in a bowl with enough water to cover them.
2. Soak on the countertop for at least two hours and drain.
3. Put everything in your Instant Pot. Close and seal the pressure cooker. Select MANUAL and then cook on HIGH pressure for 28 minutes.
4. When time is up, hit CANCEL and quick-release.
5. Taste and season more if necessary.

Nutritional Info (per serving): Calories - 322; Fat – 2; Fiber – 9; Carbs – 63; Protein – 6

Chipotle Styled Rice (veg)

(Prep + Cook Time: 35 minutes | Servings: 4)

Ingredients:

- 2 cups brown rice, rinsed
- 1 lime, juiced
- 4 small bay leaves
- 1 tsp salt
- ½ cup chopped cilantro
- 1 ½ tbsp olive oil
- 2 ¾ cups water, hot

Directions:

1. In a 6-quarts Instant Pot place rice, then add bay leaves and water.
2. Plug in and switch on the pot, select RICE option and secure pot with lid. Then position pressure indicator and let cook on default time.
3. When the timer beeps, switch off the Instant Pot and let pressure release naturally for 10 minutes and then do quick pressure release.
4. Uncover the pot, add salt, oil, lime juice and cilantro and mix until combined. Serve immediately.

Nutritional Info (per serving): Calories - 210; Fat – 4; Fiber – 1; Carbs – 40; Protein – 3.5

Dried-Fruit Wild Rice (veg)

(Prep + Cook Time: 55 minutes | Servings: 6)

Ingredients:

- 3 ½ cups water
- 1 ½ cups wild rice
- 1 cup dried, mixed fruit
- 2 peeled and chopped small apples
- 1 chopped pear
- ½ cup slivered almonds
- 2 tbsp apple juice
- 1 tbsp maple syrup
- 1 tsp veggie oil
- 1 tsp cinnamon
- ½ tsp ground nutmeg
- Salt and pepper to taste

Directions:

1. Pour water into your Instant Pot along the rice.
2. Close and seal the lid. Select MANUAL and cook for 30 minutes on HIGH pressure.
3. While that cooks, soak the dried fruit in just enough apple juice to cover everything.
4. After 30 minutes, drain the fruit. By now, the rice should be done, so hit CANCEL and wait for the pressure to come down on its own. Drain the rice and move rice to a bowl.
5. Turn your pressure cooker to SAUTE and add veggie oil. Cook the apples, pears, and almonds for about 2 minutes.
6. Pour in two tablespoons apple juice and keep cooking for a few minutes more.
7. Add syrup, the cooked rice, soaked fruit, and seasonings. Keep stirring for 2-3 minutes. Serve.

Notes: You can eat this rice as-is, or for a full meal, you can fill a partially-baked butternut squash with the rice and bake for 30-45 minutes in a 350-degree oven.

Nutritional Info (per serving): Calories - 226; Fat – 3; Fiber – 5.6; Carbs – 43; Protein – 6

Sweet Coconut Rice (veg)

(Prep + Cook Time: 30 minutes | Servings: 4)

Ingredients:

- 1 ½ cups water
- 1 cup Thai sweet rice
- ½ can full-fat coconut milk
- 2 tbsp sugar
- Dash of salt

Directions:

1. Mix rice and water in your Instant Pot.
2. Select MANUAL and cook for just 3 minutes on HIGH pressure.
3. When time is up, hit CANCEL and wait 10 minutes for a natural release.
4. In the meanwhile, heat coconut milk, sugar, and salt in a saucepan.
5. When the sugar has melted, remove from the heat.
6. When the cooker has released its pressure, mix the coconut milk mixture into your rice and stir.
7. Put the lid back on and let it rest 5-10 minutes, without returning it to pressure.
8. Serve and enjoy!

Nutritional Info (per serving): Calories - 47; Fat – 8; Fiber – 0; Carbs – 47; Protein – 4

Green Rice

(Prep + Cook Time: 40 minutes | Servings: 6)

Ingredients:

- 2 cups rice basmati
- 1 cup spinach
- 1 cup dill
- 3 oz butter
- 1 tbsp salt
- 4 cups beef broth
- 1 tbsp minced garlic
- 1 tsp olive oil
- 1 tsp dried oregano

Directions:

1. Pour the olive oil in the Instant Pot.
2. Add rice, butter, and minced garlic.
3. SAUTE the mixture for 5 minutes. Stir it frequently.

4. After this, add beef broth.
5. Wash the spinach and dill carefully. Chop the greens.
6. Transfer the chopped greens in the blender and blend them well.
7. Then add the blended greens in the rice mixture.
8. Add butter, salt, and dried oregano.
9. Mix up the mixture carefully with the help of the wooden spoon. After this, close the lid and set the Instant Pot mode RICE.
10. Cook the dish for 20 minutes.
11. When the time is over – release the remaining pressure and transfer the green rice in the serving bowl.
12. Enjoy!

Nutritional Info (per serving): Calories - 213; Fat – 17.9; Fiber – 7; Carbs – 17.56; Protein – 6

Lentil and Wild Rice Pilaf (veg)
(Prep + Cook Time: 20 minutes + 30 min. soaking | Servings: 6)

Ingredients:
For the lentils and rice (soak for 30 minutes before cooking):
- ¼ cup brown rice
- ¼ cup black/wild rice
- ½ cup black or green lentils

For the vegetables:
- 1 cup mushrooms, sliced
- 1 stalk celery, finely chopped
- ½ onion, medium-sized, finely chopped
- 3 cloves garlic, pressed/minced

For the spices:
- 1 bay leaf
- 1 tbsp Italian seasoning blend (no-salt added)
- 1 tsp dried coriander
- 1 tsp fennel seeds
- ½ tsp ground black pepper
- ¼ tsp red pepper flakes
- 2 cups vegetable broth

Directions:
1. Combine the rice and the lentils in a medium-sized bowl.
2. Let soak for 30 minutes. Drain and then rinse thoroughly.
3. Set the Instant Pot to SAUTE. Put the veggies in the inner pot and sauté for 3-5 minutes.
4. If needed, add a bit of water to prevent the veggies from burning.
5. Add the rice and lentils, vegetable broth, and spices into the pot. Close and lock the lid.
6. Press MANUAL, set the pressure to HIGH, and set the timer to 9 minutes.
7. When the timer beeps, let the pressure release naturally. Open the lid. Stir in the pilaf.
8. If liquid remains, let sit for 5 minutes uncovered to allow the pilaf to absorb more liquid.
9. Serve this dish with steamed or fresh veggies.

Notes: If you don't like fennel seeds, then use 1 tablespoon of your preferred dried herbs, such as thyme, rosemary, parsley, basil, or oregano. If you don't have black or wild rice on hand, you can use all brown rice.

Nutritional Info (per serving): Calories - 211; Fat – 2.6; Fiber – 9.3; Carbs – 35.1; Protein – 12

Rice-Stuffed Acorn Squash (veg)

(Prep + Cook Time: 20 minutes | Servings: 4)

Ingredients:

- 3 ¾ cups veggie stock
- 2 medium-sized, halved acorn squash
- 1 cup white rice
- 1 cup diced onion
- ½ cup quinoa
- ½ cup vegan cheese
- 2 minced garlic cloves
- 1 tbsp Earth Balance spread
- 1 tsp chopped rosemary
- 1 tsp chopped thyme
- 1 tsp chopped sage

Directions:

1. Turn your Instant Pot to SAUTE and melt the Earth Balance. Add onion and salt, and cook for two minutes.
2. Toss in the garlic and cook for another minute or so. Add rice, quinoa, herbs, and pour in the broth. Stir.
3. Put your de-seeded squash halves with the cut-side UP in a steamer basket.
4. Put the trivet in the cooker, and place the basket on top. Close and seal the lid.
5. Hit MANUAL and cook for 6 minutes on HIGH pressure.
6. When the timer beeps, carefully quick-release the pressure after hitting CANCEL.
7. Take out the steamer basket and drain any liquid that's hanging around in the squash.
8. Add vegan cheese to the pot and stir. Wait 5 minutes or so for the stuffing to thicken.
9. Fill the squash and sprinkle on some extra cheese. Serve!

Nutritional Info (per serving): Calories - 309; Fat – 9; Fiber – 1.7; Carbs – 54; Protein – 6

Spice Black Bean and Brown Rice Salad (veg)
(Prep + Cook Time: 35 minutes | Servings: 8)

Ingredients:
- 1 can (14 oz) black beans, drained and rinsed
- 1 cup brown rice
- 1 avocado, diced
- 1 ½ cups water
- ¼ cup cilantro, minced
- ¼ tsp salt
- 12 grape tomatoes, quartered

For the spicy dressing:
- 3 tbsp lime juice, fresh squeezed
- 3 tbsp extra-virgin olive oil
- 2 tsp Tabasco or Cholula
- 2 garlic cloves, pressed or minced
- 1/8 tsp salt
- 1 tsp agave nectar

Directions:
1. Combine the rice with the water and salt in the Instant Pot. Close and lock the lid. Set the pressure to HIGH and set the timer for 24 minutes.
2. When the timer beeps, release the pressure naturally for 10 minutes. Turn the steam valve to release any remaining pressure. Carefully open the lid.
3. Using a fork, fluff the rice and let cool to room temperature.
4. When cool, refrigerate until ready to use. In a large-sized bowl, stir the brown rice with the black beans, avocado, tomato, and cilantro.
5. In a small-sized bowl, except for the olive oil, whisk the dressing ingredients together. While continuously whisking, slowly pour in the olive oil.
6. Pour the dressing over the brown rice mix and stir to combine.

Nutritional Info (per serving): Calories - 389; Fat – 11.9; Fiber – 12.3; Carbs – 59.6; Protein – 14.6

Refried Beans (veg)

(Prep + Cook Time: 55 minutes | Servings: 8)

Ingredients:

- 2 tsp dried oregano
- 2 pounds pinto beans, dried, sorted
- 1-2 tsp sea salt
- 3 tbsp vegetable OR shortening lard
- ½ tsp ground black pepper
- 4 cups vegetable broth
- 1 jalapeno, seeds removed and chopped
- 4 cups water
- 1 ½ tsp ground cumin
- 4-5 garlic cloves, roughly chopped
- 1 ½ cups onion, chopped

Directions:

1. Put the sorted pinto beans into a large-sized mixing bowl.
2. Fill the bowl with just enough water to cover the beans by several inches. Set aside to soak for 15 minutes.
3. Meanwhile, put the garlic cloves, onion, dried oregano, jalapeno, cumin, lard, vegetable broth, black pepper, and water in the Instant Pot. Stir to mix.
4. Put the soaked beans in a colander to strain. Discard the soaking liquid. Rinse the beans with fresh water.
5. Add the beans into the pot. Stir to mix. It's ok if the lard is still a lump. It will melt as the pot heats up. Cover and lock the lid.
6. Press the BEAN/ CHILI button and adjust the time to 45 minutes.
7. When the timer beeps, let the pressure down naturally, about 40 minutes.
8. When the pressure is released, carefully open the lid and season the beans with sea salt to taste.
9. With an immersion blender, blend the beans to desired consistency. It will appear soupy, but as the beans cool, it will thicken.

Nutritional Info (per serving): Calories - 470; Fat – 7; Fiber – 18.4; Carbs – 74.5; Protein – 27.2

Steamed Green Beans (veg)

(Prep + Cook Time: 20 minutes | Servings: 4)

Ingredients:

- 1 pound green beans, washed
- 1 cup water
- 2 tbsp fresh parsley, chopped, for garnish

For the dressing:

- 1 pinch ground black pepper
- 1 pinch salt
- 2 tbsp white wine vinegar
- 3 tbsp
- 3 tbsp olive oil
- 3 cloves garlic, sliced

Directions:

1. Pour the water into the Instant Pot and set the steamer basket. Put the green beans in the basket.
2. Press MANUAL, set the pressure to HIGH and the timer to 1 minute.
3. When the timer beeps, turn the valve to VENTNG to quick release the pressure.
4. Transfer the beans into a serving bowl.
5. Toss with the dressing Ingredients and let stand for 10 minutes. Remove the slices of garlic and then garnish with the parsley. Serve.

Nutritional Info (per serving): Calories - 143; Fat – 11.5; Fiber – 4; Carbs – 9.2; Protein – 3.5

Refried Bean Nachos (veg)

(Prep + Cook Time: 35 minutes | Servings: 6)

Ingredients:

- 2 cups pinto beans dried, (rinsed well, but not soaked)
- 1 onion, large-sized, cut into fourths (or diced if you like to leave your beans chunky)
- 4 cloves garlic, peeled and roughly chopped
- 1 jalapeno pepper, seeded (more or less to taste, optional)
- 1 tsp salt
- 1 tsp paprika
- 1 tsp chili powder
- 1 tsp cumin
- ½ tsp black pepper
- ½ cup salsa Cilantro, to taste (optional)
- 3 cups vegetable broth OR water OR combination of the two

Directions:

1. Put all of the ingredients in the Instant Pot and stir well to incorporate. Close and lock the lid. Press MANUAL and set the time to 28 minutes.
2. When the timer beeps, let the pressure release naturally for 10 minutes. Turn the valve to release any remaining pressure. Carefully open the lid and stir the dish.
3. With a potato masher or in a blender, mash or blend the beans to desired consistency – be careful because the beans are hot.
4. If you prefer your beans thick, drain some of the water before mashing or blending.
5. Serve warm.

Notes: This dish is freezer-friendly. Store in portion-sized containers and freeze.

Nutritional Info (per serving): Calories - 263; Fat – 1.8; Fiber – 11.2; Carbs – 45.3; Protein – 17.1

Spicy Black Bean and Brown Rice Salad (veg)

(Prep + Cook Time: 30 minutes | Servings: 8)

Ingredients:

- 1 can (14 oz) black beans, drained and rinsed
- 1 cup brown rice
- 1 avocado, diced
- 1 ½ cups water
- ¼ cup cilantro, minced
- ¼ tsp salt
- 12 grape tomatoes, quartered

For the spicy dressing:

- 3 tbsp lime juice, fresh squeezed
- 3 tbsp extra-virgin olive oil
- 2 tsp Tabasco or Cholula
- 2 garlic cloves, pressed or minced
- 1/8 tsp salt
- 1 tsp agave nectar

Directions:

1. Combine the rice with the water and salt in the Instant Pot. Close and lock the lid. Set the pressure to HIGH and set the timer for 24 minutes.
2. When the timer beeps, release the pressure naturally for 10 minutes. Turn the steam valve to release any remaining pressure. Carefully open the lid.
3. Using a fork, fluff the rice and let cool to room temperature.
4. When cool, refrigerate until ready to use. In a large-sized bowl, stir the brown rice with the black beans, avocado, tomato, and cilantro.
5. In a small-sized bowl, except for the olive oil, whisk the dressing ingredients together.
6. While continuously whisking, slowly pour in the olive oil.
7. Pour the dressing over the brown rice mix and stir to combine.

Nutritional Info (per serving): Calories - 389; Fat – 11.9; Fiber – 12.3; Carbs – 59.6; Protein – 14.6

Green Bean Casserole

(Prep + Cook Time: 30 minutes | Servings: 4)

Ingredients:

- 16 ounces green beans (I used Frozen)
- 12 ounces mushroom, sliced
- ½ cup French's onions, for garnishing
- 1 onion, small-sized
- 1 cup heavy cream
- 1 cup chicken broth
- 2 tbsp butter

Directions:

1. Press SAUTE key of the Instant Pot.
2. Put the butter in the pot and melt. Add the onion and mushrooms; sauté for about 2-3 minutes or until the onions are soft.
3. Add the green beans, heavy cream, and chicken broth. Press the CANCEL key to stop the sauté function. Cover and lock the lid.
4. Press the MANUAL key, set the pressure to HIGH, and set the timer for 15 minutes.
5. When the Instant Pot timer beeps, press the CANCEL key and unplug the Instant Pot. Turn the steam valve to quick release the pressure. Unlock and carefully open the lid.
6. While the dish is still hot, add 2 tablespoons cornstarch to thicken.
7. Serve topped with French's onions.

Nutritional Info (per serving): Calories - 230; Fat – 17.6; Fiber – 5.4; Carbs – 14.6; Protein – 7

Red Beans Over Rice

(Prep + Cook Time: 1 hour 25 minutes | Servings: 8)

Ingredients:

- 1 pound dry red kidney beans
- 1 ½ pounds ham, smoked sausage, tasso, cut into cubes
- 1 onion, diced
- 1 pepper, diced
- 1 tsp salt
- ½ tsp black pepper
- ½ tsp dried thyme
- ¼ tsp cayenne pepper (or more if you want it spicier)
- ¼ tsp white pepper
- 2 bay leaves
- 2 tbsp oil
- 2-3 stalks celery, chopped
- 3 garlic cloves, minced
- 5 ½ cups water

Directions:

1. Set the Instant Pot to normal SAUTE mode. Put the oil in the pot and heat.
2. When hot, add the celery, onion, and pepper. Sauté for about 5 minutes or until they start to soften.
3. Add the garlic and chopped meat. Cook for about 3-4 minutes, stirring often. Rinse the kidney beans and drain.
4. Add all the ingredients into the pot. Cover and lock the lid. Press PRESSURE, set to HIGH, and set the timer to 60 minutes.
5. When the timer beeps, let the pressure release naturally for about 10-15 minutes. Open the lid.
6. With a potato masher or a wooden spoon, mash about 1/3-1/2 of the beans and stir thoroughly – the mashed beans should thicken the broth into creamy gravy.
7. Serve with rice.

Notes: If the beans are still not tender after 60 minutes, cook on HIGH for 30 minutes more.

Nutritional Info (per serving): Calories - 369; Fat – 11.4; Fiber – 10.2; Carbs – 40.1; Protein – 27.2

Black Bean + Sweet Potato Hash (veg)
(Prep + Cook Time: 15 minutes | Servings: 4)

Ingredients:
- 2 cups peeled, chopped sweet potatoes
- 1 cup chopped onion
- 1 cup cooked and drained black beans
- 1 minced garlic clove
- ⅓ cup veggie broth
- ¼ cup chopped scallions
- 2 tsp hot chili powder

Directions:
1. Prep your veggies.
2. Turn your Instant Pot to SAUTE and cook the chopped onion for 2-3 minutes, stirring so it doesn't burn.
3. Add the garlic and stir until fragrant. Add the sweet potatoes and chili powder, and stir.
4. Pour in the broth and give one last stir before locking the lid. Select MANUAL and cook on HIGH pressure for 3 minutes.
5. When time is up, quick-release the pressure carefully.
6. Add the black beans and scallions, and stir to heat everything up.
7. Season with salt and more chili powder if desired.

Nutritional Info (per serving): Calories - 133; Fiber – 9.5; Carbs – 28; Protein – 5

Bacon-y Black Beans
(Prep + Cook Time: 60 minutes | Servings: 4)

Ingredients:
- 1 pound dried black beans
- 3 strips bacon, cut into halves
- 1 small onion, cut in half
- 6 garlic cloves, crushed
- 1 orange, cut in half
- 2 bay leaves
- 2 quarts chicken stock, low-sodium
- 2 tsp kosher salt, more for seasoning

Directions:
1. Press the SAUTE key. Put the bacon in the pot and sauté for 2 minutes or until crisp and the fat is rendered.

2. Add the rest of the ingredients in the pot. Cover and close the lid.
3. Set the pressure to HIGH and the timer to 40 minutes.
4. When the timer beeps, quick release the pressure – the beans will cooked, but still firm.
5. If you want a creamier and tender beans, let the pressure release naturally. Open the lid.
6. Discard the bay leaves, orange, and onion.
7. Season with salt to taste and serve.

Notes: If you want texture and flavor in your dish, serve with orange zest, green onions, and orange slices.

Nutritional Info (per serving): Calories - 520; Fat – 8.8; Fiber – 18.9; Carbs – 81.1; Protein – 32.1

Baked Beans

(Prep + Cook Time: 60 minutes | Servings: 8)

Ingredients:
- ½ a pound of bacon
- 2 small onions
- 2 cups navy beans (dried)
- 1 tsp dry mustard
- ½ tsp salt
- 4 ounces dark molasses
- 1 ½ cups water

Directions:
1. Start by covering the beans with water in a bowl.
2. Soak the beans overnight. The next day, drain the water and rinse the beans. Remove any debris.
3. Place the beans in the pressure cooker.
4. Cover the beans with warm water. Don't fill more than halfway.
5. You should use LOW PRESSURE for 45 minutes.
6. Allow the pressure to drop naturally when the timer goes off. Carefully open the lid.
7. The beans should be soft and ready for consumption. If not, then continue cooking for a few more minutes.
8. Serve and enjoy!

Nutritional Info (per serving): Calories - 375; Fat – 13.7; Fiber – 13; Carbs – 49.2; Protein – 15.2

Beans Stew (veg)

(Prep + Cook Time: 1 hour 25 minutes | Servings: 8)

Ingredients:

- 2 carrots, chopped
- 1 plantain, chopped
- 1 pound red beans, dry
- Salt and black pepper to the taste
- 1 tomato, chopped
- Water as needed
- 2 green onions stalks, chopped
- 1 small yellow onion, diced
- ¼ cup cilantro leaves, chopped
- 2 tbsp vegetable oil

Directions:

1. Put the beans in your Instant Pot, add water to cover, cook on HIGH pressure for 35 minutes and release pressure for 10 minutes naturally.
2. Add plantain, carrots, salt and pepper to the taste, cover Instant Pot again and cook on HIGH pressure for 30 more minutes.
3. Meanwhile, heat up a pan with the vegetable oil over medium high heat, add yellow onion, stir and cook for 2 minutes.
4. Add tomatoes, green onions, some salt and pepper, stir again, cook for 3 minutes more and take off the heat.
5. Release pressure naturally from your Instant Pot, divide cooked beans amongst plates, top with tomatoes and onions mix, sprinkle cilantro at the end and serve right away.
6. Serve.

Nutritional Info (per serving): Calories - 70; Fat – 3.1; Fiber – 1; Carbs – 9.6; Protein – 2.5

Red Lentils with Sweet Potato (veg)

(Prep + Cook Time: 1 hour 30 minutes | Servings: 1)

Ingredients:

- 1 small white onion, peeled and chopped
- 1 medium-sized sweet potato, peeled and chopped
- ½ cup red lentils, rinsed
- ¼ tsp garlic powder
- ¼ tsp chipotle chili pepper
- ½ tsp ground cinnamon
- 2 tbsp apple cider vinegar
- 1 tbsp nutritional yeast
- 12 fluid ounce water

Directions:
1. In a 6-quarts Instant Pot place all the ingredients, in order, and then stir until just combined.
2. Plug in and switch on the Instant Pot, select stew/chili option and secure pot with lid.
3. Then position pressure indicator and adjust cooking time on timer pad to 5 minutes and let cook.
4. When the timer beeps, switch off the Instant Pot and do a quick pressure release.
5. Then uncover the pot and transfer to a serving dish.
6. Serve immediately.

Nutritional Info (per serving): Calories - 112; Fat – 2.3

Stewed Tomatoes and Green Beans (veg)
(Prep + Cook Time: 15 minutes | Servings: 10)

Ingredients:
- 1 pound trimmed green beans
- 2 cups fresh, chopped tomatoes
- 1 crushed garlic clove
- 1 tsp olive oil
- Salt to taste
- ½ cup water

Directions:
1. Set SAUTE setting and preheat your Instant Pot.
2. When warm, add 1 teaspoon of olive oil and garlic.
3. When the garlic has become fragrant and golden, add tomatoes and stir. If the tomatoes are dry, add ½ cup water.
4. Fill the steamer basket with the green beans and sprinkle on salt. Lower into cooker.
5. Close and seal the lid. Select MANUAL and cook for 5 minutes on HIGH pressure.
6. When the timer beeps, turn off cooker and quick-release the pressure.
7. Carefully remove the steamer basket and pour beans into the tomato sauce.
8. If the beans aren't quite tender enough, simmer in sauce for a few minutes. Serve.

Nutritional Info (per serving): Calories - 55; Fat – 3.2; Fiber – 2.6; Carbs – 6.3; Protein – 1.6

Tex Mex Pinto Beans

(Prep + Cook Time: 55 minutes | Servings: 6)

Ingredients:

- 20 ounces package pinto beans with ham
- ¼ cup cilantro, chopped
- ½ cup salsa verde
- 1 packet taco seasoning
- 1 onion
- 1 jalapeno, diced
- 1 clove garlic, diced
- 5 cups chicken broth
- Salt and pepper to taste

Directions:

1. Rinse and sort out the dried beans. Put into the Instant Pot. Pour the broth in the pot.
2. Add garlic, onion, and jalapeno. Stir in the taco seasoning. Close and lock the lid.
3. Set the pressure to HIGH and set the timer for 42 minutes.
4. When the timer beeps, let the pressure release naturally for about 15 minutes.
5. Drain excess liquid from the pot. Stir in the salsa verde, ham seasoning, and cilantro.
6. Taste and season with salt to taste.
7. Serve in tacos, over rice, or as a side dish.

Nutritional Info (per serving): Calories - 436; Fat – 5.8; Fiber – 15.2; Carbs – 67.2; Protein – 28.3

Chili Con Carne

(Prep + Cook Time: 30 minutes | Servings: 6)

Ingredients:

- 1 can (28 ounce) ground and peeled tomatoes
- 1 can (14 ounce) kidney beans, rinsed and drained
- 1 can (14 ounce) black beans, rinsed and drained
- 1 ½ pounds ground beef
- 1 ½ tsp ground cumin
- 1 ½ tsp salt
- 1 ½ cups onion, large diced
- 1 tbsp chili powder
- 1 tbsp Worcestershire Sauce
- 1 tsp dry oregano
- ½ cup fresh water
- ½ cup sweet red bell pepper, large dice
- ½ tsp freshly ground black pepper
- 1-2 jalapeños, medium-sized, stems and seeds removed, finely diced
- 2 tbsp garlic, minced
- 3 tbsp extra-virgin olive oil

Directions:

1. Press the SAUTE button. Let the Instant Pot heat. Put the oil in the pot.
2. Add the ground beef, sauté, breaking up using a wooden spoon, until the beef is slightly brown. Remove excess fat.
3. Add the onions, jalapenos, and bell pepper. Sauté for 3 minutes.
4. Add the garlic, chili powder, cumin, oregano, salt, and pepper. Sauté for 1 minute.
5. Add the beans, tomatoes, water, and Worcestershire sauce. Stir to combine. Close and lock the lid.
6. Set the pressure to HIGH and set the timer for 10 minutes.
7. When the timer beeps, let the pressure release for 10 minutes.
8. Turn the steam valve to release remaining pressure.
9. Serve immediately or simmer on less SAUTÉ for a thicker chili.

Nutritional Info (per serving): Calories - 772; Fat – 16.4; Fiber – 23.2; Carbs – 93.1; Protein – 65.7

Great Northern Bean Dip (veg)

(Prep + Cook Time: 25 minutes | Servings: 2)

Ingredients:
- ¾ cup soaked overnight Great Northern white beans
- ⅓ cup extra virgin olive oil
- 2 garlic cloves
- 3 tbsp lemon juice
- 3 tbsp minced cilantro
- 2 tsp ground cumin
- 1 ½ tsp chili powder
- Pinch of red pepper flakes
- Salt and pepper to taste
- Water as needed

Directions:
1. Drain the beans before putting them in the Instant Pot. Cover with 1 inch of fresh water. Close and seal the lid.
2. Press MANUAL and cook for 13 minutes on HIGH pressure.
3. When time is up, hit CANVEL and wait 10 minutes for a natural pressure release.
4. When the pressure is gone, drain the beans and run under cold water. In a food processor, chop up the garlic.
5. Add the rest of the ingredients (except cilantro) and puree till smooth.
6. Serve with cilantro on top.

Nutritional Info (per serving): Calories – 297.5; Fat – 18.8; Fiber – 6.35; Carbs – 25.4; Protein – 9.3

Vanilla-Infused Honey

(Prep + Cook Time: 55 minutes | Servings: 16 tbsp)

Ingredients:
- 1 cup mild honey
- 2-4 split vanilla beans
- 1 cup water

Directions:
1. Put the split vanilla beans in a half-pint Mason jar.
2. Pour in honey, leaving 1-inch of empty space at the top.
3. Get 2 round coffee filters and cut so they hang over the jar by an inch.

4. With the filters on top, screw the ring part of the Mason jar on, but not the actual lid. Pour 1 cup of water into your Instant Pot and lower in the trivet.
5. Put the jar on the trivet, and close and seal the cooker lid. Select MANUAL and cook on high pressure for 30 minutes.
6. When time is up, hit CANCEL and wait for the pressure to come down on its own.
7. When removing the jar, be careful, because the honey is very hot.
8. Carefully remove the lid with protection on your hands, and stir the honey.
9. Pour through a fine-mesh sieve into another half-pint Mason jar.
10. Throw out the vanilla beans. Store at room temperature.

Nutritional Info (per serving): Calories - 51; Fat – 0; Fiber – 0; Carbs – 13; Protein – 0

Vanilla-Bean Applesauce (veg)
(Prep + Cook Time: 20 minutes | Servings: 4)

Ingredients:
- 10 big peeled, cored, and sliced apples
- ¼ cup white sugar
- ¼ cup apple juice
- 1-2 whole split vanilla beans
- 1 tsp ground cinnamon

Directions:
1. Wash, peel, core and slice the apples.
2. Put them in the cooker along with sugar, cinnamon, apple juice, and split vanilla beans Stir before closing and sealing the lid.
3. Choose MANUAL and cook for 4 minutes on HIGH pressure.
4. When time is up, hit CANCEL and quick-release.
5. Stir the apples and pick out the vanilla beans.
6. To get the texture you want, blend with a hand blender, or move to a regular blender.
7. Be careful though, the apples are hot!

Nutritional Info (per serving): Calories - 234; Fat – 1; Fiber – 11; Carbs – 62

Delightful Rainbow Beans

(Prep + Cook Time: 35 minutes | Servings: 6)

Ingredients:

- 1 cup black beans, cooked
- ½ cup red beans, cooked
- ½ cup white beans, cooked
- 1 yellow sweet pepper
- 1 red sweet pepper
- 1 red onion
- 1 cup chicken stock
- 3 tbsp tomato paste
- 1 tbsp salt
- 1 cup water
- 1 tsp turmeric
- 3 tbsp sour cream

Directions:

1. Place the chicken stock and water in the Instant Pot. Add the black beans, red beans, and white beans.
2. Remove the seeds from the sweet yellow pepper and red pepper.
3. Peel the onion. Chop the vegetables into the medium pieces.
4. Add the chopped vegetables in the Instant Pot. After this, sprinkle the mixture with the tomato paste, salt, turmeric, and sour cream.
5. Mix up it carefully and close the lid.
6. Set the up the Instant Pot mode STEW and cook the dish for 20 minutes.
7. When the time is over – chill the dish little.
8. Then transfer it to the serving bowls.
9. Serve the dish immediately. Enjoy!

Nutritional Info (per serving): Calories - 151; Fat – 1.6; Fiber – 6; Carbs – 26.42; Protein – 9

The Whole Chicken
(Prep + Cook Time: 30 minutes | Servings: 8)

Ingredients:
- 1 medium-sized, whole chicken
- 2 cups water or broth
- 1 minced green onion
- 2 tbsp sugar
- 1 tbsp cooking wine
- 1 minced piece of ginger
- 2 tsp soy sauce
- 2 tsp salt

Directions:
1. Season the chicken thoroughly with salt and sugar.
2. Sprinkle 1 teaspoon of salt into the bottom of the Instant Pot.
3. Pour the wine, broth and soy sauce into the cooker, and add the chicken.
4. Choose POULTRY and cook.
5. When time is up, flip the chicken, and push POULTRY again.
6. Let the pressure come down naturally before opening the cooker.
7. Serve chicken pieces with green onion on top and any side dishes you'd like.

Nutritional Info (per serving): Calories - 131; Fiber – 0; Carbs – 4; Protein – 18

Sticky Sesame Chicken
(Prep + Cook Time: 30 minutes | Servings: 4)

Ingredients:
- 6 boneless chicken thigh fillets
- 4 peeled and crushed garlic cloves
- 5 tbsp hoisin sauce
- 5 tbsp sweet chili sauce
- ½ cup chicken stock
- 1 chunk of peeled, grated fresh ginger
- 1 ½ tbsp sesame seeds
- 1 tbsp rice vinegar
- 1 tbsp soy sauce

Directions:
1. Spread chicken thighs flat and place them into the Instant Pot.
2. Whisk garlic, ginger, chili sauce, hoisin, vinegar, sesame seeds, broth, and soy sauce into a sauce.
3. Pour over chicken and stir.
4. Select MANUAL and then 15 minutes on HIGH pressure.
5. When time is up, hit CANCEL and wait for a natural pressure release.
6. When all the pressure is gone, open up the cooker and serve the chicken with rice.

Nutritional Info (per serving): Calories - 428; Fiber – 1; Carbs – 52.9; Protein – 30

Salsa Verde Chicken

(Prep + Cook Time: 25 minutes | Servings: 6)

Ingredients:
- 2 ½ pounds of boneless chicken breasts
- 16 ounces of salsa verde
- 1 tsp smoked paprika
- 1 tsp cumin
- 1 tsp salt

Directions:
1. Throw everything into your Instant Pot pressure cooker.
2. Select MANUAL and then 25 minutes at HIGH pressure.
3. When the timer goes off, quick-release the pressure.
4. Carefully open the cooker and shred the chicken.
5. Serve and enjoy.

Nutritional Info (per serving): Calories - 340; Fat – 7; Fiber – 0; Carbs – 6; Protein – 59

Balsamic Chicken Thighs

(Prep + Cook Time: 25 minutes | Servings: 2)

Ingredients:

- 1 pound boneless, skinless chicken thighs
- ½ cup balsamic vinegar
- ⅓ cup cream sherry wine
- 2 tbsp chopped cilantro
- 2 tbsp olive oil
- 2 tbsp minced green onion
- 1 ½ tsp minced garlic
- 1 tsp dried basil
- 1 tsp garlic powder
- 1 tsp Worcestershire sauce
- ½ tsp black pepper

Directions:

1. Mix basil, salt, garlic, pepper, sherry, Worcestershire, onion, and vinegar in a plastic bag.
2. Add chicken and squish around, so the chicken becomes completely coated. Turn your Instant Pot on and select SAUTE.
3. Pour in the olive oil and cook the minced garlic, stirring, until fragrant.
4. Turn the pot to POULTRY and pour in the chicken and sauce.
5. Secure the lid.
6. The POULTRY setting defaults to 15 minutes, which is the correct length of time for this recipe.
7. When it beeps, quick-release the pressure.
8. Serve with chopped cilantro and a side dish like rice or veggies.

Nutritional Info (per serving): Calories - 210; Fat – 12; Fiber – 0; Carbs – 10; Protein – 14

Italian Chicken

(Prep + Cook Time: 25 minutes | Servings: 6)

Ingredients:

- 8 boneless, skinless chicken thighs
- 2 medium-sized, chopped carrots
- ½ pound stemmed and quartered cremini mushrooms
- 2 cups cherry tomatoes
- 3 smashed garlic cloves
- ½ cup pitted green olives
- ½ cup sliced fresh basil
- ¼ cup chopped fresh Italian parsley
- 1 chopped onion
- 1 tbsp olive oil
- 1 tbsp tomato paste
- ½ tsp black pepper
- Salt to taste

Directions:

1. Season the chicken thighs with salt.
2. On your Instant Pot, hit SAUTE and pour in the olive oil.
3. When shiny, toss in the carrots, mushrooms, onions, and a little salt.
4. Cook for about 3-5 minutes until soft.
5. Add the smashed garlic and tomato paste and cook for another 30 seconds.
6. Last, add the cherry tomatoes, chicken thighs, and olives.
7. Turn off SAUTE before locking the pressure cooker.
8. Hit MANUAL and choose 10 minutes on HIGH Pressure
9. When the beeper goes off, quick-release the pressure right away.
10. Take off the lid and season. Serve.

Nutritional Info (per serving): Calories - 245; Fiber – 3; Carbs – 10; Protein – 35

Honey-Sriracha Chicken
(Prep + Cook Time: 15 minutes | Servings: 4)

Ingredients:

- 4 diced chicken breasts
- ¼ cup sugar
- 5 tbsp soy sauce
- 2-3 tbsp sriracha
- 2-3 tbsp honey
- 2 tbsp cornstarch
- ¼ cup water + 2 tbsp cold water
- 1 tbsp minced garlic

Directions:

1. Mix soy sauce, honey, sriracha, sugar, ¼ cup of water, and garlic in your Instant Pot.
2. Add chicken and mix to coat in the sauce. Close and seal the lid. Select MANUAL and cook for 9 minutes on HIGH pressure.
3. When time is up, quick-release the pressure after turning the cooker off. In a cup, mix 2 tablespoons of cold water with cornstarch.
4. Turn the pot to SAUTE and pour in the cornstarch mixture.
5. Stir constantly until the pot boils and the sauce begins to thicken.
6. Serve over rice.

Nutritional Info (per serving): Calories - 419; Fat – 7; Carbs – 19; Protein – 67

Chicken, Mushroom, and Jasmine Rice in One Pot

(Prep + Cook Time: 15 minutes | Servings: 4)

Ingredients:

- 8 ounces cremini mushrooms (or your preferred kind)
- 3 pounds chicken legs and/ or thighs, skinless, boneless, any fat removed, cut into large chunks
- 3 cups Jasmine rice (18 ounces), washed until the water runs clear
- 2 ½ cups (about 24 ounces) chicken broth OR water

For the marinade:

- 1 tsp rice wine vinegar
- ¼ tsp Chinese five spice
- 2 tsp ginger, grated
- 3 tbsp black soy sauce
- 3 tbsp soy sauce (low sodium)
- Scallions, to garnish

Directions:

1. Put the chicken chunks into large-sized bowl.
2. Add the mushrooms. In another bowl, whisk together all of the marinade ingredients until well combined.
3. Pour the marinade over the chicken and mushroom. Toss to coat and marinate in the fridge for at least 30 minutes or overnight.
4. Put the rice, broth, and chicken and mushroom mixture in the Instant Pot. Cover and lock the lid.
5. Press the MANUAL key, set the pressure to HIGH, and set the timer for 10 minutes.
6. When the Instant Pot timer beeps, let the pressure release naturally for 10 minutes.

Notes: The cup I used to measure the rice is a "rice cup". If you want less rice for your dish, use 2 "rice cups" of Jasmine rice and 1 1/2 cups broth or water. You can use chicken breast for this dish – just cut it into large chunks. If you reduce this recipe tin half, reduce the cooking time to 3 minutes and release the pressure naturally.

Nutritional Info (per serving): Calories - 1024; Fat – 11.3; Fiber – 6.4; Carbs – 107.7; Protein – 113.2

Chicken, Shrimp and Broccoli Alfredo

(Prep + Cook Time: 30 minutes | Servings: 4)

Ingredients:

- 8 ounces shrimp, small-sized
- 6 ounces Parmesan cheese, fresh grated
- 4 pieces (4 ounces each) chicken breast, cubed
- 4 leaves fresh basil, chopped
- 4 cloves garlic, minced
- 2 cups heavy cream
- 2 cups broccoli
- ¼ cup fresh parsley, chopped
- 1 stick butter
- 1 bar (8 ounces) cream cheese

Directions:

1. Press the SAUTÉ key of the Instant Pot. Put the stick of butter and melt.
2. Add the cream cheese and whisk until the mixture is creamy. Slowly add the heavy cream.
3. Add the freshly grated Parmesan cheese. Add the rest of the ingredients. Cover and lock the lid.
4. Press MANUAL, set the pressure to HIGH, and set the time for 15 minutes.
5. When the timer beeps, turn the steam valve to VENTING to quick release the pressure.
6. Carefully open the lid. Serve.

Nutritional Info (per serving): Calories - 1501; Fat – 101.6; Fiber – 1.4; Carbs – 9.8; Protein – 133.9

Chicken and Corn Stew

(Prep + Cook Time: 35 minutes | Servings: 4)

Ingredients:

- 8 chicken drumsticks, skinless (28 ounces total)
- 2 corn on the cob, husked and halved
- 1 can (8 ounces) tomato sauce
- 3 scallions, chopped
- 2 cups water
- ¼ cup cilantro, chopped PLUS
- 1 tbsp, chopped, for garnish
- ½ tsp kosher salt
- ½ tsp garlic powder
- ½ tsp cumin
- ½ onion, medium-sized, chopped
- 1 tsp olive oil
- 1 tbsp chicken bouillon (I used Chicken Better than Bouillon)
- 1 plum tomato, diced
- 1 garlic, crushed

Directions:

1. Season the chicken drumsticks with garlic powder and salt. Press the SAUTÉ key of the Instant Pot.
2. When the pot is hot, add the olive oil.
3. Add the garlic, scallions, onions, and tomato. Sauté for about 2-3 minutes or until softened.
4. Add 1/4 cup of the cilantro and sauté, stirring, for 1 minute.
5. Add the water, tomato sauce, cumin, bouillon, and stir to combine. Put the chicken in the sauce.
6. Top the chicken with the corn. Cover and lock the lid.
7. Press the MANUAL key, set the pressure to HIGH, and set the timer for 20 minutes. When the Instant Pot timer beeps, turn the steam valve to VENTING to quick release the pressure.
8. Unlock and carefully open the lid.
9. Garnish with the cilantro and serve.

Nutritional Info (per serving): Calories - 405; Fat – 8.3; Fiber – 3.8; Carbs – 21; Protein – 61.5

Chicken Nachos

(Prep + Cook Time: 35 minutes | Servings: 6)

Ingredients:

- 1 ½ pound chicken thighs, boneless, skinless
- 1 package (1 ounce) taco seasoning mix
- ½ cup Herdez salsa verde (mild)
- ½ cup mild red salsa

Directions:

1. Press the SAUTE key of the Instant Pot and select the MORE option for high heat.
2. Put the oil in the pot and heat. When the oil is hot, add the chicken thighs and cook until the chicken begins to brown nicely.
3. In a bowl, combine the taco seasoning and salsa and stir to combine. Pour the salsa mixture in the pot. Stir to combine.
4. Press the CANCEL key to stop the sauté function. Cover and lock the lid.
5. Press the POULTRY key and set the timer for 15 minutes.
6. When the Instant Pot timer beeps, press the CANCEL key and unplug the Instant Pot. Let the pressure release naturally for 10-15 minutes or until the valve drops. Turn the steam valve to release remaining pressure.
7. Unlock and carefully open the lid. Shred the chicken and serve with tortilla chips.
8. Top each serving with shredded cheese, sour cream, diced green onions, black beans, and chopped cilantro to taste.

Nutritional Info (per serving): Calories - 241; Fat – 8.5; Fiber – 0; Carbs – 5.2; Protein – 33.4

Chicken Thighs with Cranberries and Pears

(Prep + Cook Time: 25 minutes | Servings: 6)

Ingredients:

- 2 pounds boneless, skinless chicken thighs
- 2 big, firm peeled and sliced
- Bosc pears
- 1 chopped shallot
- ⅔ cup chicken broth
- ¼ cup dried cranberries
- 2 tbsp balsamic vinegar
- 2 tbsp butter
- ½ tsp dried dill
- ½ tsp salt
- ½ tsp pepper

Directions:

1. Melt the butter in your Instant Pot on the SAUTE setting.
2. Season your chicken with salt and pepper.
3. In batches, brown the thighs on both sides in your pot until golden, turning once.
4. When the thighs are all browned and in a bowl, add pears and shallot to the pot.
5. Stir until the shallot is soft. Add vinegar, cranberries, and dried dill.
6. When the pot is bubbling, pour in broth and stir. Add chicken and lock and seal the lid.
7. Hit MANUAL and adjust time to 15 minutes.
8. When time is up, hit CANCEL and quick-release the pressure.
9. Stir and serve!

Nutritional Info (per serving): Calories - 265; Fat – 10; Fiber – 1.5; Carbs – 15; Protein – 30

Hot Buffalo Wings

(Prep + Cook Time: 20 minutes | Servings: 6)

Ingredients:

- 4 pounds chicken wing, sectioned, frozen or fresh
- 1-2 tbsp sugar, light brown
- ½ tsp kosher salt
- ½ cup cayenne pepper hot sauce (I used frank's red hot)
- ½ cup butter
- 1 tbsp Worcestershire sauce
- 6 ounces water

Directions:

For the sauce:

In a microwavable container, mix the hot sauce with the Worcestershire sauce, butter, salt, and brown sugar; microwave for 15 seconds or until the butter is melted.

For the wings:

1. Pour the water into the Instant Pot. Set a trivet in the bottom of the pot.
2. Put the chicken wings on the trivet. Cover and lock the lid. Press the MANUAL key, set the pressure to HIGH, and set the timer for 5 minutes.
3. When the Instant Pot timer beeps, release the pressure naturally for 5 minutes, then turn the steam valve to quick release the pressure.
4. Unlock and carefully open the lid. Put the oven rack in the center of the oven. Turn the oven to the broil.
5. Carefully transfer the chicken wings from the pot into a cookie sheet. Brush the tops of the chicken wings with the sauce.
6. Place the cookie sheet in the oven and broil for 5 minutes.
7. Turn the chicken wings and brush the other side with the remaining sauce.
8. Serve with celery sticks and blue cheese dressing.

Notes: If you want a hotter sauce, use more hot sauce. If you want a milder sauce, use more butter.

Nutritional Info (per serving): Calories - 603; Fat – 24.6; Fiber – 0; Carbs – 2.3; Protein – 87.9

Buffalo Chicken with Sweet Potatoes

(Prep + Cook Time: 35 minutes | Servings: 4)

Ingredients:

- 1 pound of large, organic chicken breasts
- 16-ounces diced sweet potatoes
- 1 diced onion
- 3 tbsp buffalo sauce
- 3 tbsp grass-fed butter
- ½ tsp garlic powder
- ½ tsp onion powder
- Salt and pepper to taste

Buffalo sauce:

- 3-4 tbsp Paleo hot sauce (like Frank's Red Hot Original Cayenne Pepper)
- 3 tbsp grass-fed butter
- 1 tbsp apple cider vinegar
- 1 tbsp lemon juice
- 1 tsp paprika
- 1 tsp garlic powder
- Salt and pepper to taste

Directions:

1. Turn your Instant Pot to SAUTE and heat 1 tablespoon of butter. Cook the onion until browned.
2. Mix the ingredients in the buffalo sauce list.
3. Add chicken, sweet potatoes, butter, 3 tablespoons of the buffalo sauce, and seasonings to the Instant Pot. Seal and close the lid.
4. Press POULTRY and cook for 18 minutes on HIGH pressure.
5. If you're using frozen breasts, select MANUAL and cook for 30 minutes.
6. When time is up, hit CANCEL and quick-release. Serve hot!

Nutritional Info (per serving): Calories - 298; Fat – 12; Fiber – 3.7; Carbs – 25; Protein – 20

Easy Spicy Chicken Wings

(Prep + Cook Time: 20 minutes | Servings: 4)

Ingredients:

- 3 pounds chicken wings
- 1½ cups chicken broth
- ¼ cup light brown sugar
- 2 tbsp olive oil
- ½ tsp garlic powder
- ½ tsp paprika
- ½ tsp cayenne pepper
- ½ tsp salt
- ½ tsp black pepper

Directions:

1. Rinse and dry the chicken wings with a paper towel. Tumble into a mixing bowl.
2. In a separate bowl, mix the seasonings. You want about 3 tablespoons total of the mixed spice rub, so feel free to add more of whatever spice you like.
3. More sugar will make it sweeter, more pepper will make it spicier.
4. Add olive oil and your spice rub to the chicken wings, and rub.
5. Pour chicken broth in your cooker and add wings. Close and seal the lid.
6. Select MANUAL and cook on HIGH pressure for 9 minutes.
7. When time is up, hit CANCEL and quick-release.
8. For really crispy skin, broil for 5-6 minutes, flipping halfway through.
9. Serve with hot sauce on the side!

Nutritional Info (per serving): Calories - 760; Fat – 51; Fiber – 0; Carbs – 14; Protein – 52

Chicken Congee

(Prep + Cook Time: 65 minutes | Servings: 7)

Ingredients:
- 6 chicken drumsticks
- 7 cups water
- 1 cup Jasmine rice
- 1 tbsp fresh ginger
- Salt to taste

Directions:
1. Rinse rice under cool water for a few minutes.
2. Pour rice, water, ginger, and drumsticks into Instant Pot. Seal the lid.
3. Hit MANUAL and adjust time to 30 minutes.
4. When time is up, hit CANCEL and wait for a natural pressure release.
5. When safe, open the lid and hit SAUTE.
6. Keep stirring while the congee thickens.
7. Season with salt.
8. Pull off the chicken with tongs, and throw away the bones.
9. Serve right away!

Nutritional Info (per serving): Calories - 248; Fat – 9; Fiber – 0; Carbs – 21; Protein – 20

Chicken Parmesan Pasta

(Prep + Cook Time: 30 minutes | Servings: 6)

Ingredients:
- 1 cup water
- 1 box linguine noodles
- 4 skinless, boneless, frozen chicken breasts
- 1 jar of spaghetti sauce
- 5 chopped garlic cloves
- 1 large onion
- 30 halved cherry tomatoes
- 1 cup Italian breadcrumbs
- ½ cup chopped parsley
- 1 tbsp butter
- Salt and crushed red pepper to taste
- ½ tsp Italian seasoning
- Parmesan cheese

Directions:

1. Put water, chicken, and noodles in your Instant Pot.
2. You'll probably have to break the noodles in half.
3. Pour in jar of sauce. Mix. Add everything else except the butter, cheese, and breadcrumbs.
4. Stir again before closing and sealing the lid.
5. Select MANUAL and cook on HIGH pressure for 20 minutes.
6. When time is up, turn off the cooker and quick-release. Toast the bread crumbs in melted butter.
7. Sprinkle on top of pasta with Parmesan cheese. Serve!

Nutritional Info (per serving): Calories - 714; Fat – 15; Fiber – 1; Carbs – 87; Protein – 54

Chicken Alfredo Pasta

(Prep + Cook Time: 5 minutes | Servings: 3)

Ingredients:

- 8-ounces fettuccine
- One 15-ounce jar of Alfredo sauce
- 2 cups water
- 1 cup cooked + diced chicken
- 2 tsp chicken seasoning

Directions:

1. Break your pasta in half so it fits in the cooker.
2. Add pasta, water, and chicken seasoning to Instant Pot.
3. Seal the lid. Hit MANUAL and adjust time to 3 minutes.
4. When the timer beeps, hit CANCEL and quick-release.
5. Drain the pasta and add to serving bowl.
6. Mix in Alfredo sauce and chicken. Serve!

Nutritional Info (per serving): Calories - 491; Fat – 16; Fiber – 0; Carbs – 59; Protein – 27

Chicken Pina Colada

(Prep + Cook Time: 35 minutes | Servings: 4)

Ingredients:

- 1 cup pineapple chunks, frozen or fresh
- 2 pounds chicken thighs, organic, cut into
- 1-inch chunks
- 1/8 tsp salt
- ½ cup green onion, chopped, for garnish
- ½ cup coconut cream, full fat
- 1 tsp cinnamon
- 2 tbsp coconut aminos

Directions:

1. Except for the green onions, put all of the ingredients in the Instant Pot. Cover and lock the lid.
2. Press the POULTRY key and cook on preset HIGH pressure and 15 minutes cooking time.
3. When the Instant Pot timer beeps, press the CANCEL key and turn off the Instant Pot.
4. Let the pressure release naturally for 10-15 minutes or until the valve drops.
5. Turn the steam valve to VENTING to release remaining pressure. Unlock and carefully open the lid. Stir to mix.
6. If you want a thick sauce, stir in 1 teaspoon arrowroot starch with 1 tablespoon water.
7. Press the SAUTÉ key of the Instant Pot.
8. Add the arrowroot starch mixture into the pot and cook until thick to preferred thickness.
9. Turn the Instant Pot off.
10. Serve garnished with green onions.

Nutritional Info (per serving): Calories - 531; Fat – 24.1; Fiber – 2; Carbs – 9; Protein – 68

Chicken Rogan Josh Curry

(Prep + Cook Time: 60 minutes | Servings: 8)

Ingredients:

- 5-pounds boneless, skinless chicken thighs
- 1/3 pound curry paste
- 1 ½ cups Greek Yogurt
- 1 tbsp vegetable oil
- 1 onion – cut into wedges
- 2 coarsely chopped large tomatoes
- 4 ounces baby spinach leaves
- 4 ounces coriander leaves

Directions:

1. First, combine the yogurt and the curry paste in a large bowl.
2. Add the chicken and toss to coat.
3. The chicken should be completely coated in the yogurt and curry mixture.
4. Leave the chicken in the bowl and cover with plastic wrap. Place the bowl in your refrigerator for about 30 minutes.
5. Heat the vegetable oil in your pressure cooker.
6. Add the onion and cook until it is golden brown. This should take about 8 to 10 minutes.
7. Add the onion and the diced tomatoes to the marinated chicken.
8. Combine the ingredients and then pour into the pressure cooker.
9. Close the lid to your pressure cooker and bring to high heat with heat pressure. Cook for 15 minutes.
10. Allow the pressure to release naturally and then serve over rice or steamed vegetables.

Nutritional Info (per serving): Calories - 423; Fat – 15.3; Fiber – 6.9; Carbs – 13.7; Protein – 58.4

Fall Off The Bone Chicken Half An Hour

(Prep + Cook Time: 45 minutes | Servings: 10)

Ingredients:

- 1 whole chicken, about
- 4 pounds, preferably organic
- 1 ½ cups chicken bone broth
- 1 tbsp coconut oil, organic virgin
- 1 tsp dried thyme
- 1 tsp paprika
- ½ tsp sea salt
- ¼ tsp black pepper, fresh ground
- 2 tbsp fresh squeezed lemon juice
- 6 cloves garlic, peeled

Directions:

1. In a small-sized bowl, combine the pepper, salt, thyme, and paprika. Rub the outside of the chicken with the spice mix.
2. Press the SAUTÉ key of the Instant Pot. Put the oil in the pot and heat until shimmering.
3. With the breast side faced down, put the chicken in the pot and cook for 6-7 minutes. Rotate the chicken.
4. Add the broth, garlic cloves, and lemon juice. Cover and lock the lid.
5. Press the MANUAL key, set the pressure to HIGH, and set the timer for 25 minutes.
6. When the timer beeps, let the pressure release naturally. Turn the steam valve to VENTING to release any remaining pressure. Carefully open the lid.
7. Transfer the chicken into a large plate and let stand for 5 minutes. Carve and serve.

Nutritional Info (per serving): Calories - 297; Fat – 7.2; Fiber – 0; Carbs – 1.1; Protein – 53.5

8-Ingredient Chicken Dinner

(Prep + Cook Time: 45 minutes | Servings: 4)

Ingredients:

- 2 pounds boneless chicken thighs
- ¼ cup coconut oil
- ¼ cup coconut aminos (or soy sauce)
- ¼ cup honey
- 3 tbsp organic ketchup
- 2 tsp garlic powder
- 1 ½ tsp sea salt
- ½ tsp black pepper

Directions:

1. Put everything in your Instant Pot. Stir, so the chicken becomes completely coated. Close and seal the lid.
2. Press MANUAL and adjust time to 18 minutes. For frozen chicken, 40 minutes.
3. When time is up, hit CANCEL and quick-release.
4. Take out the chicken and hit SAUTE.
5. Simmer for 5 minutes until the sauce has thickened nicely.
6. Serve with a vegetable side dish!

Nutritional Info (per serving): Calories - 457; Fat – 23; Fiber – 0; Carbs – 21; Protein – 44

Crack Chicken

(Prep + Cook Time: 40 minutes | Servings: 4)

Ingredients:

- 8 ounces cream cheese
- 6-8 bacon slices, cooked
- 4 ounces cheddar cheese
- 3 tbsp cornstarch
- 2 pounds chicken breast, boneless
- 1 packet ranch seasoning
- 1 cup water

Directions:

1. Put the chicken breasts and cream cheese in the Instant Pot. Sprinkle the top of the chicken and cream cheese with the ranch seasoning.
2. Pour in 1 cup of water. Cover and lock the lid.
3. Press the MANUAL key, set the pressure to HIGH, and set the timer for 25 minutes.
4. When the Instant Pot timer beeps, turn the steam valve to VENTING to quick release the pressure.
5. Carefully open the lid. Transfer the chicken into a large plate and shred the meat.
6. Press the SAUTÉ key of the Instant Pot and select LESS. Whisk in the cornstarch.
7. Add the cheese and the shredded chicken into the pot. Stir in the bacon. Serve.

Nutritional Info (per serving): Calories - 834; Fat – 48; Fiber – 0; Carbs – 8.2; Protein – 87.7

Chipotle Chicken, Rice, And Black Beans

(Prep + Cook Time: 30 minutes | Servings: 6)

Ingredients:

- 1 onion, small-sized, chopped
- 1 can black beans, organic, drained and rinsed
- 1 cup Jasmine Rice, uncooked
- 1 pound chicken thighs or breasts, boneless, skinless, cut into bite sized pieces
- 1 tbsp chipotle peppers, in adobo sauce
- ½ cup water, filtered
- ½ lime, juiced
- ½ tsp black pepper, finely ground
- 2 tbsp butter, ghee, or coconut oil
- 2 tsp real salt, OR sea salt
- 4 cups diced tomatoes in juice

Directions:

1. Put the chicken, butter, pepper, salt, rice, lime juice, water, chipotle peppers, tomatoes with its juices, and onion in the Instant Pot, stir and combine. Cover and lock the lid.
2. Press the MANUAL key, set the pressure to HIGH, and set the timer for 6 minutes.
3. When the Instant Pot timer beeps, press the CANCEL key and unplug the Instant Pot. Turn the steam valve to quick release the pressure.
4. Unlock and carefully open the lid.
5. Add the black beans into the pot and stir to combine.
6. Taste and, if needed, season with pepper and salt to taste.
7. Divide between serving bowls and garnish each serving with sour cream, shredded cheese, and guacamole.

Nutritional Info (per serving): Calories - 551; Fat – 7.9; Fiber – 14; Carbs – 78.4; Protein – 40.8

Lemon And Garlic Chicken

(Prep + Cook Time: 25 minutes | Servings: 4)

Ingredients:

- 1 lemon, large-sized, juiced, or more to taste
- 1 onion, diced
- 1 tbsp avocado oil, OR ghee, OR lard
- 1 tsp dried parsley
- 1 tsp sea salt
- ½ cup chicken broth, organic or homemade
- ¼ cup white cooking wine
- ¼ tsp paprika
- 1-2 pounds chicken, thighs or breasts
- 3-4 tsp arrowroot flour, or more
- 5 garlic cloves, minced

Directions:

1. Press the SAUTE key of the Instant Pot. Put the cooking fat and the diced onion into the pot.
2. Cook for about 5 minutes or until the onions are softened, or you can cook until they begin to brown.
3. Except for the arrowroot flour, add the rest of the ingredients into the pot. Cover and lock the lid.
4. Press the POULTRY key let cook on preset cooking time.
5. When the Instant Pot timer beeps, press the CANCEL key and unplug the Instant Pot.
6. Turn the steam valve to quick release the pressure. Unlock and carefully open the lid.
7. If you want a thick sauce, remove about 1/4 cup of the sauce, add the arrowroot flour in the cup and stir to make slurry.
8. Pour the slurry back into the pot. Stir until thicken. Serve immediately.

Nutritional Info (per serving): Calories - 539; Fat – 23.7; Fiber – 0; Carbs – 4.5; Protein – 67.7

Garlic-Ginger Drumsticks

(Prep + Cook Time: 45 minutes | Servings: 4)

Ingredients:

- 6-8 chicken drumsticks, skin on

For the sauce:

- 2 tbsp rice wine vinegar
- 2 tbsp honey
- 2 tbsp brown sugar
- 2 cloves garlic, minced
- ¼ cup water
- ½ onion, chopped
- ½ cup soy sauce
- 1 tsp fresh ginger, minced

Directions:

1. In a bowl, mix all of the sauce ingredients until well combined. Pour the sauce in the Instant Pot.
2. Add the chicken in the pot and push them down to submerge them in the sauce – they do not have to be covered completely with sauce. Cover and lock the lid.
3. Press the MANUAL key, set the pressure to HIGH, and set the timer for 15 minutes.
4. When the Instant Pot timer beeps, let the pressure release naturally for 15 minutes. Turn the steam valve to release remaining pressure. Unlock and carefully open the lid.
5. Press the SAUTE key and boil until the sauce is reduced.
6. Remove the drumsticks and transfer them into a parchment paper lined cookie sheet.
7. Broil each side of the chicken for 2 minutes.
8. Meanwhile, let the sauce cook in the Instant Pot until reduced more.
9. Remove the chicken from the oven and put on a serving platter.
10. Pour the sauce over the chicken. Serve and enjoy!

Nutritional Info (per serving): Calories - 236; Fat – 5.3; Fiber – 0.7; Carbs – 17.6; Protein – 27.6

Thai Inspired Peanut Chicken And Noodles

(Prep + Cook Time: 55 minutes | Servings: 6)

Ingredients:

- 1 ½ pounds chicken breasts, boneless, skinless
- 1 cup snow peas or sugar snap
- 1 cup Thai peanut sauce
- ¾ cup chicken broth
- 5 ounces stir-fry rice noodles

Optional garnishes:

- Peanuts, chopped
- Cilantro Green onions
- Red pepper flakes

Directions:

1. Put the chicken in the Instant Pot. Pour in the broth and add the peanut sauce. Cover and lock the lid.
2. Press the MANUAL key, set the pressure to HIGH, and set the timer for 8 minutes.
3. When the Instant Pot timer beeps, turn the steam valve to VENTING to quick release the pressure. Unlock and carefully open the lid.
4. Remove the chicken from the pot, leaving the sauce in the pot.
5. Add the noodles in the pot, making sure that all the noodles are submerged in the sauce.
6. Top with the peas. Quickly close and lock the lid of the pot.
7. Press the SLOW COOK key and set the timer for 10 minutes, cook until the noodles are soft but still firm.
8. Meanwhile, shred the chicken breast. Set aside.
9. When the cooking time is up, open the lid and stir the noodles.
10. Add the shredded chicken into the pot. Lock the lid and cook on SLOW COOK mode for 10 minutes more.
11. Serve warm.

Nutritional Info (per serving): Calories - 645; Fat – 27.2; Fiber – 4.8; Carbs – 43.1; Protein – 51

Cordon Blue Chicken Casserole

(Prep + Cook Time: 50 minutes | Servings: 8)

Ingredients:

- 1 cup panko bread crumbs
- 1 pound chicken breast, boneless, skinless, sliced into thin strips
- 1 pound ham, cubed
- 1 tbsp spicy mustard
- 16 ounces Rotini pasta
- 16 ounces Swiss cheese
- 2 cups chicken broth
- 2 tbsp butter
- 8 ounces Gouda cheese
- 8 ounces heavy cream

Directions:

1. Put the uncooked pasta in the Instant Pot. Cover the pasta with 2 cups of chicken broth.
2. Put the chicken strips and ham cubes on top. Cover and lock the lid.
3. Press the MANUAL key, set the pressure to HIGH, and set the timer for 25 minutes.
4. When the Instant Pot timer beeps, press the CANCEL key and unplug the Instant Pot. Turn the steam valve to quick release the pressure. Unlock and carefully open the lid.
5. Pour the mustard and heavy cream in the pot. Add both the cheeses in the pot and stir until smooth and creamy. In a small-sized pan, add the butter and melt.
6. When the butter is melted, add the bread crumbs and stir for about 2 to 3 minutes or until golden and toasty.
7. Serve the pasta mixture sprinkled with the toasted bread on top.

Nutritional Info (per serving): Calories - 779; Fat – 45; Fiber – 1.4; Carbs – 47.6; Protein – 44.9

Fresh Chicken Salad
(Prep + Cook Time: 35 minutes | Servings: 6)

Ingredients:
- 1 whole piece of chicken
- 1 cup of water
- 1 cup of sour cream
- 1 tsp of garlic powder
- 1 tsp of black pepper
- 3 cup of baby spinach
- 3 diced up tomatoes
- 1 sliced up avocado

Directions:
1. The first step is to open up the lid of your Instant Pot and pour in water in your inner pot. Toss in your chicken.
2. Set the Instant Pot on POULTRY mode and let it cook at HIGH pressure for about 30 minutes.
3. While that is being cooked, prepare your salad by taking a bowl and toss in the tomatoes, spinach, avocado and finely mix it.
4. Toss in your sour cream alongside garlic powder, sprinkled with black pepper.
5. By this time, the chicken should be ready.
6. Open up your Instant Pot and bring it out, only to cut it finely.
7. Once cut up, pour in your dressing and serve it warm over your prepared salad.

Nutritional Info (per serving): Calories - 417; Fat – 31; Carbs – 2.55; Protein – 29

Curry In a Hurry
(Prep + Cook Time: 25 minutes | Servings: 6)

Ingredients:
- 2 pounds chicken breast or thighs
- 2 tbsp curry powder
- 3 tbsp honey
- 6 ounces can tomato paste
- 2 cloves garlic, minced
- 16 ounces canned tomato sauce
- 16 ounces canned coconut milk
- 1 tsp salt
- 1 cup onion, chopped OR
- ¼ cup dry minced onion

Directions:

1. Except for the chicken, put all of the ingredients into the Instant Pot.
2. Stir to combine and then add the chicken. Cover and lock the lid.
3. Press the MANUAL key, set the pressure to HIGH, and set the timer for 15 minutes.
4. When the Instant Pot timer beeps, press the CANCEL key and unplug the Instant Pot. Let the pressure release naturally for 10-15 minutes or until the valve drops. Turn the steam valve to release remaining pressure.
5. Unlock and carefully open the lid. Serve with rice and/ or peas.

Nutritional Info (per serving): Calories - 319; Fat – 20.8; Fiber – 5.1; Carbs – 25.6; Protein – 12.9

Picadillo Pizza
(Prep + Cook Time: 50 minutes | Servings: 4)

Ingredients:
- 1 cup salsa
- 1 piece (about 17.75-ounces) pizza crust (already made or dough that is ready to bake)
- 1 tbsp cilantro, chopped
- ½ cup dried cranberries
- ½ cup green olives, chopped
- ¼ cup onion, chopped
- ¼ tsp ground cinnamon
- ¼ tsp ground cumin
- 2 chicken breasts, boneless, skinless
- 2 cups Monterey Jack cheese, shredded

Directions:
1. Put the chicken breast in the Instant Pot and add 1/2-1 cup water. Cover and lock the lid.
2. Press the POULTRY key and set the timer for 5 minutes.
3. While the chicken is cooking, prepare your pizza dough and the ingredients that need to be chopped.
4. When the Instant Pot timer beeps, press the CANCEL key and unplug the Instant Pot. Turn the steam valve to quick release the pressure.

5. Unlock and carefully open the lid. Remove the chicken from the pot and shred or chop.
6. Mix the salsa with the cinnamon and cumin. Spread the salsa mixture over the prepared crust.
7. Sprinkle 1 cup shredded Monterey Jack cheese over the salsa.
8. Sprinkle with the chicken, cried cranberries, green olives, and onions.
9. Top with the remaining cheese and then sprinkle the top with cilantro.
10. Bake in a preheated 400F oven for 15 minutes. When baked, remove the pizza from the oven, slice, and serve.

Notes: The olives are fabulous on this pizza. You can also add sliced or slivered almonds on top to add a delightful crunch on your pizza.

Nutritional Info (per serving): Calories - 785; Fat – 31.2; Fiber – 4.4; Carbs – 67.9; Protein – 57.7

Turkey Verde and Rice
(Prep + Cook Time: 35 minutes | Servings: 4)

Ingredients:
2/3 cup chicken broth
1 ½ pounds turkey tenderloins (I used Jennie-O)
1 ¼ cup long grain brown rice
1 yellow onion, small-sized, sliced
½ cup salsa verde
½ tsp salt

Directions:
1. Put the rice in the Instant Pot. Pour in the broth.
2. Top the mix with the onion, turkey, and then the salsa. Sprinkle with the salt.
3. Cover and lock the lid. Press the MANUAL key, set the pressure to HIGH, and set the timer for 8 minutes.
4. When the Instant Pot timer beeps, let the pressure release naturally for 8 minutes. Turn the steam valve to release remaining pressure. Unlock and carefully open the lid.
5. Garnish each serving with fresh cilantro.

Nutritional Info (per serving): Calories - 421; Fat – 4.1; Fiber – 2.7; Carbs – 49.2; Protein – 48.1

Turkey Drumsticks

(Prep + Cook Time: 40 minutes | Servings: 5)

Ingredients:

- 6 turkey drumsticks
- 2 tsp brown sugar, packed tight
- ½ tsp garlic powder
- ½ cup water
- ½ cup soy sauce
- 1 tsp black pepper, fresh ground
- 1 tbsp kosher salt

Directions:

1. In a small-sized bowl, combine the garlic powder, pepper, brown sugar, and salt, breaking any clump of sugar.
2. Season the turkey drumsticks with the seasoning mix. Pour the water in the Instant Pot. Add the soy sauce.
3. Add the seasoned drumsticks with any remaining seasoning mix.
4. Cover and lock the lid. Press the MANUAL key, set the pressure to HIGH, and set the timer for 25 minutes.
5. When the Instant Pot timer beeps, let the pressure release naturally for 15 minutes. Turn the steam valve to release remaining pressure. Unlock and carefully open the lid.
6. Using tongs, carefully transfer the drumsticks into a serving plate – be very careful because the drumsticks are cooked to fall-off-the-bone tender.
7. If you have time, pour the cooking liquid into a fat strainer. Let the fat float to the top.
8. Pass the defatted cooking liquid at the table as a sauce.

Notes: If you want crispy turkey skin, brush the drumsticks with the cooking liquid and broil them until browned. This dish was cooked in a 6-quart Instant Pot. If the turkey legs are short, then you can stack them in the pot without any trouble. Longer turkey legs will take some working out. You may have to stack them like a jigsaw puzzle. Don't worry about the max fill line. You can stack them in the pot as long as you can close and lock the lid afterwards. The cooking liquid is also delicious with baked potatoes.

Nutritional Info (per serving): Calories - 209; Fat – 0; Fiber – 0; Carbs – 3; Protein – 34.6

Turkey Legs With Gravy

(Prep + Cook Time: 45 minutes | Servings: 4)

Ingredients:

- 2 pieces turkey legs
- 1 cup chicken stock, homemade, unsalted
- 1 dash sherry wine
- 1 onion, small-sized, sliced
- 1 pinch rosemary
- 1 pinch thyme
- 1 stalk celery, chopped
- 1 tbsp light soy sauce
- 1 tbsp olive oil
- 2 bay leaves
- 3 cloves garlic, roughly minced
- Kosher salt and ground black pepper, to taste

Directions:

1. Generously season the turkey legs with salt and pepper. Press the SAUTÉ key of the Instant Pot and select the MORE option.
2. Wait for the indicator to show HOT. When the pot is hot, put in the 1 tablespoon olive oil, making sure the bottom of the pot is coated. Add the turkey legs into the pot. Cook or about 2 to 3 minutes each side or until browned.
3. Transfer onto a plate. Set aside until ready to use. Press the CANCEL key to the sauté function and then press the SAUTE function again to set the heat MEDIUM. Stir in the onion in the pot.
4. Season with a pinch of salt and pepper and cook for 1 minute or until the onion is soft.
5. Add the garlic and sauté for about 30 seconds or until fragrant.
6. Add the celery and sauté for 1 minute. If desired, season with another pinch of salt and pepper.
7. Add the bay leaves. Slightly scrunch the thyme and the rosemary and then add them in the pot. Stir to combine.

8. Pour in 1 dash wine to deglaze the pot, scraping any browned bit off the bottom using a wooden spoon. Let cook until the alcohol is evaporated.
9. Add the stock. Stir in the soy sauce. Taste and, if needed, season to taste with salt and pepper. Press CANCEL to stop the sauté function. Cover and lock the lid.
10. Press the MANUAL key, set the pressure to HIGH, and set the timer for 18 or 20 minutes. When the Instant Pot timer beeps, let the pressure release naturally for 10 minutes. Turn the steam valve to VENTING to quick release the pressure. Unlock and carefully open the lid.
11. Remove the turkey legs. If desired, filter the turkey gravy.
12. If you want a thicker sauce, mix 3 tablespoons cornstarch with 1 tablespoon water. Pour about 1/ 3 of the mixture at a time into the pot until the sauce reaches your desired thickness.

Nutritional Info (per serving): Calories - 295; Fat – 13.1; Fiber – 1.7; Carbs – 8.4; Protein – 35.1

Stuffed Turkey Tenderloin

(Prep + Cook Time: 30 minutes | Servings: 6)

Ingredients:
- 2 turkey breast tenderloins
- 2 cups white rice
- 2 bacon slices, diced
- 1-2 sprigs fresh rosemary, optional
- ½ cup dry white wine
- 1 tsp fresh rosemary, chopped
- 1 cup fresh cranberries
- 1 ½ cups butternut squash, diced, frozen or fresh
- 3 ½ cups chicken broth OR water

Directions:

1. Press the SAUTE key of the Instant Pot.
2. Add the bacon in the pot and sauté until some of the fat rendered and the edges start to crisp.
3. Add the squash and cranberries, along with the rosemary. Sauté until the edges of the squash are golden and the bacon is crisp. Turn the Instant Pot off.
4. Butterfly the turkey tenderloins by slicing them gently lengthwise, going almost all the way through the other edge, making sure to leave the other edge intact. Open the tenderloins like a butterfly.
5. When the butternut mix is cooked, gently spoon the mix into the center of each butterflied turkey. Fold the tenderloin back.
6. Weave a rosemary sprig through the open edge of the tenderloin to seal. Alternatively, you can use a cooking twine. Press the SAUTÉ key of the Instant Pot.
7. When the pot is hot, cook the tenderloins for about 3 to 4 minutes per side or until both sides are golden.
8. Remove the browned tenderloins from the pot.
9. Add the rice in the pot and sauté for about 1 to 2 minutes or just until the rice begins to smell nutty.
10. Add the white wine in the pot to deglaze, stirring and scraping the browned bits off the bottom using a wooden spoon.
11. Add the broth and water in the pot. Place the stuffed tenderloin on top of the rice.
12. If desired, add the rosemary sprigs in the pot. Cover and lock the lid. Press the RICE key.
13. When the Instant Pot timer beeps, release the pressure naturally for 10 minutes.
14. Turn the steam valve to VENTING to release remaining pressure. Unlock and carefully open the lid. Remove the rosemary sprigs and then slice the tenderloin. Serve.

Nutritional Info (per serving): Calories - 447; Fat – 5.5; Fiber – 2.5; Carbs – 56.7; Protein – 38.1

Turkey-Stuffed Bell Peppers

(Prep + Cook Time: 35 minutes | Servings: 4)

Ingredients:

- 1 pound ground turkey
- 4 big bell peppers (red or green)
- One 4 1/2 -ounce can of mild green chiles
- 1 cup shredded sharp cheddar cheese
- 1 chopped yellow onion
- ½ cup corn kernels
- 2 tbsp butter
- 2 tsp minced garlic
- 1 tsp ground cumin
- 1 tsp dried oregano
- 1 cup water
- ¼ tsp salt
- ¼ tsp (or less) cayenne

Directions:

1. Melt the butter in your Instant Pot on the SAUTE setting.
2. Cook the onion until it becomes soft in about 3 minutes.
3. Add the ground turkey, breaking it up with a spatula, and cook for 3 minutes.
4. Add cayenne, garlic, oregano, cumin, and salt.
5. After half a minute of stirring, move everything to a large bowl to cool for 20 minutes.
6. Stir in the corn, cheese, and chiles into the turkey.
7. Prep your peppers by cutting off the tops and scraping out the seeds. Stuff the peppers with the turkey filling.
8. Wipe the inside of the cooker with a paper towel and lower in the steamer rack.
9. Pour in 1 cup of water and arrange the peppers on top of the rack. Lock and seal the lid.
10. Hit MANUAL and cook for 7 minutes on HIGH pressure.
11. When the timer beeps, turn off the cooker and quick-release. Serve!

Nutritional Info (per serving): Calories - 371; Fat – 18; Fiber – 2; Carbs – 17; Protein – 35

Whole Turkey with Apricot Glaze

(Prep + Cook Time: 1 hour | Servings: 8)

Ingredients:

- 9 ½ pound turkey
- 1 cup chicken stock
- 1 peeled and diced onion
- 1 diced carrot
- 5-ounces apricot jam
- 1 tsp salt
- 1 tsp black pepper
- ½ tsp cumin
- ½ tsp coriander
- ½ tsp turmeric

Directions:

1. Mix the jam, pepper, cumin, coriander, and turmeric together.
2. Rinse the bird and pat dry. Rub the glaze all over the turkey.
3. Pour broth and veggies into the pot, before putting the turkey on top. Close and seal the lid.
4. Select POULTRY and adjust time to 30 minutes.
5. When time is up, hit CANCEL and wait for a natural release.
6. Remove the turkey and serve!

Nutritional Info (per serving): Calories - 880; Fat – 19; Fiber – 0; Carbs – 101; Protein – 101

Tomato Sauce Turkey Meatballs

(Prep + Cook Time: 40 minutes | Servings: 4)

Ingredients:

- 1 pound ground turkey, 93 % lean
- 1 jar (24-ounce) of your preferred pasta sauce
- 1 onion, medium-sized, diced
- 1 tsp Italian Seasoning (I used Penzey's Pasta Sprinkle)
- 1 tsp kosher salt
- ½ cup rice, long grain
- ½ cup water
- 2 tbsp fresh basil, chopped, optional
- 2 tbsp olive oil
- 2 zucchini, medium-sized, sliced
- 8 ounces cremini mushrooms, sliced

Directions:

1. Press the SAUTE key of the Instant Pot. Add the oil and onions; sauté for about 5 minutes or until the onions are soft.
2. Add the mushrooms and zucchini; sauté for about 3 minutes or until the mushrooms start to soften and release some of their liquid.
3. Add the water and pasta sauce in the pot. Stir well to combine.
4. While waiting for the sauce to simmer, form meatballs. In a medium-sized mixing bowl, combine the ground turkey with the rice, salt, and Italian herbs.
5. Combine well and then roll the mixture into 1 dozen meatballs that are just slightly larger than a golf ball.
6. Drop the meatballs gently into the simmering sauce into the Instant Pot. Spoon some sauce over the top of each meatball. Press the CANCEL key to stop the sauté function. Cover and lock the lid.
7. Press the POULTRY key.
8. When the Instant Pot timer beeps, turn the steam valve to VENTING to quick release the pressure. Unlock and carefully open the lid. Serve topped with fresh basil.
9. Serve over spaghetti squash.

Notes: To make a spaghetti squash, slice a spaghetti squash lengthwise. With the cut side faced down, put on a microwavable baking dish; microwave for 5 minutes. If the squash is not easily pierced using a fork, microwave for 2 to 5 minutes more or until fork soft. Let cool enough to handle, turn over, and scoop out the spaghetti squash strands with a fork.

Nutritional Info (per serving): Calories - 544; Fat – 24.8; Fiber – 6.4; Carbs – 47.9; Protein – 37.2

Mustard Beer Pulled Turkey

(Prep + Cook Time: 65 minutes | Servings: 4)

Ingredients:

- 2 pieces (1¼ to 1½ -pound each) turkey thighs, bone-in, skin removed
- 1 bottle (12-ounce) dark beer, preferably a porter
- 1 tbsp mustard, whole-grain
- 1 tbsp tomato paste, canned variety
- 1 tsp dry mustard
- 1 tsp ground black pepper
- 1 tsp salt
- ½ tsp garlic powder
- 2 tbsp apple cider vinegar
- 2 tbsp packed dark brown sugar
- 2 tsp ground coriander

Directions:

1. In a small-sized bowl, mix the coriander with the garlic powder, pepper, salt, and dry mustard.
2. Rub the seasoning mix all over the turkey thighs thoroughly and evenly coating them.
3. Pour the beer into the Instant Pot. Nestle the seasoned turkey thighs in the beer. Cover and lock the lid.

4. Press the MANUAL key, set the pressure to HIGH, and set the timer for 45 minutes.
5. When the Instant Pot timer beeps, turn the steam valve to quick release the pressure. Unlock and carefully open the lid.
6. Transfer the turkey onto a chopping board and let cool for a couple minutes.
7. Remove the bones and save to make bone broth. Chop the meat into small pieces. Press the SAUTE key of the Instant Pot.
8. Bring the liquid to a simmer and cook for about 4 minutes until reduced by half.
9. Stir in the tomato paste, mustard, vinegar, and brown sugar until the sauce is smooth, cooking for 1 minute and stirring all the time.
10. Add the turkey pieces into the pot and stir well to combine.
11. Turn off the Instant Pot and wait until the turkey is heated through.

Nutritional Info (per serving): Calories - 560; Fat – 15.3; Fiber – 0.9; Carbs – 10.1; Protein – 84.6

Marsala Turkey with Mushrooms

(Prep + Cook Time: 45 minutes | Servings: 4)

Ingredients:

- 1 ¼ pounds boneless, skinless turkey breasts
- 6 ounces sliced white mushrooms
- 3 tbsp chopped shallots
- 3 tbsp heavy cream
- 2 tbsp olive oil
- 1 minced garlic clove
- ⅔ cup chicken stock
- ⅓ cup dry Marsala wine
- 1 ½ tbsp cornstarch
- ½ tsp dried thyme
- Salt and pepper to taste

Directions:

1. Trim the turkey and cut away the sinews, which are silver-colored.
2. With string, tie the roasts crosswise every 2 inches. Season with salt and pepper.
3. In your cooker, heat 1 tablespoon of oil and when hot, brown the breasts on both sides for 3 minutes. Move to a plate.
4. Pour in the rest of the oil and cook shallots, thyme, garlic, and mushrooms.
5. When mushrooms are softening, add the turkey back into the cooker. Pour in wine and broth. Close and seal the lid.
6. Select MANUAL and cook on HIGH pressure for 15-20 minutes.
7. When time is up, turn off the cooker and quick-release.
8. Turkey should be 160-degrees. If cooked through, tent with foil on a carving board.
9. Turn the cooker back on to SAUTE and bring to a boil. In a small bowl, mix cornstarch and heavy cream until smooth.
10. Pour into cooker and let the sauce thicken.
11. Season with more salt and pepper and move sauce to a serving bowl.
12. Cut the string off the roasts and slice into ½-inch pieces. Serve with sauce!

Nutritional Info (per serving): Calories - 192; Fat – 5; Fiber – 1; Carbs – 5; Protein – 15

Thanksgiving Turkey Casserole

(Prep + Cook Time: 45 minutes | Servings: 4)

Ingredients:

- 4 turkey breasts, boneless (about 2 pounds), or chicken breasts
- 2 small-sized cans cream of mushroom soup
- 1 stalk celery
- 1 onion, sliced
- 1 cup chicken broth
- 1 bag Pepperidge farms stuffing cubes
- 1 bag frozen mixed veggies

Directions:

1. Put the turkey breasts in the Instant Pot.
2. Add the broth, mixed vegetables, celery, and onion. Cover and lock the lid. Press the MANUAL key, set the pressure to HIGH, and set the timer for 25 minutes. Alternatively, you can press the POULTRY setting and adjust the timer for 25 minutes.
3. When the Instant Pot timer beeps, turn the steam valve to quick release the pressure. Unlock and carefully open the lid.
4. Add the stuffing cubes in the pot on top of the cooked mix. Pour in the cream of mushroom soup.
5. Press the SAUTE key and cook for 8 minutes.
6. Press CANCEL to stop the sauté function. Shred the turkey breast right in the pot. Serve.

Nutritional Info (per serving): Calories - 650; Fat – 20.1; Fiber – 7.2; Carbs – 66.6; Protein – 48.7

Ducks Legs in Orange Sauce

(Prep + Cook Time: 60 minutes | Servings: 4)

Ingredients:

- 4 duck legs
- 3 chopped garlic cloves
- ½ cup dry white wine
- ¼ cup chopped celery
- ¼ cup chopped shallots
- ¼ cup chopped carrot
- ¼ cup triple sec
- 2 tbsp chopped parsley

- 2 tbsp sherry vinegar
- Juice and zest from 1 orange
- ½ tbsp olive oil
- ½ tsp salt
- ⅛ tsp sage
- ⅛ tsp thyme
- Salt and pepper to taste

Directions:

1. Rinse the duck legs before patting dry and seasoning with pepper. Turn your Instant Pot to SAUTE and add oil.
2. When hot, brown legs all over, starting with the skin first. When golden, plate legs for now.
3. Get rid of any extra duck fat before adding celery, garlic, shallots, and carrot to the pot.
4. Cook for just a few minutes before pouring in triple sec, white wine, salt, sage, and thyme.
5. Sprinkle in ⅓ of the orange zest.
6. When the liquid is boiling, return the duck legs. Close and seal the lid.
7. Select MANUAL and cook on HIGH pressure for 45 minutes.
8. When the beeper sounds, turn off the cooker and quick-release the pressure.
9. Take out the legs and tent to keep them warm.
10. Add the rest of the zest to your pot and using a hand blender, puree the contents.
11. Pour in orange juice, vinegar, and salt and pepper. Add parsley and serve!

Nutritional Info (per serving): Calories - 531; Fat – 35; Fiber – 1; Carbs – 37; Protein – 35

Duck Fat Risotto

(Prep + Cook Time: 25 minutes | Servings: 4)

Ingredients:
- 4 cups warm chicken broth
- 2 cups Arborio rice
- ½ cup white wine
- 8-ounces sliced white mushrooms
- 4-ounces chopped prosciutto
- 3 tbsp duck fat
- 2 tbsp chopped shallot
- 2 minced garlic cloves
- 1 tbsp orange zest
- 1 tbsp chopped parsley
- Salt and pepper to taste

Directions:
1. Turn your Instant Pot to SAUTE and melt the duck fat until it's fragrant.
2. Add shallot and cook for 3 minutes before adding garlic. Cook for another 30 seconds before tossing in mushrooms.
3. When they have softened a bit (it should take around 4 minutes), add the rice and stir.
4. Keep stirring until the rice has become toasty. Pour in the wine and stir until the wine is almost all evaporated.
5. Add broth and (still) keep stirring until well-combined.
6. Close and seal the pressure cooker lid. Select MANUAL and cook on HIGH pressure for 5 minutes.
7. When the timer beeps, hit CANCEL and quick-release. Take off the lid and hit SAUTE again.
8. Keep stirring for 3-5 minutes until the liquid is absorbed into the rice.
9. Serve with orange zest, parsley, prosciutto, salt, and pepper.

Nutritional Info (per serving): Calories - 437; Fat – 11; Fiber – 1; Carbs – 77; Protein – 8

Duck a L'Orange

(Prep + Cook Time: 1 hour 15 minutes | Servings: 4)

Ingredients:

- 2 halved duck breasts
- 2 halved duck legs
- 2 cups fresh orange juice
- 9 spring onions, green and white parts divided
- 3 tbsp fresh chopped ginger
- 2 tbsp fish sauce
- 2 tbsp white sugar
- 2 red chilies
- 1 whole star anise
- ½ tbsp dried lemongrass
- Black pepper to taste

Directions:

1. Turn your Instant Pot to SAUTE to heat up.
2. When hot, add duck skin-side down first and fry until the skin becomes crispy, and the fat has rendered out.
3. Skim out the fat, leaving a few tablespoons, and add garlic until it becomes fragrant.
4. Add the rest of the ingredients (minus spring onions). Put the duck back in the cooker. Close and seal the lid.
5. Hit MANUAL and cook on HIGH pressure for 30 minutes. Hit CANCEL when time is up, and let the pressure come down naturally.
6. Turn the cooker back to SAUTE. Add the white parts of the spring onion to the cooker and simmer until they've softened.
7. Take out the duck and skim out the layer of fat on the top.
8. Let the sauce keep simmering until it has become reduced and thick.
9. Serve duck with plenty of sauce and the green parts of the onion sprinkled on top.

Nutritional Info (per serving): Calories - 467; Fat – 23.7; Fiber – 1; Carbs – 6.4; Protein – 51

Hard-Boiled Eggs

(Prep + Cook Time: 9 minutes | Servings: 6)

Ingredients:
- 12 large white eggs
- 1 cup of water

Directions:
1. In the Instant Pot Pour down about 1 cup of water into the bowl.
2. Place stainless steamer basket inside the pot.
3. Place the eggs in the steamer basket.
4. Boil 7 minutes on manual HIGH pressure
5. Then release the pressure through the quick release valve.
6. Open up the lid and take out the eggs using tongs and dunk them into a bowl of cold water.

Soft-Boiled Egg

(Prep + Cook Time: 6 minutes | Servings: 2)

Ingredients:
- 4 eggs
- 1 cup of water
- Two toasted English muffins
- Salt and pepper to taste

Directions:
1. Pour 1 cup of water into the Instant Pot and insert the steamer basket. Put four canning lids into the basket before placing the eggs on top of them, so they stay separated.
2. Secure the lid.
3. Press the STEAM setting and choose 4 minutes.
4. When ready, quick-release the steam valve.
5. Take out the eggs using tongs and dunk them into a bowl of cold water.
6. Wait 1-2 minutes.
7. Peel and serve with one egg per half of a toasted English muffin.
8. Season with salt and pepper.

Delightful Soft Eggs

(Prep + Cook Time: 10 minutes | Servings: 4)

Ingredients:

- 3 eggs
- 6 oz ham
- 1 tsp salt
- ½ tsp ground white pepper
- 1 tsp paprika
- ¼ tsp ground ginger
- 2 tbsp chives

Directions:

1. Take the small ramekins and beat the eggs in them.
2. Sprinkle the eggs with the salt, ground black pepper, and paprika.
3. Transfer the ramekins to the Instant Pot and set the mode STEAM. Close the lid and cook the dish for 4 minutes.
4. Meanwhile, chop the ham and chives and combine the ingredients together.
5. Add ground ginger and stir the mixture carefully.
6. Transfer the mixture to the serving plates.
7. When the time is over – remove the eggs from the Instant Pot and put them over the ham mixture.
8. Serve the dish immediately. Enjoy!

Nutritional Info (per serving): Calories - 205; Fat – 11.1; Fiber – 1; Carbs – 6.47; Protein – 19

French Toast Bake

(Prep + Cook Time: 35 minutes | Servings: 4)

Ingredients:

- 3 big, beaten eggs
- 3 cups stale cinnamon-raisin bread, cut into cubes
- 1 ½ cups water
- 1 cup whole milk
- 2 tbsp maple syrup
- 1 tsp butter
- 1 tsp sugar
- 1 tsp pure vanilla extract

Directions:

1. Pour the water into your Instant Pot and lower in the steam rack.

2. Grease a 6-7 inch soufflé pan.
3. In a bowl, mix milk, vanilla, maple syrup, and eggs.
4. Add the bread cubes and let them soak for 5 minutes.
5. Pour into the pan, making sure the bread is totally submerged.
6. Set in the pressure cooker.
7. Hit MANUAL and adjust the time to 15 minutes on HIGH pressure
8. Quick-release the pressure when time is up.
9. Sprinkle the top with sugar and broil in the oven for 3 minutes.

Nutritional Info (per serving): Calories - 183; Fat – 3; Fiber – 0; Carbs – 21; Protein – 8

Poached Tomato Eggs
(Prep + Cook Time: 15 minutes | Servings: 4)

Ingredients:
- 4 eggs
- 3 medium tomatoes
- 1 red onion
- 1 tsp salt

- 1 tbsp olive oil
- ½ tsp white pepper
- ½ tsp paprika
- 1 tbsp fresh dill

Directions:
1. Spray the ramekins with the olive oil inside.
2. Beat the eggs in every ramekin.
3. Combine the paprika, white pepper, fresh dill, and salt together in the mixing bowl. Stir the mixture.
4. After this, chop the red onion.
5. Chop the tomatoes into the tiny pieces and combine them with the onion. Stir the mixture.
6. Then sprinkle the eggs with the tomato mixture.
7. Add spice mixture and transfer the eggs to the Instant Pot.
8. Close the lid and set the Instant Pot mode STEAM.
9. Cook the dish for 5 minutes. Then remove the dish from the Instant Pot and chill it little.
10. Serve the dish immediately. Enjoy!

Nutritional Info (per serving): Calories - 194; Fat – 13.5; Fiber – 2; Carbs – 8.45; Protein – 10

Poached Eggs With Ham and Hollandaise Sauce

(Prep + Cook Time: 10 minutes | Servings: 2)

Ingredients:

- 2 eggs
- 2 tbsp water
- 2-3 slices ham
- 2 tbsp hollandaise sauce

Equipment:

- 2 glass egg poachers or small ramekins

Directions:

1. Crack an egg into each poachers, making sure the yolks stay intact.
2. Add 1 tablespoon water into each. Place the egg poachers into a handy rack. Put into the Instant Pot.
3. Pour water into the bottom of the Instant Pot, making sure the water does not touch the rack or the poachers.
4. Set the timer for 2 minutes on steam. When the timer beeps, open for quick release.
5. When the Instant Pot is depressurized, open it and take out the poachers; scoop the eggs out from the poachers, leaving the water out.
6. Put the slices into the handy rack.
7. If the hollandaise sauce is cold, put about 2 tablespoons into a small ramekin.
8. Set the timer to zero on steam; this will heat both the sauce and the slices of ham.
9. Serve the poached eggs with the ham and the sauce.

Nutritional Info (per serving): Calories - 271; Fat – 16.2; Fiber – 1.1; Carbs – 5.2; Protein – 25.3

Scrambled Eggs

(Prep + Cook Time: 15 minutes | Servings: 4)

Ingredients:

- 7 eggs
- ½ cup milk
- 1 tbsp butter
- 1 tsp basil
- ¼ cup fresh parsley
- 1 tsp salt
- 1 tsp paprika
- 4 oz bacon
- 1 tbsp cilantro

Directions:

1. Beat the eggs in the mixing bowl and whisk them well.
2. Then add milk, basil, salt, paprika, and cilantro. Stir the mixture. Chop the bacon and parsley.
3. Set the Instant Pot mode SAUTE and transfer the chopped bacon. Cook it for 3 minutes.
4. Then add whisked egg mixture and cook the dish for 5 minutes more.
5. After this, mix up the eggs carefully with the help of the wooden spoon.
6. Then sprinkle the dish with the chopped parsley and cook it for 4 minutes more.
7. When the eggs are cooked – remove them from the Instant Pot.
8. Serve the dish immediately. Enjoy!

Nutritional Info (per serving): Calories - 290; Fat – 23.4; Fiber – 1; Carbs – 4.53; Protein – 16

Aromatic Bacon Eggs

(Prep + Cook Time: 15 minutes | Servings: 4)

Ingredients:

- 7 oz bacon
- 4 eggs, boiled
- 1 tsp cilantro
- ½ cup spinach
- 2 tsp butter
- ½ tsp ground white pepper
- 3 tbsp cream

Directions:
1. Slice the bacon and sprinkle it with the ground white pepper, and cilantro. Stir the mixture.
2. Peel eggs and wrap them in the spinach leaves.
3. Then wrap the eggs in the sliced bacon.
4. Set the Instant Pot mode MEAT/STEW and transfer the wrapped eggs.
5. Add butter and cook the dish for 10 minutes.
6. When the time is over – remove the eggs from the Instant Pot and sprinkle them with the cream.
7. Serve the dish hot.

Nutritional Info (per serving): Calories - 325; Fat – 28.4; Fiber – 2; Carbs – 5.24; Protein – 15

Cheesy Sausage Frittata
(Prep + Cook Time: 45 minutes | Servings: 4)

Ingredients:
- 1 ½ cups water
- 4 beaten eggs
- ½ cup cooked ground sausage
- ¼ cup grated sharp cheddar
- 2 tbsp sour cream
- 1 tbsp butter
- Salt to taste
- Black pepper to taste

Directions:
1. Pour water into the Instant Pot and lower in the steamer rack.
2. Grease a 6-7 inch soufflé dish.
3. In a bowl, whisk the eggs and sour cream together.
4. Add cheese, sausage, salt, and pepper. Stir.
5. Pour into the dish and wrap tightly with foil all over.
6. Lower into the steam rack and close the pot lid.
7. Hit MANUAL and then 17 minutes on LOW pressure.
8. Quick-release the pressure. Serve hot!

Nutritional Info (per serving): Calories - 282; Fat – 12; Fiber – 0; Carbs – 1; Protein – 16

Savory Breakfast Egg Porridge

(Prep + Cook Time: 60 minutes | Servings: 4)

Ingredients:

- 2 cups chicken broth
- 2 cups water
- 4 eggs
- 4 chopped scallions
- ½ cup rinsed and drained white rice
- 1 tbsp sugar
- 1 tbsp olive oil
- 2 tsp soy sauce
- ½ tsp salt
- Black pepper

Directions:

1. Pour water, broth, sugar, salt, and rice into the Instant Pot. Close the lid.
2. Hit PORRIDGE and 30 minutes on HIGH pressure.
3. While that cooks, heat oil in a saucepan.
4. Crack in the eggs one at a time, so they aren't touching each other.
5. Cook until the whites become crispy on the edges, but the yolks are still runny. Sprinkle on salt and pepper.
6. When the Instant Pot timer goes off, hit CANCEL and wait for the pressure to go down on its own.
7. If the porridge isn't thick enough, hit SAUTE and cook uncovered for 5-10 minutes.
8. Serve with scallions, soy sauce, and an egg per bowl.

Nutritional Info (per serving): Calories - 214; Fat – 2; Fiber – 1; Carbs – 24; Protein – 10

Bacon and Cheese Egg Muffins

(Prep + Cook Time: 25 minutes | Servings: 8)

Ingredients:

- 4 eggs
- 4 slices bacon, cooked and crumbled
- 4 tbsp cheddar or pepper jack cheese, shredded
- 1 green onion, diced
- ¼ tsp lemon pepper seasoning
- 1 ½ cup water

Directions:

1. Pour the water into the Instant Pot container and then put a steamer basket into the pot. In a large-sized measuring bowl with a pour pout, break the eggs.
2. Add the lemon pepper and beat well. Divide the bacon, cheese, and green onion between 4 silicone muffin cups.
3. Pour the egg mix into each muffin cups; with a fork, stir using a fork to combine. Put the muffin cups onto the steamer basket, cover and lock the pot lid in place.
4. Set the pressure on HIGH pressure and the timer to 8 minutes.
5. When the timer beeps, turn off the pot, wait for 2 minutes, and then turn the steam valve to quick release the pressure. Carefully open the pot lid, lift the steamer basket out from the container, and then remove the muffin cups.
6. Serve immediately.

Notes: These muffins can be stored in the refrigerator for more than 1 week. When ready to serve, just microwave for 30 seconds on HIGH to reheat.

Nutritional Info (per serving): Calories - 127; Fat – 9.4; Fiber – 0; Carbs – 0.9; Protein – 9.7

Eggs En Cocotte

(Prep + Cook Time: 15 minutes | Servings: 4)

Ingredients:

- 3 eggs, pasture raised, fresh
- 3 tbsp cream
- 1 tbsp chives
- 1 cup water, for the pot
- Butter, at room temperature
- Sea salt and freshly ground pepper

Directions:

1. With a paper towel, wipe the bottoms and sides of 3 pieces 4-5 ounces ramekins with butter.
2. Pour 1 tablespoon cream into each ramekin.
3. Carefully crack 1 egg into each, making sure not to break the yolks, and then sprinkle with chives.
4. Pour the water into the bottom of the Instant Pot and then put a rack with handle or a trivet into the bottom of the pot.
5. Put the ramekins onto the rack. Close the lid and make sure the valve is closed.
6. Plug the pot, set to MANUAL, the pressure to LOW, and the timer to 2 minutes for runny yolks or 4 minutes for firm yolks. The pot will beep and the display ON. After a few minutes, the timer will display 2 minutes.
7. When the timer beeps, turn the steam valve to quick release the pressure and let the steam dissipate.
8. Carefully open the lid and with a kitchen towel or a hot pad, carefully remove the rack with the handle or, if using trivet, the ramekins.
9. Season the eggs en cocotte with salt and pepper. Enjoy as is or on toasts.

Notes: If you are cooking less than 3 eggs, fill the remaining ramekins with water, and put in the pot as well. Otherwise, the eggs will cook too fast.

Nutritional Info (per serving): Calories - 173; Fat – 16.6; Fiber – 0; Carbs – 0.8; Protein – 5.8

Spinach Tomato Crustless Quiche

(Prep + Cook Time: 35 minutes | Servings: 6)

Ingredients:

- 12 large eggs
- ¼ tsp fresh ground black pepper
- 3 cups fresh baby spinach, roughly chopped
- ¼ cup Parmesan cheese, shredded
- 3 large green onions, sliced
- ½ tsp salt
- 4 tomato slices, for topping the quiche
- ½ cup milk
- 1 cup tomato, seeded, diced
- 1 ½ cup water

Directions:

1. Pour the water into the Instant Pot container. In a large-sized bowl, whisk the eggs with the milk, pepper, and salt.
2. Add the tomato, spinach, and the green onions into a 1 1/2 quart-sized baking dish; mix well to combine.
3. Pour the egg mix over the vegetables; stir until combined. Put the tomato slices gently on top.
4. Sprinkle with the shredded parmesan cheese. Put the baking dish into the rack with a handle.
5. Put the rack into the Instant Pot and then lock the lid. Set the pressure to HIGH and the timer to 20 minutes.
6. When the timer beeps, wait for 1o minutes, then turn the steamer valve to VENTING to release remaining pressure. Open the pot lid carefully.
7. Hold the rack handles and lift the dish out from the pot.
8. Broil till the top of the quiche is light brown, if desired.

Notes: You can cover the baking dish with foil to prevent moisture from gathering on the quiche top. You can cook uncovered; just soak the moisture using a paper towel.

Nutritional Info (per serving): Calories - 178; Fat – 11.2; Fiber – 1.2; Carbs – 5; Protein – 15.3

Eggs, Bacon and Sausage Omelet

(Prep + Cook Time: 50 minutes | Servings: 6)

Ingredients:

- 6-12 eggs
- ½ cup milk
- 6 slices bacon, cooked
- 6 sausages links, sliced
- 1 onion, diced Garlic powder
- Salt to taste
- Pepper to taste
- Olive oil cooking spray

Equipment:

- 1 ½ quart ceramic baking dish or Pyrex

Directions:

1. Crack the eggs into a large measuring cup. Add ½ cup milk into the egg.
2. With a hand mixer, whisk the eggs and the milk until well combined.
3. Add the sausages and add the onion. Season with garlic powder, salt, and pepper to taste Spray a Pyrex glass bowl with cooking spray; use a deep one that will fit your Instant Pot. Pour the egg mix into the Pyrex; cover tightly with foil.
4. Add 16 ounces water into the Instant Pot. Put the bowl into a handy rack and put into the Instant Pot.
5. Press MANUAL and set the timer to 25 minutes. When cooked, let the pressure release naturally. Remove the foil.
6. The egg may pop-out of the bowl; just push it back. Layer the cooked back on top of the egg and then cover with shredded cheese.
7. Set the timer for another 5 minutes on manual. Take out from the Instant Pot.
8. Sprinkle with a bit of dried oregano. Slice into servings and enjoy.

Nutritional Info (per serving): Calories - 222; Fat – 15.5; Fiber – 0; Carbs – 3.5; Protein – 16.8

Egg Roll Soup

(Prep + Cook Time: 50 minutes | Servings: 8)

Ingredients:

- 32 ounces (4 cups) chicken broth, OR beef broth
- 2/3 cup coconut aminos
- 2 cups carrots, shredded
- ½ head cabbage, chopped
- 1 tsp sea salt
- 1 tsp onion powder
- 1 tsp ground ginger
- 1 tsp garlic powder
- 1 tbsp ghee, OR avocado oil, OR olive oil
- 1 pound ground pork, pastured
- 1 onion, large-sized, diced

Optional:
- 2-3 tbsp tapioca starch

Directions:

1. Press the SAUTE key of the Instant Pot. Put your choice of cooking fat in the fat and add the ground pork and diced onion. Sauté until the meat is no longer pink. Add the rest of the ingredients into the pot.
2. Press the CANCEL key to stop the sauté function. Cover and lock the lid.
3. Press the MANUAL key, set the pressure to HIGH, and set the timer for 25 minutes.
4. When the Instant Pot timer beeps, press the CANCEL key and unplug the Instant Pot. Turn the steam valve to quick release the pressure.
5. Unlock and carefully open the lid. Ladle the soup into serving bowls and serve.
6. If you want to thicken the soup, remove 1/4 cup of broth from the pot and stir in 2 to 3 tablespoons tapioca starch to make slurry.
7. Pour the slurry back into the pot and stir well for a couple of minutes or until thick.

Nutritional Info (per serving): Calories - 283; Fat – 2.90; Fiber – 2.4; Carbs – 9.1; Protein – 20.7

Easy Cheesy Hash Brown Bake
(Prep + Cook Time: 10 minutes | Servings: 8)

Ingredients:

- 8 eggs
- 6 slices chopped bacon
- 2 cups frozen hash browns
- 1 cup shredded cheddar cheese
- ¼ cup milk
- 1 tsp salt
- ½ tsp black pepper

Directions:

1. Turn your Instant Pot to SAUTE and cook the bacon until it becomes crispy.
2. Add hash browns and stir for 2 minutes, or until they start to thaw.
3. In a bowl, whisk eggs, milk, cheese, and seasonings.
4. Pour over the hash browns in the pot, and lock and seal lid.
5. Press MANUAL and adjust time to 5 minutes.
6. When time is up, hit CANCEL and quick-release the pressure. Serve in slices.

Nutritional Info (per serving): Calories - 164; Fat – 11; Fiber – 0; Carbs – 7; Protein – 12

Spinach-Feta Egg Cups
(Prep + Cook Time: 10 minutes | Servings: 4)

Ingredients:

- 6 eggs
- 1 cup water
- 1 cup chopped baby spinach
- 1 chopped tomato
- ½ cup mozzarella cheese
- ¼ cup feta cheese
- 1 tsp black pepper
- ½ tsp salt

Directions:

1. Pour water into the Instant Pot and lower in trivet.
2. Layer silicone ramekins with spinach.
3. In a bowl, mix the rest of the ingredients and pour into cups, leaving ¼-inch of head room.
4. Put in pressure cooker (you may have to cook in batches) and adjust time to 8 minutes on HIGH pressure.
5. When time is up, turn off the cooker and quick-release.

Nutritional Info (per serving): Calories - 114; Fat – 7; Fiber – 3; Carbs – 2; Protein – 11

Spinach-Tomato Crustless Quiche

(Prep + Cook Time 40 minutes | Servings: 6)

Ingredients:

- 12 large eggs
- ¼ tsp fresh ground black pepper
- 3 cups fresh baby spinach, roughly chopped
- ¼ cup Parmesan cheese, shredded
- 3 large green onions, sliced
- ½ tsp salt
- 4 tomato slices, for topping the quiche
- ½ cup milk
- 1 cup tomato, seeded, diced
- 1 ½ cup water

Directions:

1. Pour the water into the Instant Pot container. In a large-sized bowl, whisk the eggs with the milk, pepper, and salt.
2. Add the tomato, spinach, and the green onions into a 1 1/2 quart-sized baking dish; mix well to combine.
3. Pour the egg mix over the vegetables; stir until combined. Put the tomato slices gently on top.
4. Sprinkle with the shredded parmesan cheese.
5. Put the baking dish into the rack with a handle.
6. Put the rack into the Instant Pot and then lock the lid. Set the pressure to HIGH and the timer to 20 minutes.
7. When the timer beeps, wait for 1o minutes, then turn the steamer valve to release remaining pressure.
8. Open the pot lid carefully. Hold the rack handles and lift the dish out from the pot.
9. Broil till the top of the quiche is light brown, if desired.

Notes: You can cover the baking dish with foil to prevent moisture from gathering on the quiche top. You can cook uncovered; just soak the moisture using a paper towel.

Nutritional Info (per serving): Calories - 179; Fat – 11.2; Fiber – 1.2; Carbs – 5; Protein – 15.3

Aromatic Egg Side Dish

(Prep + Cook Time 20 minutes | Servings: 6)

Ingredients:

- 1 tbsp mustard
- ¼ cup cream
- 1 tsp salt
- 8 eggs
- 1 tsp mayo sauce
- ¼ cup dill
- 1 tsp ground white pepper
- 1 tsp minced garlic
- 1 cup water

Directions:

1. In the Instant Pot pour down about 1 cup of water into the bowl.
2. Place stainless steamer basket inside the pot.
3. Place the eggs in the steamer basket.
4. Cook the eggs at the high pressure for 5 minutes.
5. Then remove the eggs from the Instant Pot and chill.
6. Peel the eggs and cut them into 2 parts.
7. Discard the egg yolks and mash them.
8. Then add the mustard, cream, salt, mayo sauce, ground white pepper, and minced garlic in the mashed egg yolks.
9. Chop the dill and sprinkle the egg yolk mixture with the chopped dill.
10. Mix up it carefully until you get smooth and homogenous mass.
11. Then transfer the egg yolk mixture to the pastry bag.
12. Fill the egg whites with the yolk mixture.
13. Serve the dish immediately. Enjoy!

Nutritional Info (per serving): Calories - 170; Fat – 12.8; Fiber – 0; Carbs – 2.42; Protein – 11

Eggs De Provence

(Prep + Cook Time 40 minutes | Servings: 6)

Ingredients:

- 1 cup kale leaves, fresh, chopped
- 1 cup cheddar cheese
- ½ cup heavy cream
- 1 onion, small, chopped
- 6 eggs, large
- 1 tsp Herbes de Provence
- ⅛ tsp sea salt & pepper
- 1 cup bacon or ham, cooked
- 1 cup water

Directions:
1. Whisk the eggs together with the heavy cream in a large bowl.
2. Add in the remaining ingredients; mix well.
3. Transfer the mixture into a dish, preferably heat proof & then cover.
4. Add a cup of water into the bottom of your Instant Pot. Place the steamer basket or trivet inside.
5. Tightly close the lid & close the vent valve. Select the MANUAL option and set the cooking time to 20 minutes, preferably on HIGH pressure.
6. Once you are done with the cooking process, let the pressure to release naturally.
7. Serve immediately.

Nutritional Info (per serving): Calories - 220; Fat – 16.3; Fiber – 0.9

Breakfast In a Jar
(Prep + Cook Time 25 minutes | Servings: 3)

Ingredients:
- 3 pieces mason jars
- 6 eggs
- 1 ¼ cups water
- Tater tots
- 9 slices sharp cheese or shredded cheese, divided
- 6 tbsp peach-mango salsa, divided
- 6 pieces bacon, cooked of your preferred breakfast meat, such as sausage

Directions:
1. Put 1 ¼ cups water into the Instant Pot. Put enough tater tots to cover the bottom of the mason jars.
2. Crack 2 eggs into each Mason jar. Poke the egg yolks using a fork or the tip of a long knife.
3. Add a couple of your preferred meat into the mason jars. Put 2 slices of cheese in each Mason jar, covering the ingredients.
4. Add 2 tablespoons salsa into each jar, on top of the cheese. Add a couple more tater tots on top of the salsa.
5. Then top 1 slice of cheese on top. Cover each jar with foil, making sure to cover tightly to prevent moisture from going into the jars.

6. Place the jars right into the water in the Instant Pot. Cover the Instant Pot and close.
7. Set on HIGH pressure and set the timer to 5 minutes; make sure the valve of the Instant Pot is in pressure cooker mode.
8. When the timer beeps, turn the steam valve to release pressure.
9. Open the Instant Pot. Carefully take the jars out.

Nutritional Info (per serving): Calories - 632; Fat – 45.6; Fiber – 1.6; Carbs – 15.8; Protein – 38

Meat Lover's Crustless Quiche
(Prep + Cook Time: 45 minutes | Servings: 4)

Ingredients:

- 6 large eggs, well beaten
- ½ cup milk
- ¼ tsp salt
- 1/8 tsp ground black pepper
- 4 slices bacon, cooked and then crumbled
- 1 cup ground sausage, cooked
- ½ cup ham, diced
- 2 large green onions, chopped
- 1 cup cheese, shredded
- 1 ½ cups water

Directions:
1. Pour the water into the Instant Pot container and put a stainless steel rack with handle into the bottom of the pot.
2. In a large-sized bowl, whisk the eggs with the milk, salt, and pepper.
3. Add the sausage, bacon, ham, cheese, and green onions into a 1-quart soufflé dish; mix well.
4. Pour the egg mix over the meat; stir well to combine.
5. With an aluminum foil, loosely cover the dish. Put onto the rack. Lock the pot lid.
6. Set the pressure to HIGH and the timer to 30 minutes.
7. When the timer beeps, turn the pot off, let the pressure release naturally for 10 minutes, and then turn the valve to release remaining pressure. Carefully open the pot lid. Lift out the rack with the dish.
8. Remove the foil covering and, if desired, sprinkle the top of the quiche with additional cheese and broil until melted and slightly browned.
9. Serve immediately.

Nutritional Info (per serving): Calories - 419; Fat – 32; Fiber – 0.6; Carbs – 4.1; Protein – 29.6

Marinated Steak

(Prep + Cook Time: 45 minutes | Servings: 4)

Ingredients:
- 2 pounds flank steak
- 2 tbsp onion soup mix, dried
- ¼ cups apple cider vinegar
- ½ cups olive oil
- 1 tbsp Worcestershire sauce

Directions:
1. Press the SAUTE key of the Instant Pot.
2. Put the flank steak in the pot and cook each side until browned.
3. Add the Worcestershire sauce, vinegar, onion soup mix, and olive oil.
4. Press the CANCEL key to stop the sauté function. Cover and lock the lid.
5. Press the MEAT/ STEW key, set the pressure to HIGH, and set the timer for 35 minutes.
6. When the Instant Pot timer beeps, turn the steam valve to quick release the pressure.
7. Unlock and carefully open the lid. Serve!

Nutritional Info (per serving): Calories - 684; Fat – 44.1; Fiber – 0; Carbs – 5.5; Protein – 63.6

Beef Stroganoff

(Prep + Cook Time: 10 minutes | Servings: 4)

Ingredients:

- 1 pound steak, thin-cut
- 1 cup sour cream
- 1 onion, small-sized
- 16 ounces egg noodles
- 4 cups beef broth
- 4 tbsp butter
- 8 ounces mushrooms, sliced

Directions:

1. Dice the onion into small-sized pieces. Cut the steak into thin pieces. Press the SAUTÉ key of the Instant Pot.
2. Add the butter, onion, and steak and wait until the butter is melted. Add the mushrooms, broth, and egg noodle.
3. Press the CANCEL key to stop the sauté function. Cover and lock the lid. Press the MANUAL key, set the pressure to HIGH, and set the timer for 4 minutes.
4. When the Instant Pot timer beeps, turn the steam valve to quick release the pressure. Unlock and carefully open the lid.
5. Stir in the sour cream and serve.

Nutritional Info (per serving): Calories - 669; Fat – 33.1; Fiber – 2.5; Carbs – 36.3; Protein – 55

Garlic Teriyaki Beef

(Prep + Cook Time: 55 minutes | Servings: 4)

Ingredients:

- 1 piece (2 pounds) flank steak

For the teriyaki sauce:

- 2 tbsp fish sauce
- ¼ cup maple syrup
- ¼ cup coconut aminos OR soy sauce instead
- 2 cloves garlic, finely chopped

- 1 tbsp raw honey
- 1 ½ tsp ground or fresh ginger, optional

Directions:

1. Slice the flank steak into 1/2-inch strips.
2. In a bowl, put all of the teriyaki sauce and mix until combined.
3. Put the steak strips and the sauce in the Instant Pot – there is no need to brown the meat. Cover and lock the lid.
4. Press the MANUAL key, set the pressure to HIGH, and set the timer for 40 minutes.

Nutritional Info (per serving): Calories - 351; Fat – 12.7; Fiber – 0; Carbs – 13.2; Protein – 43.7

Beef And Broccoli
(Prep + Cook Time: 50 minutes | Servings: 4)

Ingredients:
- 1 pound stew beef meat
- 1 bag (10-12 ounces) frozen broccoli
- 1 clove garlic, pressed
- 1 onion, quartered
- 1 tsp ground ginger
- ½ cup beef or bone broth
- ½ tsp salt
- ¼ cup coconut aminos
- 2 tbsp fish sauce

Directions:
1. Except for the broccoli, put the rest of the ingredients in the Instant Pot. Cover and lock the lid.
2. Press the MEAT/ STEW key, and cook on pre-set time.
3. When the Instant Pot timer beeps, press the OFF key and turn the steam valve to quick release the pressure. Unlock and carefully open the lid.
4. Add the broccoli, loosely cover with the lid, and let sit for 15 minutes. Serve!

Nutritional Info (per serving): Calories - 267; Fat – 7.5; Fiber – 2.7; Carbs – 9.3; Protein – 39.7

Italian Beef
(Prep + Cook Time: 40 minutes | Servings: 6)

Ingredients:
- 3 ½ pounds beef roast
- 16 ounces whole tomatoes, canned
- 2 whole bay leaves
- 2 tsp bouillon, beef, granules
- ¼ tsp black pepper
- ¼ cups water
- ½ tsp pickling spice
- ½ tsp garlic, minced, #1
- 1 tsp salt
- 1 tbsp wine vinegar
- 3 cloves garlic

Directions:
1. Trim the fat off the beef and cut to fit inside the inner pot.
2. Put the rest of the ingredients in the pot, placing them over the beef. Cover and lock the lid.
3. Press the MEAT/ STEW key, set the pressure to HIGH, and set the timer for 35 minutes.
4. When the Instant Pot timer beeps, turn the steam valve to quick release the pressure. Unlock and carefully open the lid.
5. Remove the bay leaf and serve.

Nutritional Info (per serving): Calories - 515; Fat – 16.8; Fiber – 1.4; Carbs – 7.6; Protein – 81.4

Korean Beef

(Prep + Cook Time: 75 minutes | Servings: 6)

Ingredients:

- 4 pounds bottom roast, cut into cubes
- 1 apple, Granny Smith or pear, peeled and then chopped
- 2 tablespoons olive oil
- ½ cup soy sauce
- 1 tablespoon ginger, fresh grated
- 1 large orange OR
- 2 small orange, juice only
- 1 cup beef broth
- 5 cloves garlic, minced
- Salt and pepper to taste

Directions:

1. Season the roast cubes generously with pepper and salt. Press the SAUTE key of the Instant Pot.
2. When the pot is hot, coat with the olive oil. In batches, cook the meat until all sides are browned –transfer the browned meat into a plate while cooking.
3. When all the meat is browned, pour the beef broth in the pot and deglaze the pot – scrape the browned bits off from the bottom of the pot.
4. Pour the soy sauce in the pot and stir to mix. Return all the browned meat into the pot.
5. Add the ginger, garlic, and pear /apple on top of the meat. Lightly stir to combine slightly.
6. Add the orange juice.
7. Press the CANCEL key to stop the sauté function. Cover and lock the lid. Press the MANUAL key, set the pressure to HIGH, and set the timer for 45 minutes.
8. When the Instant Pot timer beeps, turn the steam valve to VENTING to quick release the pressure. Unlock and carefully open the lid.
9. Serve over rice or cauliflower rice.

Nutritional Info (per serving): Calories - 654; Fat – 23.9; Fiber – 1.8; Carbs – 10.4; Protein – 94.5

Mongolian Beef

(Prep + Cook Time: 25 minutes | Servings: 4)

Ingredients:

- 1 ½ pounds Flank steak
- 1 carrot, shredded
- 1 garlic clove, minced
- 1 green onion, sliced, for garnish
- 1 tbsp olive oil
- ½ cup brown sugar
- ½ tsp fresh ginger, minced
- ¼ cup water
- ¾ cup soy sauce

To thicken the sauce:

- 3 tbsp water
- 3 tbsp cornstarch

Directions:

1. Slice the flank into the strips. In a bowl, combine the soy sauce with the oil, garlic, ginger, sugar, and water.
2. Pour the sauce in the Instant Pot.
3. Add the shredded carrot and beef strips, and mix until the beef is coated with the sauce. Cover and lock the lid.
4. Press the MANUAL key, set the pressure to HIGH, and set the timer for 8 minutes.
5. When the Instant Pot timer beeps, press the CANCEL key and unplug the Instant Pot.
6. Let the pressure release naturally for 10-15 minutes or until the valve drops.
7. Using an oven mitt or a long handled spoon, turn the steam valve to release remaining pressure. Unlock and carefully open the lid. In a small-sized water, combine the cornstarch with the water until there are no more lumps.
8. Press the SAUTÉ key and pour cornstarch mixture into the pot. Boil for about 1 to 2 minutes or until the sauce is thick.
9. Serve on a platter and garnish with chopped green onions.

Nutritional Info (per serving): Calories - 486; Fat – 17.7; Fiber – 1; Carbs – 29.1; Protein – 50.6

Grandma's Italian Beef

(Prep + Cook Time: 45 minutes | Servings: 6)

Ingredients:

- 3 ½ pounds beef roast
- 16 ounces whole tomatoes, canned
- 2 whole bay leaves
- 2 tsp bouillon, beef, granules
- ¼ tsp black pepper
- ¼ cups water
- ½ tsp pickling spice
- ½ tsp garlic, minced
- 1 tsp salt
- 1 tbsp wine vinegar
- 3 cloves garlic, medium-sized

Directions:

1. Trim the fat off the beef and cut to fit inside the inner pot.
2. Put the rest of the ingredients in the pot, placing them over the beef. Cover and lock the lid.
3. Press the MEAT/ STEW key, set the pressure to HIGH, and set the timer for 35 minutes.
4. When the Instant Pot timer beeps, turn the steam valve to quick release the pressure.
5. Unlock and carefully open the lid.
6. Remove the bay leaf and serve.

Nutritional Info (per serving): Calories - 515; Fat – 16.8; Fiber – 1.4; Carbs – 7.6; Protein – 81.4

Beef Short Ribs

(Prep + Cook Time: 60 minutes | Servings: 6)

Ingredients:

- 4 pounds beef short ribs
- 4-6 carrots, cut into bite sized pieces
- 3 cloves garlic, minced
- 2 tbsp olive oil
- 2 cups onions, diced
- 1 tbsp dried thyme
- 1 ½ cups beef broth
- Kosher salt and fresh cracked pepper

Directions:

1. Press the SAUTE key of the Instant Pot. Pat dry the short ribs and generously season with the pepper and salt.
2. Drizzle olive oil in the pot and, in one single layer at a time, put the ribs in the pot and cook for about 4-5 minutes each side or until all the sides are browned – do not crowd the pot, so brown the short ribs in batches.
3. Transfer the browned short ribs into a plate and set aside.
4. Put the garlic in the pot and sauté, constantly stirring, for about 1 minute. Add the onion, carrot, and thyme. Season to taste with more salt and pepper.
5. Cook for about 4 to 5, occasionally stirring, until the veggies are soft. Return the browned short ribs into the pot. Press the CANCEL key to stop the sauté function. Cover and lock the lid.
6. Press the MANUAL key, set the pressure to HIGH, and set the timer for 35 minutes.
7. When the Instant Pot timer beeps, release the pressure naturally for 10-15 minutes or until the valve drops.
8. Turn the steam valve to release remaining pressure.
9. Unlock and carefully open the lid. Serve hot.

Nutritional Info (per serving): Calories - 705; Fat – 32.3; Fiber – 2; Carbs – 8.6; Protein – 89.4

Beefy Lasagna

(Prep + Cook Time: 40 minutes | Servings: 6)

Ingredients:

- 2 pounds ricotta cheese
- 1 pound of ground beef
- 24-ounces pasta sauce
- 8-ounces of no-boil lasagna noodles
- 1 package shredded mozzarella cheese
- 2 big eggs
- ¼ cup water
- ⅓ cup grated Parmesan
- 1 diced onion
- 1 tbsp olive oil
- 2 tsp minced garlic
- 1 tsp Italian seasoning
- Salt and pepper to taste

Directions:

1. Pour olive oil in your Instant Pot and heat until it starts to smoke.
2. Quickly add the ground beef, onions, salt, and pepper.
3. When the meat is brown and onions clear, pour in the water and pasta sauce.
4. Stir before pouring out into a bowl.
5. In a separate bowl, mix the ricotta, garlic, Italian seasoning, eggs, Parmesan, salt, and pepper together.
6. Fill the pressure cooker with ¼ inch of water.
7. Layer ⅙ of the beef mixture into the bottom before adding the noodles.
8. Pour in ⅓ of the ricotta mixture, and then more beef sauce.
9. Top with noodles, and keep going until you've used everything. The last layer should be beef sauce.
10. Close the Instant Pot lid.
11. Select MANUAL, and then 7 minutes on HIGH pressure.
12. When the beep sounds, press CANCEL and quick-release the pressure.
13. Open the lid and sprinkle on the mozzarella.
14. Cool for a few minutes before serving.

Nutritional Info (per serving): Calories - 408; Fat – 22.1; Fiber – 2.6; Carbs – 27.4; Protein – 25.1

Beef and Noodles

(Prep + Cook Time: 1 hour 10 minutes | Servings: 4)

Ingredients:

- 3 pounds boneless beef chuck roast
- 8-ounces egg noodles
- 1 cup water
- 1 chopped onion
- 2 minced garlic cloves
- 2 tbsp veggie oil
- Salt and pepper to taste

Directions:

1. Cube roast into bite-sized pieces. Add oil to your Instant Pot, and turn to the SAUTE setting.
2. Brown meat before adding garlic, onion, salt, and pepper. Pour in water and seal the lid.
3. Select MANUAL and cook for 37 minutes on HIGH pressure.
4. When time is up, hit CANCEL and wait for a natural pressure release.
5. Take out the meat. Pour another cup of water into the cooker and turn back to SAUTE. Bring liquid to a boil.
6. Add the noodles and cook, lowering the SAUTE heat if possible to thicken the liquid into a gravy.
7. When noodles are done, add meat, and stir. Serve!

Nutritional Info (per serving): Calories – 627.4; Fat – 28.7; Carbs – 18.2; Protein – 74.8

Swedish Meatballs

(Prep + Cook Time: 20 minutes | Servings: 4)

Ingredients:

- 16 ounces egg noodles
- 1 ½ cups beef broth, low sodium
- 1 cup sour cream
- 1 cup milk
- 1 bag (24 Ounces) Johnsonville Home-style Meatballs, fully cooked or frozen
- 2 boxes (12 ounces) cream of mushroom soup (mix with 12 ounces water for both)

Directions:

1. Put the cream of mushroom soup, milk, beef broth, and water in the pot. Add the package of egg noodles.
2. In a single layer, layer the meatballs on top of the egg noodles. Cover and lock the lid.
3. Press the MANUAL key, set the pressure to HIGH, and set the timer for 12 minutes.
4. When there are only 2 minutes left of cooking time, turn the steam valve to VENTING. Unlock and carefully open the lid when all the steam is released.
5. Stir in 1 cup sour cream and mix thoroughly. Now you have dreamy, creamy, delicious Swedish meatballs.

Nutritional Info (per serving): Calories - 740; Fat – 45.4; Fiber – 3.4; Carbs – 52.1; Protein – 42.5

Balsamic Maple Beef

(Prep + Cook Time: 55 minutes | Servings: 6)

Ingredients:

- 3 pounds chuck steak, boneless, fat trimmed, sliced into ½-inch strips
- 2 tbsp avocado oil OR olive oil
- ½ cup balsamic vinegar
- 1 tsp ground ginger
- 1 tsp garlic, finely chopped
- 1 cup maple syrup
- 1 cup bone broth
- 1 ½ tsp salt

Directions:

1. Trim the fat off from the joint the beef and slice the meat into 1/2-inch thin strips. In a bowl, mix the ground ginger with the salt. Season the meat with the ginger mix.
2. Press the SAUTE key of the Instant Pot. Put the oil in the pot and heat.
3. When the oil is hot and shimmery, but not smoking, add the beef and cook until all sides are browned – you will have to cook in batches.
4. Transfer the browned beef into a plate and set aside. Put the garlic in the pot and sauté for about 1 minute.
5. Add the broth, maple syrup, and balsamic vinegar. Stir to mix. Return the browned beef into the pot.
6. Press the CANCEL key to stop the sauté function. Cover and lock the lid.
7. Press the MANUAL key, set the pressure to HIGH, and set the timer for 35 minutes.
8. When the Instant Pot timer beeps, turn the steam valve to VENTING to quick release the pressure.
9. Unlock and carefully open the lid. If desired, you can thicken the sauce. Press the SAUTE key.
10. Mix 4 tablespoons arrowroot or tapioca starch with 4 tablespoons water until smooth and then add into the pot; cook for about 5 minutes or until the sauce is thick. Serve!

Nutritional Info (per serving): Calories - 721; Fat – 30.5; Fiber – 0; Carbs – 36.1; Protein – 71

Beef Bourguignon

(Prep + Cook Time: 1 hour 15 minutes | Servings: 4)

Ingredients:

- 1 pound flank steak or stewing steak
- ½ pound bacon tips or rashers
- 5 carrots, medium-sized, cut into sticks
- 2 sweet potato, large white, peeled and cubed
- 1 cup red wine
- 1 red onion, large-sized, peeled and sliced
- 1 tbsp avocado oil or olive oil
- 1 tbsp maple syrup
- ½ cup beef broth or stock
- 2 cloves garlic, minced
- 2 tbsp parsley, dried or fresh
- 2 tbsp thyme, dried or fresh
- 2 tsp ground black pepper
- 2 tsp rock salt

Directions:

1. Press the SAUTE key of the Instant Pot. Put 1 tablespoon oil in the pot and heat.
2. Pat the beef dry and season with salt and pepper.
3. Working in batches, cook the beef in the pot until all sides are browned. Set aside. Slice the bacon into strips and put into the pot.
4. Add the onions. Sauté until the onions are translucent and soft. Return the browned beef in the pot.
5. Add the remaining ingredients.
6. Press the CANCEL key to stop the sauté function. Cover and lock the lid. Press the MANUAL key, set the pressure to HIGH, and set the timer for 30 minutes.
7. When the Instant Pot timer beeps, turn the steam valve to VENTING to quick release the pressure.
8. Unlock and carefully open the lid. Enjoy!

Nutritional Info (per serving): Calories - 701; Fat – 34; Fiber – 5.4; Carbs – 30.1; Protein – 55.7

Classic Corned Beef and Cabbage

(Prep + Cook Time: 1 hour 35 minutes | Servings: 6)

Ingredients:

- 4 cups water
- 3 pounds corned beef
- 3 pounds cabbage, cut into eight wedges
- 1 ½ pounds new potatoes
- 1 pound peeled and cut carrots
- 1 quartered onion
- 1 quartered celery stalk
- 1 corned beef spice packet

Directions:

1. Rinse the beef. Put in the Instant Pot along with onion and celery.
2. Add in the spice packet and pour in water. Close and seal the lid.
3. Press MANUAL and cook for 90 minutes on HIGH pressure.
4. When time is up, hit CANCEL and very carefully quick-release the pressure.
5. Plate beef and keep celery and onion in the pot.
6. Add potatoes, carrots, and cabbage - in that order - in the pot. Close and seal lid again.
7. Select MANUAL and cook for just 5 minutes.
8. When time is up, turn off cooker and quick-release. Move veggies to plate with the corned beef.
9. Pour pot liquid through a gravy strainer.
10. Serve beef and veggies with a bit of broth on top, and the rest in a gravy boat.

Nutritional Info (per serving): Calories - 464; Fat – 30; Fiber – 7; Carbs – 17; Protein – 30

Mississippi Pot Roast

(Prep + Cook Time: 1 hour 55 minutes | Servings: 6)

Ingredients:

- 5-6 pounds beef, arm or chuck roast
- ½ cup beef broth
- ½ cup pepperoncini juice
- 1 envelope ranch dressing mix
- 1 envelope au jus gravy mix (or brown gravy mix)
- ¼ cup butter
- 6-8 pepperoncini

Directions:

1. Pour the pepperoncini juice and the broth in the pot.
2. Add the roast beef. Sprinkle the gravy and the dressing mix over the roast, and then top with the butter and pepperoncini. Cover and lock the lid.
3. Press the MANUAL key, set the pressure to HIGH, and set the timer for 90 minutes.
4. When the Instant Pot timer beeps, turn off the pot, release the pressure naturally for 10-15 minutes or until the valve drops.
5. Turn the steam valve to release remaining pressure.
6. Unlock and carefully open the lid.

Nutritional Info (per serving): Calories - 828; Fat – 32; Fiber – 1.7; Carbs – 11.4; Protein – 116.9

Instant Pot Roast

(Prep + Cook Time: 55 minutes | Servings: 8)

Ingredients:

- 4 pounds beef chuck roast, cut into cubes (2 inches)
- 1 cup beef broth
- 5 minced garlic cloves
- 1 peeled and chopped Granny Smith apple
- 1 thumb of grated ginger
- ½ cup soy sauce Juice of one big orange
- 2 tbsp olive oil
- Salt and pepper to taste

Directions:

1. Season the roast with salt and pepper. Turn on your Instant Pot to SAUTE.
2. When hot, pour in the olive oil and brown the roast all over.
3. Move the meat to a plate.
4. Pour in the beef broth and scrape any stuck bits of meat.
5. Pour in soy sauce and stir.
6. Put the roast back into the pot.
7. Arrange the cut apple, garlic, and ginger on top.
8. Pour in the orange juice. Close the pressure cooker lid.
9. Select MANUAL and then 45 minutes on HIGH pressure.
10. Hit CANCEL and quick-release the pressure when the timer beeps. Serve!

Nutritional Info (per serving): Calories - 492; Fat – 37; Fiber – 0; Carbs – 3; Protein – 46

Very Tender Pot Roast

(Prep + Cook Time: 50 minutes | Servings: 6)

Ingredients:

- 2-3 pounds beef, chuck roast
- 4 potatoes, large-sized, cut into large cubes
- 4 carrots, chopped
- 3 tbsp steak sauce, optional
- 3 cloves garlic
- 2 tbsp olive oil
- 2 tbsp Italian Seasonings
- 2 stalks celery, chopped
- 1 onion
- 1 cups beef broth
- 1 cup red wine

Directions:

1. Press the SAUTE key of your Instant Pot. Pour in the olive oil.
2. Add the roast beef and cook each side for about 1 to 2 minutes or until browned. Transfer the browned beef into a plate.
3. Put the celery, carrots, and potatoes in the pot. Top with the garlic and onion.
4. Pour the beef broth and the wine in the pot. Put the roast on top of the vegetables.
5. Spread the seasonings over the top of the roast and then spread with the steak sauce. Press the CANCEL key to stop the sauté function. Cover and lock the lid.
6. Press the MANUAL key, set the pressure to HIGH, and set the timer for 35 minutes.
7. When the Instant Pot timer beeps, release the pressure naturally for 10-15 minutes or until the valve drops.
8. Turn the steam valve to release remaining pressure. Unlock and carefully open the lid. Serve!

Nutritional Info (per serving): Calories - 499; Fat – 15.9; Fiber – 4.9; Carbs – 30.4; Protein – 49.8

Teriyaki Short Ribs

(Prep + Cook Time: 45 minutes | Servings: 4)

Ingredients:
- 4 big beef short ribs
- 1 cup water
- ¾ cup soy sauce
- 1 big, halved orange
- ½ cup brown sugar
- 1 full garlic bulb, peeled and crushed
- 1 large thumb of peeled and crushed fresh ginger
- ½ tbsp sesame oil
- Dried pepper flakes
- A bunch of chopped green onions

Directions:
1. In a Ziploc bag, mix water, sugar, and soy sauce.
2. Squish around until the sugar has dissolved.
3. Add the orange juice and stir, before adding the orange slices as well.
4. Lastly, throw in the garlic, ginger, onions, and dried pepper flakes.
5. Stir before adding the ribs.
6. Stir one last time and marinate in the fridge for at least 4 hours.
7. When ready to cook the ribs, coat the bottom of the Instant Pot with olive oil and heat.
8. Remove the ribs from the bag (save the liquid!) with tongs and quickly sear for 2-3 minutes on both sides.
9. Pour in the marinade and close the lid.
10. Select the MEAT/STEW setting and select 30 minutes.
11. When time is up, press CANCEL and quick-release the pressure. Serve!

Nutritional Info (per serving): Calories - 603; Fat – 10; Fiber – 1; Carbs – 76; Protein – 43

Sweet-Spicy Meatloaf

(Prep + Cook Time: 55 minutes | Servings: 4)

Ingredients:

- 1 pound lean ground beef
- ⅔ cup bread crumbs
- ⅔ cup diced onion
- 6 sliced black olives
- 1 egg white
- 2 tbsp ketchup
- 2 fresh, chopped basil leaves
- 1 tsp minced garlic
- ½ tsp salt
- Black pepper
- ¼ cup ketchup
- 1 tbsp brown sugar
- 1 tbsp spicy brown mustard

Directions:

1. Prepare a round, one-quart dish with a bit of olive oil.
2. Mix everything in the first ingredient list and form a loaf in the dish.
3. In a separate bowl, mix the brown sugar, ketchup, and spicy brown mustard together.
4. Brush on top of the meatloaf.
5. Cover the dish tightly with foil.
6. Pour one cup of water into the pressure cooker and lower in the trivet.
7. Place the meatloaf dish on top and close the Instant Pot lid.
8. Select MEAT/STEW, and then 45 minutes.
9. When the beep sounds, quick-release.
10. Carefully take out the hot dish.
11. Holding the meat in place, pour out any excess liquid.
12. Rest the meat before serving.

Nutritional Info (per serving): Calories - 261; Fat – 7.5; Fiber – 0; Carbs – 19.2; Protein – 25

Herbs and Meatloaf

(Prep + Cook Time: 55 minutes | Servings: 2)

Ingredients:

- 2 pound of ground beef
- 2 pieces of eggs
- 1 cup of almond flour
- 1 tsp of thyme
- 1 tsp of rosemary
- 1 tsp of garlic powder
- 3 tbsp of olive oil

Directions:

1. The first step here is to take a bowl and toss in your eggs, beef, flour alongside the seasoning in a large sized mixing bowl.
2. Take a wooden spoon and mix them very gently.
3. Open up the lid of your Instant Pot and grease up the inner pot with olive oil.
4. Gently place the meatloaf mixture in your greased up Instant Pot and firmly pack it up with your hand to make sure it's even.
5. Set the Instant Pot to normal pressure setting and choose MEAT mode.
6. Let it cook for about 40 minutes.
7. Once done, wait for about 10 minutes and manually release the pressure of your Instant Pot.
8. Open it up and serve the meal with salad and mashed potatoes.

Nutritional Info (per serving): Calories - 263; Fat – 14; Carbs – 2; Protein – 9

Stuffed Rigatoni

(Prep + Cook Time: 45 minutes | Servings: 6)

Ingredients:

- 1 pound rigatoni, cooked
- ½ pound ground beef
- ½ pound hot sausage
- 16 ounces mozzarella
- 16 ounces ricotta cheese
- 2 eggs
- 1 tbsp garlic powder
- 1 tbsp parsley
- 32 ounces of your favorite sauce

Equipment:

- Spring-form pan

Directions:

1. In a large-sized bowl, mix the ricotta cheese with the mozzarella cheese, 2 eggs, parsley, and garlic powder. Set aside.
2. Press the SAUTE key of the Instant Pot.
3. Brown the sausage and the ground beef in the pot, breaking up the sausages in the process.
4. Add into the bowl with the sauce and mix well. Turn off the pot for the time being.
5. Coat the bottom of the spring-form pan with the meat-sauce mix. In a standing up position, place the pasta in the pan.
6. Spoon the cheese mix into a plastic bag. Poke a hole in one corner of the plastic bag and squeeze the cheese mix inside each rigatoni. Top the sauce mix with additional mozzarella cheese.
7. Set a trivet in the Instant Pot and pour in 1 cup of water. Place the spring-form pan in the trivet. Cover and lock the lid.
8. Press the MANUAL key, set the pressure to HIGH, and set the timer for 20 minutes.
9. When the Instant Pot timer beeps, turn the steam valve to quick release the pressure.
10. Unlock and carefully open the lid. Let the pan sit in the pot for 10 minutes or until the dish settles. Serve!

Nutritional Info (per serving): Calories - 696; Fat – 35.2; Fiber – 2.8; Carbs – 94; Protein – 60.6

Beef Stew

(Prep + Cook Time: 1 hour 35 minutes | Servings: 4)

Ingredients:

- 1 ½ pound whole beef brisket
- 1 tbsp flour
- 2 bay leaves
- 2 carrots, chopped
- 2 onions, small-sized, finely chopped
- 2 stalks celery, chopped
- 2 tbsp olive oil, divided
- 3 cloves garlic, crushed and then chopped
- 3 russet potatoes, cubed (OR 3 Yukon gold potatoes)
- Couple pinches dried thyme
- Dash sherry wine
- Kosher salt and pepper

For the chicken stock mixture:

- 1 tbsp fish sauce
- 1 tbsp light soy sauce
- 1 tbsp Worcestershire sauce
- 2 cups chicken stock, homemade, unsalted OR chicken stock, low sodium
- 3 tbsp tomato paste

Directions:

1. In a medium-sized bowl, combine the tomato paste with the fish sauce, light soy sauce, Worcestershire sauce, and chicken stock.
2. Trim any excess fat off from the beef brisket and then generously season with salt and pepper.
3. Press the SAUTE key of the Instant Pot. Add 1 tablespoon oil.
4. Sear both sides of the beef for about 5 minutes each side. Transfer into a chopping board and let rest.
5. Add 1 tablespoon of olive oil in the Instant Pot. Add the onion, season with salt and pepper, and cook until tender and browned.
6. Add the garlic and stir until fragrant. Add the carrot, celery, season with pinch of salt and pepper, and cook for 2 minutes.

7. Add a dash of wine to deglaze the pot and cook until the wine is reduced. Add the chicken stock mix in the pot.
8. Cut the beef into 1 to 1 1/2-inch cube chunks.
9. Toss with the flour and then add into the pot, spreading them out so each chunk can soak the stock mix.
10. Do not stir. You don't want too much flour mix with the stock. Add the bay leaves.
11. Rub the dried thyme with your fingers and sprinkle in the pot.
12. Add the potato on top of the beef chunks.
13. Lock the lid and close the steam valve. Cook for 70 minutes on HIGH pressure.
14. When the timer beeps, let the pressure release naturally.
15. Carefully open the lid, taste, and adjust the salt and pepper to taste.
16. Serve immediately as is or with rice or pasta.

Notes: If you want more texture in your soup, add parboiled potatoes, chopped celery and carrots in the stew, and cook until the veggies are tender.

Nutritional Info (per serving): Calories - 556; Fat – 18,2; Fiber – 6,7; Carbs – 40; Protein – 56,9

Easy Teriyaki Beef

(Prep + Cook Time: 45 minutes | Servings: 6)

Ingredients:
2 pounds flank steak
½ cup + 3 tbsp of good-quality teriyaki sauce
2-4 chopped garlic cloves
1 ½ tsp ground ginger
Rice to serve

Directions:
1. Cut the steak into ½-inch strips.
2. Put all the ingredients in your Instant Pot and seal the lid.
3. Hit MANUAL and cook for 40 minutes.
4. When time is up, hit CANCEL and quick-release.
5. Serve with rice!

Nutritional Info (per serving): Calories - 487; Fat – 21; Fiber – 0; Carbs – 23; Protein – 51

Beef Curry

(Prep + Cook Time: 60 minutes | Servings: 4)

Ingredients:

- 1 ½ cups jarred tikka masala or madras curry sauce
- 1 ½ pounds of beef chuck steak (trimmed to ¼" fat), cut into cubes
- 1 cup beef broth
- ½ cup coconut milk
- Salt and pepper, to taste

Optional toppings:

- sliced green chilis
- chopped coriander or basil leaves

Directions:

1. Season the beef with salt and pepper.
2. In the inner pot of the pressure cooker, press the SAUTE button and add the beef.
3. Cook until evenly browned on all sides. Stir in the remaining ingredients and mix until well combined.
4. Press the CANCEL button.
5. Close the lid completely and position the steam release handle to sealing position.
6. Press the MANUAL button and set the pressure cooking time to 25 minutes.
7. When the pressure cooking cycle is completed, slide the steam release handle to venting position to fully release the pressure.
8. Open the lid when the float valve has dropped down.
9. Serve over rice with any additional toppings you desire.

Easy Seasoned Italian Beef

(Prep + Cook Time: 1 hour 55 minutes | Servings: 6)

Ingredients:

- 3 pounds of grass-fed chuck roast
- 6 garlic cloves
- 1 cup beef broth
- ¼ cup apple cider vinegar
- 2 tsp garlic powder
- 1 tsp oregano
- 1 tsp onion powder
- 1 tsp Himalayan pink salt
- 1 tsp marjoram
- 1 tsp basil
- ½ tsp ground ginger

Directions:

1. Cut a series of slits in the meat, and press the garlic cloves inside.
2. In a bowl, mix the onion powder, garlic powder, salt, ginger, basil, oregano, and marjoram.
3. Rub into the meat and put in your Instant Pot. Pour in the apple cider vinegar and broth.
4. Close and seal the lid. Hit MANUAL and adjust time to 90 minutes.
5. When time is up, hit CANCEL and wait for a natural release.
6. When all the pressure is gone, open the lid and shred the beef on a plate.
7. Serve over salad, cauliflower rice, cooked sweet potatoes, and so on.

Nutritional Info (per serving): Calories - 408; Fat – 26; Fiber – 0; Carbs – 2; Protein – 40

Shredded Pepper Steak

(Prep + Cook Time: 1 hour 40 minutes | Servings: 6)

Ingredients:

- 3-4 pounds beef
- 1 16-oz jar Mild Pepper Rings (banana peppers or pepperocini)
- ½ cup salted beef broth
- 1 tbsp garlic powder
- Red chili flakes to taste

Directions:

1. Season beef with garlic powder and red chili flakes before adding to cooker.
2. Pour peppers and broth into cooker, too. Seal the lid.
3. Hit MANUAL and cook for 70 minutes.
4. When the timer beeps, hit CANCEL and wait for a natural pressure release.
5. When safe, open the cooker and shred the meat. Serve!

Nutritional Info (per serving): Calories - 442; Fat – 18; Fiber – 0; Carbs – 3; Protein – 65

Pasta with Meat Sauce

(Prep + Cook Time: 15 minutes | Servings: 4)

Ingredients:

- 1 ½ pounds ground beef
- 8-ounces dried pasta
- 24-ounces pasta sauce
- 12-ounces water
- Italian seasoning to taste

Directions:

1. Turn your cooker to SAUTE.
2. Add ground beef to brown, breaking it up with a spatula as it cooks.
3. When browned, hit CANCEL and pour in pasta, sauce, and water.
4. You'll probably have to break the pasta in half.
5. Seal the lid and hit MANUAL, cooking for 5 minutes.
6. When time is up, hit CANCEL and quick-release.
7. Season with Italian seasoning to taste and serve!

Nutritional Info (per serving): Calories - 590; Fat – 17; Fiber – 0; Carbs – 58; Protein – 47

The Ultimate Pot Roast

(Prep + Cook Time: 50 minutes | Servings: 6)

Ingredients:

- 2-3 pounds beef, chuck roast
- 4 potatoes, large-sized, cut into large cubes
- 4 carrots, chopped
- 3 tbsp steak sauce, optional
- 3 cloves garlic
- 2 tbsp olive oil
- 2 tbsp Italian Seasonings
- 2 stalks celery, chopped
- 1 onion
- 1 cups beef broth
- 1 cup red wine

Directions:

1. Press the SAUTE key of your Instant Pot.
2. Pour in the olive oil. Add the roast beef and cook each side for about 1 to 2 minutes or until browned.
3. Transfer the browned beef into a plate.
4. Put the celery, carrots, and potatoes in the pot. Top with the garlic and onion.
5. Pour the beef broth and the wine in the pot. Put the roast on top of the vegetables.
6. Spread the seasonings over the top of the roast and then spread with the steak sauce.
7. Press the CANCEL key to stop the sauté function. Cover and lock the lid. Turn the steam valve to SEALING.
8. Press the MANUAL key, set the pressure to HIGH, and set the timer for 35 minutes.
9. When the Instant Pot timer beeps, release the pressure naturally for 10-15 minutes or until the valve drops.
10. Turn the steam valve to VENTING to release remaining pressure. Unlock and carefully open the lid. Serve!

Nutritional Info (per serving): Calories - 499; Fat – 15.9; Fiber – 4.9; Carbs – 30.4; Protein – 49.8

Corned Beef And Cabbage

(Prep + Cook Time: 1 hour 30 minutes | Servings: 4)

Ingredients:
- 1 head cabbage, cut into wedges (8 cups)
- 4 pounds corned beef brisket
- 4 cloves garlic
- 4 celery stalks OR 1 cup, chopped
- 4 carrots OR 1 cup, sliced into thirds
- 2 tsp black peppercorns
- 2 tsp dried mustard
- 2 onions OR
- 1 cup sliced
- 6 cups water

Directions:
1. Put the beef into the Instant Pot. Discard the spice packet that comes with the beef. Pour the water in the pot.
2. Add more water as needed to cover the beef. Add the spices into the pot. Cover and lock the lid.
3. Press the MEAT/ STEW key, set the pressure to HIGH, and set the timer for 60 minutes.
4. When the Instant Pot timer beeps, press the CANCEL key. Let the pressure release naturally for 10-15 minutes or until the valve drops. Turn the steam valve to release remaining pressure. Unlock and carefully open the lid.
5. Remove the beef and keep warm.
6. Add the vegetables into the pot. Cover and lock the lid. Turn the steam valve to SEALING.
7. Press the SOUP key and set the timer for 15 minutes.
8. When the Instant Pot timer beeps, turn the steam valve to quick release the pressure. Unlock and carefully open the lid.
9. Return the beef into the pot and let warm through. Serve immediately.

Nutritional Info (per serving): Calories - 317; Fat – 9.7; Fiber – 2.7; Carbs – 8.1; Protein – 47.3

Hamburger Helper

(Prep + Cook Time: 20 minutes | Servings: 8)

Ingredients:

- 1 pound ground beef
- 1 tbsp garlic powder
- 1 tbsp onion powder
- 16 ounces cheddar cheese
- 16 ounces elbow macaroni
- 2 cups beef broth
- 4 ounces American cheese
- 8 ounces milk, OR heavy cream

Directions:

1. Press the SAUTE key of the Instant Pot. Put the beef in the pot. Add the onion powder and garlic powder. Sauté until the beef is no longer pink and browned, crumbling the meat in the process.
2. When the beef is browned, pour in the broth, milk, and add the uncooked pasta.
3. Press the CANCEL key to stop the sauté function. Cover and lock the lid.
4. Press the MANUAL key, set the pressure to HIGH, and set the timer for 4 minutes.
5. When the Instant Pot timer beeps, press the CANCEL key and unplug the Instant Pot. Turn the steam valve to quick release the pressure.
6. Unlock and carefully open the lid. Stir in the cheeses until mixed. Serve!

Nutritional Info (per serving): Calories - 705; Fat – 37.5; Fiber – 2; Carbs – 46.6; Protein – 43.4

Cheesy Beef Pasta

(Prep + Cook Time: 30 minutes | Servings: 8)

Ingredients:

- 1 ¼ pounds ground beef
- 1 pound elbow macaroni
- 1 packet onion soup mix
- 3 ½ cups hot water
- 3 beef bouillon cubes
- 8 ounces sharp cheddar

Directions:

1. Press the SAUTE key of the Instant Pot. Add the beef and sauté until browned.
2. While the beef is cooking, combine the bouillon cubes with the hot water, and onion soup mix in a bowl and stir until well mixed.
3. When the beef is cooked and browned.
4. Add the liquid mixture and the pasta in the pot and stir well to combine. Cover and lock the lid.
5. Press the MANUAL key, set the pressure to HIGH, and set the timer for 5 minutes.
6. When the Instant Pot timer beeps, press the CANCEL key. Turn the steam valve to quick release the pressure. Unlock and carefully open the lid.
7. Add the shredded cheese, press the SAUTE key, and sauté for about 1 to 2 minutes or until the cheese is melted. Serve immediately.

Nutritional Info (per serving): Calories - 462; Fat – 14.8; Fiber – 1.9; Carbs – 43.6; Protein – 36.3

Cheesy Taco Pasta

(Prep + Cook Time: 10 minutes | Servings: 8)

Ingredients:

- 1 pound ground beef
- 1 packet taco seasoning
- 16 ounces salsa
- 16 ounces pasta (I used ruffles)
- 16 ounces canned black beans
- 2 cups Doritos
- 16 ounces cheddar cheese
- 3 cups water
- Sour cream, for topping

Directions:

1. Press the SAUTE key of the Instant Pot.
2. Put the beef in the pot and add the taco seasoning. Sauté for about 1 to 2 minutes or until the beef is just crumbled.
3. Add the salsa, and black beans/ refried beans, uncooked pasta and water in the pot.
4. Press the CANCEL key to stop the sauté function. Cover and lock the lid.
5. Press the MANUAL key, set the pressure to HIGH, and set the timer for 4 minutes.
6. When the Instant Pot timer beeps, press the CANCEL key and unplug the Instant Pot. Turn the steam valve to quick release the pressure. Unlock and carefully open the lid.
7. Add 1/ 2 of the cheese and stir. Crumble the Doritos and line the bottom of the baking pan.
8. Pour the pasta over the Doritos, top with the rest of the cheddar cheese, and then with crumbled Doritos.
9. Bake in a preheated oven 350F for about 3-4 minutes or until the cheese is just melted.

Nutritional Info (per serving): Calories - 772; Fat – 28; Fiber – 10.4; Carbs – 78.2; Protein – 52.6

Homemade Pastrami

(Prep + Cook Time: 30 minutes | Servings: 8)

Ingredients:
- 3-4 pounds corned beef
- 2 cups water
- 3 tbsp black pepper
- 2 tbsp ground coriander
- 1 tbsp kosher salt
- 1 tbsp onion powder
- 1 tbsp garlic powder
- 1 tbsp brown sugar
- 2 tsp paprika
- ¼ tsp cloves
- ¼ tsp ground allspice
- Vegetable oil

Directions:
1. Take out the beef and rinse. Pour 2 cups of water in your cooker and lower in the trivet.
2. Put the meat, fatty side up, on the trivet and close and seal the lid.
3. Hit MANUAL and cook for 45 minutes on HIGH pressure.
4. When time is up, hit CANCEL and wait for a natural pressure release.
5. When that's done, take off the lid and wait another 20 minutes.
6. When cool, take out the meat and throw out the water. Pat dry and coat with veggie oil.
7. In a bowl, mix the spices and press on the meat. Store in a fridge wrapped in plastic wrap at least for the night, or as long as a few days.

Nutritional Information (1 slice per serving): Calories - 41; Fat – 1.6; Fiber – 0; Carbs – 6; Protein – 6

Grain-Free Paleo Meatballs

(Prep + Cook Time: 35 minutes | Servings: 2)

Ingredients:

- 1 pound grass-fed ground beef
- 5 tbsp 100% grape jelly
- 1 egg
- ½ cup chili sauce
- ¼ cup arrowroot
- 1 tsp garlic salt
- ½ tsp paprika
- ½ tsp chili powder

Directions:

1. Mix the meat, garlic salt, egg, arrowroot, and pepper in a bowl with your hands.
2. Form meatballs about the size of a golf ball.
3. Put chili sauce, jelly, paprika, and chili powder in your Instant Pot.
4. Put the meatballs inside, turning to coat in the sauce, before sealing the lid.
5. Set your pressure cooker on LOW pressure, and cook for 30 minutes.
6. When time is up, hit CANCEL and quick-release the pressure.
7. Serve meatballs with sauce.

Nutritional Info (per serving): Calories - 583; Fat – 19; Fiber – 0; Carbs – 26; Protein – 51

Beef 'n Bean Pasta Casserole

(Prep + Cook Time: 20 minutes | Servings: 4)

Ingredients:

- 1 pound lean ground beef
- One 28-ounce can of diced tomatoes
- 2 cups corn kernels
- One 15-ounce can of drained and rinsed kidney beans
- One 12-ounce bottle brown ale
- 8-ounces pasta shells
- 1 chopped yellow onion
- 1 seeded and chopped green bell pepper
- 2 tbsp sweet paprika
- 1 tbsp olive oil
- 1 tbsp minced garlic
- 1 tsp dried oregano
- 1 tsp ground cumin
- ½ tsp chipotle pepper
- ½ tsp salt

Directions:

1. Heat your oil in the Instant Pot on the SAUTE setting.
2. When hot, add garlic, bell pepper, and onion. Stir until the onion becomes clear.
3. Add the ground beef, breaking it up with a spatula if necessary.
4. Keep stirring and browning, which should take about 4 minutes.
5. Add the corn, tomatoes, beans, and seasonings. Pour in the beer. Stir until the beer foam has gone down.
6. Add the pasta and stir so it becomes coated. Close and seal the lid.
7. Select MANUAL and adjust time to 8 minutes.
8. When time is up, hit CANCEL and carefully quick-release the pressure. Stir the casserole before serving.

Nutritional Info (per serving): Calories - 638; Fat – 14; Fiber – 6; Carbs – 88; Protein – 44

Teriyaki Pork Tenderloin

(Prep + Cook Time: 30 minutes | Servings: 4)

Ingredients:

- 2 pork tenderloins, cut into half
- 2 cups teriyaki sauce (if using a thick kind, thin it out some water so prevent it from burning on the bottom of the pot)
- 2 green onions, chopped
- 2 tbsp canola oil OR a similar oil
- Generous amounts salt and pepper
- Sesame seeds, toasted

Directions:

1. Press the SAUTE button of your Instant Pot and put the oil in the pot.
2. When the pot is hot, put about 1-2 tenderloins in the pot and lightly brown a few sides of the tenderloins.
3. When the meat is browned, lay the roast down and pour the sauce over the top of the tenderloins. Cover and lock the lid.
4. Press the MANUAL key, set the pressure to HIGH, and set the timer for 20 minutes.
5. When the Instant Pot timer beeps, release the pressure naturally for 10 minutes. Turn the steam valve to release remaining pressure.
6. Unlock and carefully open the lid. Slice the meat into pieces.
7. Serve with steamed broccoli and jasmine rice.
8. Garnish with chopped green onions and toasted sesame seeds.

Nutritional Info (per serving): Calories - 538; Fat – 20.2; Fiber – 0.7; Carbs – 45.9; Protein – 40.1

Pork Ribs BBQ

(Prep + Cook Time: 30 minutes | Servings: 4)

Ingredients:

- 1 pork spare rib (about 6 pounds)
- ½ cup Knob Creek Bourbon (optional)
- ½ cup water
- Barbecue sauce
- Onion powder
- Garlic powder Chipotle

Directions:

1. Set a steamer rack in the Instant Pot and pour in the water and bourbon.
2. Sprinkle the pork ribs with the onion powder, garlic, and chipotle.
3. Coil into a circle and vertically place on the steamer rack. Cover and lock the lid.
4. Press the MANUAL key, set the pressure to HIGH, and set the timer for 25 minutes.
5. When the Instant Pot timer beeps, release the pressure naturally for 15 minutes.
6. Turn the steam valve to release remaining pressure. Unlock and carefully open the lid.
7. Transfer the pork ribs on a baking sheet lined with foil and coat with barbecue sauce.
8. Broil for a couple minutes to caramelize the sauce. Cut the ribs in-between the bones. Serve with additional sauce.

Nutritional Info (per serving): Calories - 1986; Fat – 120.5; Fiber – 0; Carbs – 0; Protein – 180.2

☐

Honey Pork Chops

(Prep + Cook Time: 25 minutes | Servings: 4)

Ingredients:

- 2 pounds pork chops, boneless
- 2 tbsp Dijon mustard
- ¼ tsp cloves, ground
- ¼ tsp black pepper
- ¼ cups honey
- ½ tsp sea salt
- ½ tsp fresh ginger, peeled and minced
- ½ tsp cinnamon
- ½ tbsp maple syrup

Directions:

1. Sprinkle the pork chops with pepper and salt.
2. Put the seasoned pork in the pot.
3. Press the SAUTE key and brown both sides of the pork chops in the pot.
4. In a bowl, combine the honey with the maple syrup, Dijon mustard, cloves, and cinnamon.
5. Pour the mix over the pork chops.
6. Press the CANCEL key to stop the sauté function. Cover and lock the lid. Press the MANUAL key, set the pressure to HIGH, and set the timer for 15 minutes.
7. When the Instant Pot timer beeps, release the pressure naturally or quickly. Unlock and carefully open the lid. Serve.

Nutritional Info (per serving): Calories - 804; Fat – 56.7; Fiber – 0.5; Carbs – 20.1; Protein – 51.4

Pork Chops With Mushroom Gravy

(Prep + Cook Time: 35 minutes | Servings: 4)

Ingredients:

- 4 pork chops, bone-in thick
- 2 tbsp vegetable oil
- 1 can condensed cream of mushroom soup
- 1 ½ cups water
- Lemon pepper

Directions:

1. Pat the pork chops dry and then liberally season with lemon pepper or your preferred seasoning. Put the oil in the in the pot and press the SAUTE key.
2. When the oil starts to sizzle, brown both sides of the pork chops in the pot. When browned, transfer into a platter.
3. When all the pork chops are browned, pour the water in the pot to deglaze the pot.
4. Stir and scrape any browned bits off from the bottom of the pot.
5. Stir in the mushroom soup and then return the browned pork chops into the pot, along with any meat juices that accumulated on the platter.
6. Press the CANCEL key to stop the sauté function. Cover and lock the lid.
7. Press the MANUAL key, set the pressure to HIGH, and set the timer for 18 minutes.
8. When the Instant Pot timer beeps, release the pressure naturally for 10-15 minutes or until the valve drops.
9. Turn the steam valve to release remaining pressure. Unlock and carefully open the lid.
10. Transfer the pork chops into a large-sized serving bowl. If needed, thicken the gravy in the pot with a slurry of flour and water.
11. Pour the thick gravy over the chops. Serve.

Nutritional Info (per serving): Calories - 381; Fat – 31.2; Fiber – 0; Carbs – 0; Protein – 19.2

Pork Fried Rice

(Prep + Cook Time: 40 minutes | Servings: 4)

Ingredients:

- 3 cups + 2 tbsp water
- 2 cups white rice
- 8-ounces thin pork loin, cut into ½-inch slices
- 1 beaten egg
- ½ cup frozen peas
- 1 chopped onion
- 1 peeled and chopped carrot
- 3 tbsp olive oil
- 3 tbsp soy sauce
- Salt and pepper to taste

Directions:

1. Turn your Instant Pot to SAUTE.
2. Pour in 1 tablespoon of oil and cook the carrot and onion for 2 minutes.
3. Season the pork. Cook in the pot for 5 minutes.
4. Hit CANCEL and take out the onion, carrot, and pork.
5. Deglaze with the water. Add rice and a bit of salt. Lock the lid.
6. Hit RICE and cook for the default time.
7. When time is up, press CANCEL and wait 10 minutes.
8. Release any leftover steam.
9. Stir the rice, making a hollow in the middle so you can see the bottom of the pot.
10. Hit SAUTE and add 2 tablespoons of oil.
11. Add the egg in the hollow and whisk it around to scramble it while it cooks. When cooked, pour in peas, onion, carrot, and pork.
12. Stir until everything has warmed together.
13. Stir in soy sauce, press CANCEL, and serve.

Nutritional Info (per serving): Calories - 547; Fat – 2; Fiber – 3; Carbs – 81; Protein – 22

Pork Carnitas

(Prep + Cook Time: 60 minutes | Servings: 4)

Ingredients:

- 4 pounds pork roast
- 4 cloves garlic, minced
- 2 tsp salt
- 2 tbsp cumin
- 2 tbsp chili powder
- 1 tsp black pepper
- 1 tbsp oregano
- 1 tbsp ghee OR coconut oil
- 1 orange, cut in half
- 1 onion, chopped
- 1 jalapeno pepper, deseeded and diced
- Small gluten-free OR corn tortillas

Directions:

1. Press the SAUTE key of the Instant Pot and wait until hot.
2. Combine the chili powder, cumin, oregano, pepper, and salt to make a rub.
3. Rub the pork the spice rub mix, coating all the surface of the meat and using all the seasoning.
4. Put the oil in the pot and add the pork. Sear each side of the pork for a couple of minutes until all the sides are beginning to get crispy.
5. Add the rest of the ingredients into the pot. Gently mix and spread out the ingredients with a spoon.
6. Squeeze the orange juice over the pork and add the orange back in in the pot to cook with the meat. Press the CANCEL key. Cover and lock the lid.
7. Press the MANUAL key, set the pressure to HIGH, and set the timer for 50 minutes.
8. When the Instant Pot timer beeps, release the pressure naturally for 10 minutes to let the meat absorb the flavor.
9. Turn the steam valve to release remaining pressure. Unlock and carefully open the lid.
10. Shred the pork carnitas and serve on quesadillas, tortillas, burritos, or top of a salad.
11. If serving on tortillas, top with avocado and sprinkle with cilantro and a dash of paprika.

Nutritional Info (per serving): Calories - 1033; Fat – 47.5; Fiber – 4.1; Carbs – 13.6; Protein – 131.4

Pork Cutlets With the Plum Sauce

(Prep + Cook Time: 40 minutes | Servings: 6)

Ingredients:

- 12 oz ground pork
- 1/3 cup lemon juice
- 6 oz plums, pitted
- 1 tbsp sugar
- 1 tsp cilantro
- ½ tsp thyme

- 1 egg
- 1 tbsp cornstarch
- 1 tbsp ground ginger
- 1 tbsp olive oil
- 1 tbsp flour
- 1 tsp paprika

Directions:

1. Combine the ground pork with the cilantro, thyme, cornstarch, paprika, and egg.
2. Mix up the mixture carefully till you get homogenous mass.
3. Then make the medium cutlets from the ground meat mixture.
4. Pour the olive oil in the Instant Pot and add the pork cutlets. Cook the cutlets at the SAUTE mode for 10 minutes.
5. Stir the cutlets till all the sides are golden brown.
6. Meanwhile, put the plums in the blender and blend them until smooth. Then add sugar, ground ginger, flour, sugar, and lemon juice.
7. Blend the mixture for 1 minute more.
8. When the cutlets are cooked – pour the plum sauce in the Instant Pot.
9. Close the lid and cook the dish at the STEW mode for 10 minutes.
10. Then remove the pork cutlets from the Instant Pot, sprinkle them with the plum sauce.
11. Serve the dish hot!

Nutritional Info (per serving): Calories - 234; Fat – 9.7; Fiber – 1; Carbs – 14.5; Protein – 23

Cilantro Pork Tacos

(Prep + Cook Time: 45 minutes | Servings: 6)

Ingredients:

- 1 tbsp cilantro
- 10 oz ground pork
- 1 tbsp tomato paste
- 1 red onion
- 1 tsp salt
- 1 tsp basil
- 1 tbsp butter
- 1 cup lettuce
- 7 oz corn tortilla
- 1 tsp paprika

Directions:

1. Combine the ground pork, salt, cilantro, paprika, and basil together in the mixing bowl.
2. Add butter and tomato paste. Stir the mixture well.
3. After this, place the ground pork mixture in the Instant Pot and close the lid.
4. Cook the dish at the MEAT mode for 27 minutes.
5. Meanwhile, chop the lettuce and peel the onion. Slice the onion.
6. When the meat is cooked – remove it from the Instant Pot and transfer in the corn tortillas.
7. Then add chopped lettuce and sliced onion. Wrap the tacos.
8. Serve the dish immediately.

Nutritional Info (per serving): Calories - 189; Fat – 6.4; Fiber – 3; Carbs – 17.5; Protein – 17

Pork Satay

(Prep + Cook Time: 35 minutes | Servings: 6)

Ingredients:

- 12 oz pork loin
- 3 tbsp apple cider vinegar
- 1 tbsp olive oil
- 1 tbsp sesame oil
- 1 tsp turmeric
- ½ tsp cayenne pepper
- 1 tsp cilantro
- 1 tsp basil
- 1 tsp brown sugar
- 1 tsp soy sauce
- 11 tbsp fish sauce

Directions:

1. Chop the pork loin into the medium pieces.
2. Place the chopped pork lion in the mixing bowl. Sprinkle the meat with the apple cider vinegar, olive oil, sesame oil, turmeric, cayenne pepper, cilantro, basil, brown sugar, soy sauce, and fish sauce. Mix up the mixture.
3. Then screw the meat into the skewers.
4. Place the skewers in the Instant Pot.
5. Cook the pork satay for 25 minutes at the MEAT mode.
6. When the dish is cooked – remove the pork satay from the Instant Pot.
7. Chill the dish little.
8. Serve the pork satay immediately. Enjoy!

Nutritional Info (per serving): Calories - 214; Fat – 12.1; Fiber – 0; Carbs – 4.3; Protein – 21

Pulled pork

(Prep + Cook Time: 40 minutes | Servings: 8)

Ingredients:
- 2-pound pork shoulder
- ½ cup tomato paste
- ½ cup cream
- ¼ cup chicken stock
- 1 tbsp salt
- 1 tsp ground black pepper
- 1 tsp cayenne pepper
- 3 tbsp olive oil
- 1 tbsp lemon juice
- 1 tsp garlic powder
- 1 onion

Directions:
1. Peel the onion and transfer it to the blender.
2. Blend the onion till it is smooth. Pour the olive oil in the Instant Pot and add pork shoulder and roast the meat at the SAUTÉ mode for 10 minutes.
3. Then add tomato paste, cream, chicken stock, ground black pepper, cayenne pepper, lemon juice, and garlic powder.
4. Mix up the mixture and close the Instant Pot lid. Cook the dish at the HIGH pressure mode for 15 minutes.
5. When the time is over – remove the pork shoulder from the Instant Pot and shred it with the help of the folk.
6. After this, return the shredded pork back in the Instant Pot and mix up the mixture carefully.
7. Cook the dish at the manual mode for 2 minutes more.
8. Then transfer the cooked dish in the serving plate.
9. Serve the dish immediately.

Nutritional Info (per serving): Calories - 403; Fat – 28.3; Fiber – 1; Carbs – 6.3; Protein – 30

Pulled BBQ Pork

(Prep + Cook Time: 1 hour 45 minutes | Servings: 4)

Ingredients:

- 2.6 pounds pork roast
- 2 cups chicken stock OR water
- ¼ cup vegetable oil
- Any of your preferred spices (Worcestershire sauce, pepper, salt)
- BBQ sauce, optional

Directions:

1. Slice the roast into halves to make it easier to handle and fit in the pot.
2. Season and spice the roast with your choice of spices or seasoning or marinade; let sit for about 20 minutes, if desired.
3. Press the SAUTE key. Put the vegetable oil in the pot and heat. When the oil is hot, add the pork and sear each side for 3 minutes.
4. Add 2 cups of liquid – stock or water – into the pot. Press the CANCEL key to stop the sauté function. Cover and lock the lid.
5. Press the MEAT/STEW key and set the timer for 90 minutes
6. When the Instant Pot timer beeps, release the pressure naturally for 10 minutes.
7. Turn the steam valve to release remaining pressure. Unlock and carefully open the lid. Transfer the pork into a plate and shred.
8. At this point, you can eat this dish as is or continue to the BBQ option. Make sure that there is 1/2 cup water in the pot.
9. Add your preferred BBQ sauce into the pot. Return the shredded pork into the pot. Stir to mix. Cover and lock the lid.
10. Press the MANUAL key, set the pressure to HIGH, and set the timer for 5 minutes.
11. When the Instant Pot timer beeps, turn the steam valve to VENTING to quick release the pressure. Unlock and carefully open the lid.
12. Serve with your favorite bread.

Nutritional Info (per serving): Calories - 783; Fat – 30; Fiber – 0.5; Carbs – 3; Protein – 120

Pulled Pork Tacos

(Prep + Cook Time: 70 minutes | Servings: 8)

Ingredients:

For the pork:

- 1 ½ tsp sea salt
- 1 cup chicken broth, OR beef broth
- 1 piece (4 lbs) pork shoulder (a.k.a pork butt, bone out or in)
- 1 tsp freshly ground pepper
- 1 yellow onion, large-sized, peeled and thinly sliced
- ½ tsp chipotle chili powder
- ½ tsp cumin
- ½ tsp garlic powder
- Your favorite or preferred tortillas

Garnish:

- Purple cabbage, sliced
- Cilantro, chopped
- Lime

Directions:

1. In a bowl, combine all of the spices until well mixed.
2. Put the onion in the Instant Pot and pour in the broth.
3. Rub all the sides of the pork with the spice mixture and then put the spice-rubbed pork into the pot. Cover and lock the lid.
4. Press the MEAT key and set the timer for 60 minutes.
5. When the Instant Pot timer beeps, press the CANCEL key and unplug the Instant Pot. Turn the steam valve to quick release the pressure. Unlock and carefully open the lid.
6. Transfer the meat into a cutting board, discard the onion and the cooking liquid.
7. With 2 forks, shred the meat, discarding the fat in the process.
8. If you want crispy, browned edges, you can sear the shredded meat in a hot pan or broil in the oven for a couple of minutes.
9. Use the shredded meat to make tacos, garnishing with sliced purple cabbage and chopped cilantro.
10. Top with your favorite guacamole and salsa.

Nutritional Info (per serving): Calories - 681; Fat – 48.9; Fiber – 0.6; Carbs – 3.2; Protein – 53.8

Cranberry BBQ Pulled Pork

(Prep + Cook Time: 55 minutes | Servings: 10)

Ingredients:

- 3-4 pounds pork shoulder or roast, boneless, fat trimmed off

For the sauce:

- 3 tbsp liquid smoke
- 2 tbsp tomato paste
- 2 cups fresh cranberries
- ¼ cup buffalo hot sauce
- 1/3 cup blackstrap molasses
- ½ cup water
- ½ cup apple cider vinegar
- 1 tsp salt, or more to taste
- 1 tbsp adobo sauce
- 1 cup tomato puree
- 1 chipotle pepper in adobo sauce, diced

Directions:

1. Cut the pork against the grain in halves or thirds and set aside.
2. Press the SAUTE key of the Instant Pot.
3. When the pot is hot, add the cranberries and the water.
4. Let simmer for about 4 to 5 minutes or until the cranberries start to pop. Add the remaining sauce ingredients in the pot and continue simmering for 5 minutes more.
5. Add the pork in the pot. Press the CANCEL key to stop the sauté function. Cover and lock the lid.
6. Press the MANUAL key, set the pressure to HIGH, and set the timer for 40 minutes.
7. When the Instant Pot timer beeps, turn the steam valve to VENTING to quick release the pressure. Unlock and carefully open the lid.
8. With a fork, pull the pork apart into shreds.
9. Serve the pork with plenty of sauce on rolls or bread or over your favorite greens.

Nutritional Info (per serving): Calories - 1150; Fat – 73; Fiber – 3.7; Carbs – 35.4; Protein – 80.9

Memphis-Rub BBQ Pork

(Prep + Cook Time: 1 hour 15 minutes | Servings: 10)

Ingredients:

- 8 pounds pork butt roast
- 25 grinds of fresh black pepper
- 1 tbsp veggie oil
- 2 tsp paprika
- 2 tsp ground cumin
- 2 tsp sugar
- 2 tsp dry oregano
- 1 tsp cayenne pepper

Directions:

1. Rub the pork with oil and then seasonings evenly all over. Put in your Instant Pot and pour in enough water to cover. Seal and close the lid.
2. Select MANUAL and cook for 65-70 minutes.
3. When time is up, hit CANCEL and carefully quick-release. Remove the pork and save 2 cups of liquid. Shred the pork with two forks.
4. Mix in with BBQ sauce, adding pot liquid as desired to get the right consistency.
5. Serve and enjoy!

Nutritional Info (per serving): Calories - 971; Fat – 70; Fiber – 0; Carbs – 1; Protein – 85

Spare Ribs and Black Bean Sauce

(Prep + Cook Time: 5 minutes | Servings: 4)

Ingredients:

- 1 pound pork spareribs, cut into pieces
- 1 tbsp corn starch
- 1 tbsp oil
- 1 tsp fish sauce, optional
- 1-2 tsp water
- Green onions as garnish

For the black bean marinade:

- 1 tbsp black bean sauce
- 1 tbsp ginger, grated
- 1 tbsp light soy sauce
- 1 tbsp Shaoxing wine
- 1 tsp sesame oil
- 1 tsp sugar
- 3 cloves garlic, minced
- A pinch white pepper

Directions:

1. In an oven-safe bowl, combine all the marinade ingredients.
2. Add the pork and marinate for 25 minutes in the refrigerator.
3. When marinated, mix 1 tablespoon oil into the pork and then add the cornstarch.
4. Mix well. Add 1 to 2 teaspoon water and mix well. Pour 1 cup water into the Instant Pot.
5. Put a steamer rack in the pot and put the bow with the marinated spare ribs on the rack.
6. Press the CANCEL key to stop the sauté function. Cover and lock the lid. Turn the steam valve to SEALING. Press the MANUAL key, set the pressure to HIGH, and set the timer for 15 minutes.
7. When the Instant Pot timer beeps, release the pressure naturally for 10-15 minutes or until the valve drops.
8. Turn the steam valve to release remaining pressure. Unlock and carefully open the lid.
9. Taste and, if desired, add 1 teaspoon fish sauce and garnish with green onions.

Nutritional Info (per serving): Calories - 778; Fat – 49.7; Fiber – 0.7; Carbs – 17.6; Protein – 61.8

Mexican Pulled-Pork Lettuce Wraps

(Prep + Cook Time: 1 hour 40 minutes | Servings: 6)

Ingredients:

- 4 pounds pork roast
- 1 head washed and dried butter lettuce
- 2 grated carrots
- 2 tbsp oil
- 2 lime wedges
- 1 chopped onion
- 1 tbsp salt
- 2-3 cups water
- 1 tbsp unsweetened cocoa powder
- 2 tsp oregano
- 1 tsp red pepper flakes
- 1 tsp garlic powder
- 1 tsp white pepper
- 1 tsp cumin
- ⅛ tsp cayenne
- ⅛ tsp coriander

Directions:

1. Marinate the pork the night before by mixing all the ingredients in the second list and rubbing into the pork. Store in the fridge.
2. The next day, turn your Instant Pot to SAUTE. When warm, brown roast all over.
3. Pour in 2-3 cups of water, so the roast is almost totally submerged. Close and seal the lid.
4. Select MANUAL and cook on HIGH pressure for 55 minutes.
5. When time is up, hit CANCEL and wait for the pressure to decrease naturally.
6. When ready, take out the meat and pull with two forks.
7. Turn the cooker back to SAUTE and reduce the liquid by half.
8. Strain and skim off any excess fat. If you want crispy pork, fry in a pan with some oil until it becomes light brown.
9. Mix pork with the cooking liquid before serving in the lettuce with grated carrots, a squirt of lime, and any other toppings.

Nutritional Info (per serving): Calories – 175.9; Fat – 13; Fiber – 2; Carbs – 13; Protein – 18

Pork Chops And Applesauce

(Prep + Cook Time: 40 minutes | Servings: 4)

Ingredients:

- 1 ½ pounds boneless pork chops
- 6 cups apples, sliced
- ½ cup brown sugar
- 2 tbsp flour
- 1 tsp cinnamon
- ½ cup water
- drizzle olive oil
- Salt and black pepper to taste

Directions:

1. In the inner pot of the pressure cooker, press the SAUTE button and add the oil.
2. Season the pork chops with salt and pepper, then place in the pot. Brown on both sides, then remove from the pot. Press the CANCEL button.
3. In a separate bowl, toss together the apples, flour, brown sugar and cinnamon.
4. Add the water to the inner pot and scrape at any browned bits left from the pork.
5. Pour the apples into the pot and place the pork on top.
6. Close the lid completely and position the steam release handle to sealing position.
7. Press the MANUAL button and set the pressure cooking time to 10 minutes.
8. When the pressure cooking cycle is completed, allow the pressure to release for 5-10 minutes.
9. Then slide the steam release handle to venting position to fully release the pressure. Open the lid when the float valve has dropped down.
10. Transfer the pork chops to a plate and serve covered in the apple mixture.

Pork Sauerkraut

(Prep + Cook Time: 40 minutes | Servings: 6)

Ingredients:

- 1 pounds country pork ribs
- 1 tbsp brown sugar
- 1 tbsp oil
- ½ tsp salt
- 1/3 cup water
- ¼ tsp pepper
- 14 ounces kielbasa, sliced
- 24 ounces sauerkraut

Directions:

1. Press the SAUTE key of the Instant Pot and wait until hot. Add the oil.
2. Add all the pork ribs in the pot, sprinkle with salt and pepper, and cook until browned.
3. Add the sauerkraut and then sprinkle the top with the brown sugar.
4. Put the kielbasa on top and pour the water in the pot.
5. Press the CANCEL key to stop the sauté function. Cover and lock the lid.
6. Press the MANUAL key, set the pressure to HIGH, and set the timer for 15 minutes.
7. When the Instant Pot timer beeps, press the CANCEL key and unplug the Instant Pot. Turn the steam valve to quick release the pressure or let the pressure release naturally. Unlock and carefully open the lid.
8. Mix the sauerkraut around a bit and serve.
9. You can enjoy this dish as is for a low carb meal or serve with mashed potatoes.

Nutritional Info (per serving): Calories - 403; Fat – 27.5; Fiber – 3.3; Carbs – 9; Protein – 29.1

Pork-and-Egg Fried Rice

(Prep + Cook Time: 40 minutes | Servings: 4)

Ingredients:
- 3 cups + 2 tbsp water
- 2 cups long-grain white rice
- 1 beaten egg
- 1 finely-chopped onion
- 1 peeled and finely-chopped carrot
- ½ cup frozen peas
- 8-ounces sliced pork loin chop (½-inch pieces)
- 3 tbsp soy sauce
- 3 tbsp veggie oil
- Salt and pepper to taste

Directions:
1. Preheat the cooker to SAUTE function and add 1 tablespoon of oil. Stir the onion and carrot for about 2 minutes.
2. Add pork after seasoning with salt and pepper. Cook for 5 minutes or until the meat is cooked all the way through.
3. Hit CANCEL and take out the onion, carrot, and pork. Pour in water and deglaze, scraping up any bits.
4. Pour in rice, salt, and seal the lid. Hit RICE and cook for whatever the default time is.
5. When time is up, hit CANCEL and wait 10 minutes for a natural release. Quick-release any leftover steam.
6. Create a hole in the rice, and pour in the rest of the olive oil before hitting SAUTE. Add egg and scramble.
7. When the egg is just about ready, add the peas, onion, carrot, and pork.
8. Keep stirring for a few minutes until everything is mixed in well.
9. Serve with soy sauce!

Nutritional Info (per serving): Calories - 547; Fat – 2; Fiber – 3; Carbs – 81; Protein – 22

First Timer's Pork Belly

(Prep + Cook Time: 1 hour 10 minutes | Servings: 4)

Ingredients:

- 1 pound pork belly
- ½-1 cup white wine
- 1 garlic clove
- Enough olive oil to coat the bottom
- Rosemary sprig
- Salt to taste
- Black pepper to taste

Directions:

1. Put oil in your cooker and turn to the SAUTE setting.
2. When hot, add pork and sear 2-3 minutes on each side until golden and crispy.
3. Pour in wine, about a quarter inch. Season pork with salt, pepper, and garlic.
4. Add garlic clove. Turn on the cooker to SAUTE to boil the liquid.
5. When boiling, lock the lid. Select MANUAL and cook on HIGH pressure for 40 minutes.
6. If you want the pork to be more like steak, cook for 30 minutes.
7. When time is up, hit CANCEL and wait for the pressure to go down on its own.
8. When the pork is room-temperature, slice and season to taste with more salt.

Nutritional Info (per serving): Calories - 610; Fat – 61; Fiber – 0; Carbs – 0; Protein – 31

French Onion Pork Chops

(Prep + Cook Time: 30 minutes | Servings: 4)

Ingredients:

- 4 boneless center-cut pork loin chops
- One 10.5-ounce French Onion soup
- One 10.5-ounce Campbell's chicken broth
- ½ cup sour cream

Directions:

1. Pour broth into the Instant Pot and lay in pork chops. Seal the lid.
2. Hit MANUAL and cook for 12 minutes.
3. When time is up, hit CANCEL and allow a natural pressure release.
4. Pork should be cooked to 145-degrees.
5. Mix sour cream and French Onion soup together.
6. Put pork chops in a baking dish and slather with mixture.
7. Broil in the oven for 3-5 minutes.
8. Serve!

Nutritional Info (per serving): Calories - 485; Fat – 28; Fiber – 0; Carbs – 11; Protein – 37

Seasoned Pork Chops with Cherry-Jam Sauce

(Prep + Cook Time: 40 minutes | Servings: 4)

Ingredients:
- Two 1 ¼-2 inch thick pork loin chops (bone-in and trimmed)
- 1 cup pearl onions
- ½ cup sour cherry jam
- ¼ cup medium-dry red wine
- 2 tbsp olive oil
- 1 tbsp butter
- ½ tsp ground cinnamon
- ¼ tsp ground coriander
- ¼ tsp ground ginger
- ¼ tsp ground cardamom
- ¼ tsp salt

Directions:
1. Mix dry spices in a bowl and coat both sides of the pork chops.
2. In your Instant Pot, melt butter on the SAUTE setting.
3. When melted, add one chop at a time and brown lightly on both sides. You want a nice golden color, not too dark, because you don't want the spice rub to burn.
4. When both chops are browned and plated, add onions to the pressure cooker.
5. Stir and cook for about 4 minutes, or until they are browned. Add jam and wine, and deglaze.
6. When the jam has dissolved, add both chops and turn to coat in the sauce. Close and seal the lid.
7. Select MANUAL and cook for 24 minutes on HIGH pressure.
8. When the timer beeps, quick-release the pressure after hitting CANCEL.
9. Cut the chops into strips to serve, with sauce on top.

Nutritional Info (per serving): Calories - 425; Fat – 19; Fiber – 1; Carbs – 22; Protein – 47

Southern Pork-Sausage Gravy

(Prep + Cook Time: 35 minutes | Servings: 8)

Ingredients:

- 1 pound pork sausage
- 2 cups whole milk
- 4 minced garlic cloves
- ¼ cup flour
- Water as needed

Directions:

1. Turn your Instant Pot to SAUTE and add garlic. If they start to stick, pour in a little water.
2. When fragrant and golden, add the meat. Cook until brown, breaking up with a spatula.
3. Add 1 ½ cups milk and seal the lid.
4. Hit MANUAL and cook for 5 minutes.
5. When time is up, turn off the cooker and carefully quick-release the pressure.
6. If it sprays too much, wait 5 minutes or so. Mix flour and remaining milk in a bowl until smooth.
7. Hit SAUTE again on the open cooker, and slowly add into the gravy.
8. When it starts to bubble and thicken, it's ready to serve!

Nutritional Info (per serving): Calories - 247; Fat – 18; Fiber – 0; Carbs – 9; Protein – 14

Milk-Braised Pork

(Prep + Cook Time: 55 minutes | Servings: 4)

Ingredients:

- 2 pounds of pork loin roast, tied together with kitchen string
- 2 ½ cups milk
- 2 tbsp olive oil
- 2 tbsp butter
- 1 bay leaf
- 2 tsp salt
- 2 tsp ground pepper

Directions:

1. Melt the butter in your Instant Pot on SAUTE. Add oil. Put in the meat, fatty-side down, and brown all over.
2. Sprinkle in salt, pepper, bay leaf, and pour in milk. The roast should be half-covered. Close and seal the lid.
3. Hit MANUAL and cook for 30 minutes.
4. When time is up, hit CANCEL and wait for the pressure to come down.
5. After 10 minutes, quick-release leftover pressure.
6. Transfer roast to a dish and tent with foil.
7. Wait for the sauce to cool in the pot, and then skim off the fat. Pick out the bay leaf.
8. Turn the pot to sauté and reduce if you want it to be thicker.
9. If there are milk clusters and you don't want them, whisk in a little bit of milk to smooth.
10. Serve roast slices with sauce poured on top.

Nutritional Info (per serving): Calories - 382; Fat – 19; Fiber – 0; Carbs – 4; Protein – 45

Pork Roast with Cranberries, Honey, and Herbs

(Prep + Cook Time: 1 hour 25 minutes | Servings: 4)

Ingredients:

- 2 pounds boneless pork roast
- 12-ounces frozen cranberries
- 10-ounces bone broth
- 2 tbsp apple cider vinegar
- 2 tbsp chopped herbs
- 1 tbsp honey
- 1 tbsp grass-fed butter
- ¼ tsp cinnamon
- ¼ tsp ground garlic
- ⅛ tsp cinnamon
- Salt to taste

Directions:

1. Turn your cooker on to the SAUTE setting and add butter.
2. When the butter is melted and coats the bottom, salt the pork and add to the pot. Sear for 2 minutes on each side.
3. Pour in broth and cranberries.
4. Add in vinegar, honey, and herbs. Close and seal the lid.
5. Press MANUAL and cook for 70 minutes on HIGH pressure.
6. When time is up, hit CANCEL and carefully quick-release. Take out the pork and shred. Return to the pot and add more salt.
7. Seal the lid again and press MANUAL and cook for 10 more minutes.
8. Serve pork with cooked cranberries, cloves, garlic, and cinnamon.

Nutritional Info (per serving): Calories - 689; Fat – 38; Fiber – 3.9; Carbs – 31; Protein – 45

Ham and Peas

(Prep + Cook Time: 50 minutes | Servings: 10)

Ingredients:

- 5 ounces ham, diced
- 1 pound dried peas, use black-eyed (rinse, but do not pre-soak)
- 6 ½ cups stock (vegetable or chicken)

Directions:

1. Put all of the ingredients into the pot. Cover and lock the lid.
2. Press the MANUAL key, set the pressure to HIGH, and set the timer to 30 minutes.
3. When the Instant Pot timer beeps, press the CANCEL key and unplug the Instant Pot.
4. Let the pressure release naturally for 10-15 minutes or until the valve drops.
5. Unlock and carefully open the lid. Taste and season with salt and pepper as needed.

Note: The cooking time indicated for this dish cooked the peas well-done and soft, with a couple falling apart. If you want the peas to be more firm, then reduce the cooking time for a couple of minutes.

Nutritional Info (per serving): Calories - 85; Fat – 2.3; Fiber – 2.5; Carbs – 7.7; Protein – 8

Glazed Honey Ham

(Prep + Cook Time: 35 minutes | Servings: 8)

Ingredients:

- 6-7 pound ham, boneless
- ½ cup honey
- 1 cup brown sugar
- 1 tsp ground cloves
- 4 tbsp crushed pineapple, juice included
- 1 cup water

Directions:

1. Prepare the ham by slicing it as you would for serving. This will help distribute the glaze.
2. In the inner pot of the pressure cooker, add 1 cup of water and the steam rack.
3. Create a sling using tin foil to help remove the ham when it is done cooking.
4. Place the sliced ham in a tinfoil packet. Sprinkle with brown sugar and drizzle with the honey.
5. Distribute the cloves evenly and top with the pineapple and juice. close the packet and place on the steam rack.
6. Close the lid completely and position the steam release handle to sealing position.
7. Press the MANUAL button and set the pressure cooking time to 10 minutes.
8. When the pressure cooking cycle is completed, slide the steam release handle to venting position to fully release the pressure. Open the lid when the float valve has dropped down.
9. Transfer the ham to a serving platter and serve immediately with the sauce in a separate serving sauce bowl.

Holiday Brussels Sprouts

(Prep + Cook Time: 35 minutes | Servings: 6)

Ingredients:

- 6 cups Brussels sprouts, chopped
- 5 slices bacon, chopped
- 2 tbsp water
- 2 tbsp balsamic reduction
- ¼ tsp salt
- ¼ cup soft goat cheese, optional
- Pepper, to taste

Directions:

1. Press the SAUTE key of the Instant Pot. Add the bacon and sauté until desired crispiness is achieved.
2. Add the Brussels sprouts and stir to coat with the scrumptious bacon fat.
3. Add the water and sprinkle with pepper and salt. Cook for about 4 to 6 minutes, stirring occasionally, and continue sautéing until the Brussel sprouts are crisp. Transfer into a serving dish.
4. Drizzle with balsamic reduction and, if desired, sprinkle with crumbled goat cheese.

Notes: If a bit of bacon stuck in the inner pot, put 1 cup of soapy water in the pot and PRESS SAUTÉ. The browned bits will come right off. Easy to clean up afterwards.

Nutritional Info (per serving): Calories - 140; Fat – 8.1; Fiber – 3.3; Carbs – 8.4; Protein – 9.9

Turnip Greens With Bacon

(Prep + Cook Time: 50 minutes | Servings: 4)

Ingredients:

- 1 bag (1-pound) turnip greens
- ½-1 cup smoked ham hocks or necks
- 3-4 slices bacon, cut into small pieces
- 2 cups chicken broth
- ½ cup onion, diced (I use frozen)
- Splash extra-virgin olive oil
- Salt and pepper, to taste

Directions:

1. Set the Instant Pot to SAUTE. Pour a splash of olive oil. Add the bacon, the smoked ham, and onion.

2. Season with salt and pepper and sauté until the fat is rendered and the meat is cooked.
3. Add the broth and the greens. Close and lock the lid. Turn the steam release valve to SEALING. Set to pressure and cook on HIGH for 30 minutes.
4. When the timer beeps, quick release the pressure and serve warm.

Nutritional Info (per serving): Calories - 192; Fat – 10.4; Fiber – 4.2; Carbs – 10.8; Protein – 14.1

Collard Greens With Bacon

(Prep + Cook Time: 40 minutes | Servings: 6)

Ingredients:

- ¼ pound bacon, cut into 1-inch pieces
- 1 pound collard greens, cleaned and then stems trimmed
- ½ tsp kosher salt
- ½ cup water
- Fresh ground black pepper

Directions:

1. Spread the bacon in the bottom of the Instant Pot inner pot.
2. Press the SAUTÉ button and cook for about 5 minutes, occasionally stirring until the bacon is crispy and browned.
3. Stir in a big handful of collard greens to coat with bacon grease until slightly wilted. Pack in the rest of the collards.
4. The pot will be filled –just pack them enough to close the lid since they will quickly wilt.
5. Sprinkle the greens with salt and pour water over everything. Close and lock the lid. Turn the steam release valve to SEALING, set the pressure to HIGH, and the timer to 20 minutes.
6. When the timer beeps, turn the steam valve to VENTING to quick release the pressure. Carefully open and remove the lid.
7. Pour the collard into a serving dish.
8. Sprinkle with freshly ground black pepper and then serve.

. *Nutritional Info (per serving):* Calories - 123; Fat – 8.4; Fiber – 2.5; Carbs – 4.4; Protein – 8.7

Meat Lover's Crustless Quiche

(Prep + Cook Time: 50 minutes | Servings: 4)

Ingredients:

- 6 large eggs, well beaten
- ½ cup milk
- ¼ tsp salt
- 1/8 tsp ground black pepper
- 4 slices bacon, cooked and then crumbled
- 1 cup ground sausage, cooked
- ½ cup ham, diced
- 2 large green onions, chopped
- 1 cup cheese, shredded
- 1 ½ cups water

Directions:

1. Pour the water into the Instant Pot container and put a stainless steel rack with handle into the bottom of the pot. In a large-sized bowl, whisk the eggs with the milk, salt, and pepper.
2. Add the sausage, bacon, ham, cheese, and green onions into a 1-quart soufflé dish; mix well.
3. Pour the egg mix over the meat; stir well to combine.
4. With an aluminum foil, loosely cover the dish. Put onto the rack. Lock the pot lid. Set the pressure to HIGH and the timer to 30 minutes.
5. When the timer beeps, turn the pot off, let the pressure release naturally for 10 minutes, and then turn the valve to VENTING to release remaining pressure.
6. Carefully open the pot lid. Lift out the rack with the dish.
7. Remove the foil covering and, if desired, sprinkle the top of the quiche with additional cheese and broil until melted and slightly browned.
8. Serve immediately.

Nutritional Info (per serving): Calories - 419; Fat – 31.3; Fiber – 0.6; Carbs – 4.1; Protein – 29.6

Thyme Lamb

(Prep + Cook Time: 55 minutes | Servings: 8)

Ingredients:

- 1 cup fresh thyme
- 1 tbsp olive oil
- 2-pound lamb
- 1 tsp oregano
- 1 tbsp ground black pepper
- 1 tsp paprika
- ¼ cup rice wine
- 1 tsp sugar
- 4 tbsp butter
- ¼ cup chicken stock
- 1 tbsp turmeric

Directions:

1. Chop the fresh thyme and combine it with the oregano, ground black pepper, paprika, rice wine, sugar, chicken stock, and turmeric.
2. Mix up the mixture.
3. Sprinkle the lamb with the spice mixture and stir it carefully.
4. After this, transfer the lamb mixture in the Instant Pot and add olive oil.
5. Close the Instant Pot lid and cook the dish at the MEAT mode for 45 minutes.
6. When the meat is cooked – remove it from the Instant Pot.
7. Chill the lamb little and slice it. Enjoy!

Nutritional Info (per serving): Calories - 384; Fat – 27.6; Fiber – 2; Carbs – 5.15; Protein – 29

Lamb Shanks

(Prep + Cook Time: 1 hour 10 minutes | Servings: 4)

Ingredients:

- 3 pounds lamb shanks
- 3 carrots, peeled and chopped
- 1 can (14 ounces) fire-roasted tomatoes
- ¼ tsp pepper
- ½ tsp salt
- ½ tsp crushed red pepper flakes
- 1 yellow onion, diced
- 1 tbsp tomato paste
- 1 tbsp coconut oil
- 1 tbsp balsamic vinegar
- 1 cup beef stock
- 3 stalks celery, diced
- 4 cloves garlic, minced Italian parsley, chopped, for garnish

Directions:

1. Sprinkle the lamb shanks with pepper and salt.
2. Press the SAUTE key of the Instant Pot and wait until hot.
3. Add the coconut oil and heat.
4. When the oil hot, cook the lamb shanks for about 8 to 10 or until all sides are browned. Transfer into a platter.
5. Add the garlic, onion, celery, and carrots in the pot.
6. Season with pepper and salt. Cook, frequently stirring, until the onion is translucent – be careful not to burn the garlic.
7. Add the fire-roasted tomatoes and the tomato paste. Stir to mix. Return the lamb shanks in the pot. Add the beef stock and balsamic vinegar.
8. Press the CANCEL key to stop the sauté function. Cover and lock the lid.
9. Press the MANUAL key, set the pressure to HIGH, and set the timer for 45 minutes.
10. When the Instant Pot timer beeps, release the pressure naturally for 10-15 minutes or until the valve drops.
11. Turn the steam valve to release remaining pressure. Unlock and carefully open the lid.
12. Transfer the lamb shanks in a serving plate. Ladle the sauce over the shanks.
13. Garnish with chopped fresh parsley.

Nutritional Info (per serving): Calories – 405; Fat – 28.8; Fiber – 3.4; Carbs – 13.3; Protein – 98.3☐

Lamb and Avocado Salad

(Prep + Cook Time: 45 minutes | Servings: 10)

Ingredients:

- 1 avocado, pitted
- 1 cucumber
- 8 oz lamb fillet
- 3 cups water
- 1 tsp salt
- 1 tsp chili pepper
- 3 tbsp olive oil
- 1 garlic clove
- 1 tsp basil
- 1 tbsp sesame oil
- 1 cup lettuce

Directions:

1. Place the lamb fillet in the Instant Pot and add water.
2. Sprinkle the mixture with the salt.
3. Peel the garlic clove and add it to the lamb mixture. Close the lid and cook the dish at the MEAT mode for 35 minutes.
4. Meanwhile, slice the cucumbers and chop the avocado. Combine the ingredients together in the mixing bowl.
5. Chop the lettuce roughly and add it to the mixing bowl.
6. After this, sprinkle the mixture with the chili pepper, olive oil, basil, and sesame oil.
7. When the meat is cooked – remove it from the Instant Pot and chill it well.
8. Chop the meat roughly and add it to the mixing bowl.
9. Mix up the salad carefully and transfer it to the serving bowl.
10. Serve the dish warm. Enjoy!

Nutritional Info (per serving): Calories - 203; Fat – 17.5; Fiber – 2; Carbs – 3.5; Protein – 9

Ground Lamb Curry

(Prep + Cook Time: 55 minutes | Servings: 4)

Ingredients:

- 1 pound ground lamb
- 3 carrots, chopped
- 1 can (13.5 ounce) tomato sauce
- 2 potatoes, chopped
- 1 cup frozen peas, rinsed
- 1 onion, diced
- 1 tbsp coriander powder
- 1 tsp meat masala, homemade
- 1 tsp paprika
- 1 tsp salt
- ½ tsp cumin powder
- ½ tsp Kashmiri chili powder (or 1/4 tsp cayenne)
- ½ tsp black pepper
- ¼ tsp turmeric powder
- 1-2 Serrano peppers, minced, or more to taste
- 1-inch fresh ginger, minced
- 2 tbsp ghee OR grass-fed butter
- 4 garlic cloves, minced
- 4 tomatoes, chopped
- Cilantro, garnish

Directions:

1. Press the SAUTE key of the Instant Pot.
2. Add the ghee and the onions. Cook until the onion starts to brown.
3. Add the garlic, ginger, and Serrano pepper. Stir-fry for 1 minute.
4. Add the tomatoes. Cook for5 minutes or until the tomatoes begin to break down.
5. Add the spice and stir-fry for 1 minute.
6. Add the ground lamb and cook until the meat is browned.

7. Add the potatoes, carrots, peas, and tomato sauce. Mix well until combined. Press the CANCEL key to stop the sauté function. Cover and lock the lid.
8. Press the CHILI key and cook on preset time, which is 30 minutes.
9. When the Instant Pot timer beeps, release the pressure naturally for 10-15 minutes or until the valve drops.
10. Turn the steam valve to VENTING to release remaining pressure.
11. Unlock and carefully open the lid. Serve.

Nutritional Info (per serving): Calories - 460; Fat – 15.6; Fiber – 10; Carbs – 42.1; Protein – 39.2

Lamb Shanks With Figs And Ginger

(Prep + Cook Time: 1 hour 50 minutes | Servings: 4)

Ingredients:

- 2 tbsp coconut oil
- 4 pieces (12-ounce) lamb shanks
- 1 onion, large-sized, sliced thinly pole-to-pole
- 2 tbsp fresh ginger, minced
- 2 tbsp coconut aminos
- 2 tbsp apple cider vinegar
- 2 tsp fish sauce
- 2-3 cloves garlic, finely minced
- 1 ½ cups bone broth
- 10 dried figs, stems cut off and cut lengthwise into halves

Directions:

1. Press the SAUTE key of the Instant Pot.
2. When hot, put in 1 tablespoon coconut oil in the pot.

3. Put 2 pieces lamb shanks in the pot and cook until all sides are browned, occasionally turning the meat.
4. Transfer into a bowl or a plate. Repeat the process with the remaining tablespoon coconut oil and lamb shanks.
5. Put the ginger and the onion in the pot. Cook, stirring often, for about 3 minutes or until the onion is soft. Stir in the garlic, fish sauce, vinegar, and coconut aminos.
6. Stir in the broth and scrape the browned bits off from the bottom of the pot.
7. Add the figs as return the brown shanks, along with the meat juices collected in the bowl/ plate, in the pot.
8. Make sure that the meaty part of the shanks are at least partially submerged in the cooking liquid. Press the CANCEL key to stop the sauté function. Cover and lock the lid.
9. Press the MANUAL key, set the pressure to HIGH, and set the timer for 1 hour.
10. When the Instant Pot timer beeps, turn off and release the pressure naturally for 10-15 minutes or until the valve drops. Turn the steam valve to VENTING to release remaining pressure. Unlock and carefully open the lid.
11. Transfer the shanks into a serving platter. Skim the fat off from the surface of the sauce and discard.
12. Alternatively, you can pour the sauce in a fat separator. Ladle the de-fatted sauce over the shanks.
13. Serve with cauliflower rice or white rice.

Nutritional Info (per serving): Calories - 855; Fat – 32.9; Fiber – 5.7; Carbs – 36.3; Protein – 100.7

Braised Lamb Shanks With Carrots And Tomatoes

(Prep + Cook Time: 50 minutes | Servings: 4)

Ingredients:

- 2 pounds lamb shanks
- 2 carrots, peeled and sliced
- 2 cups whole canned tomatoes, sliced
- 1 white onion, large
- 3 sprigs fresh oregano, chopped
- 3 sprigs fresh rosemary, chopped
- 3 sprigs fresh thyme, chopped
- 6 cloves garlic, sliced
- 6 tbsp oil
- 1½ cups veal stock or beef stock
- Flour, for dredging
- Salt and pepper to taste

Directions:

1. Press the SAUTE key of the Instant Pot.
2. Dredge the lamb shanks with flour and cook in the pot until all the sides are browned.
3. When the lamb shanks are browned, add all the ingredients in the pot, except for the canned tomatoes. Press the CANCEL key to stop the sauté function. Cover and lock the lid.
4. Press the MANUAL key, set the pressure to HIGH, and set the timer for 25 minutes.
5. When the Instant Pot timer beeps, turn the steam valve to VENTING to quick release the pressure. Unlock and carefully open the lid. Add the canned tomatoes. Cover and lock the lid again.
6. Press the MANUAL key, set the pressure to HIGH, and set the timer for 5 minutes.

7. When the Instant Pot timer beeps, turn the steam valve to VENTING to quick release the pressure. Unlock and carefully open the lid. If desired, thicken the gravy.
8. Pour the gravy over the lamb shanks and other food.
9. Serve!

Nutritional Info (per serving): Calories - 703; Fat – 38.1; Fiber – 5.8; Carbs – 17.7; Protein – 72

Indian Curry Lamb Spareribs

(Prep + Cook Time: 40 minutes | Servings: 4)

Ingredients:

For the lamb:
- 2 ½ pounds lamb spare ribs, pastured
- 1 tbsp curry powder (I used Maharajah Style Curry Powder)
- 2 teaspoons kosher salt

For the sauce:
- 1 ¼ cup cilantro, chopped, divided
- 1 large yellow onion, coarsely chopped
- 1 lemon, juice only
- 1 tbsp coconut oil
- 1 tbsp curry powder (I used Maharajah Style Curry Powder)
- 1 tbsp kosher salt
- ½ pound ripe tomatoes
- 4 scallions, thinly sliced
- 5 cloves garlic, minced

Directions:

1. Season the spare ribs with 2 teaspoons salt and 1 tablespoon curry powder.

2. Use your hands to massage the meat to coat the ribs thoroughly. Cover and refrigerate for at least 4 hours up to 1 day.
3. When ready to cook, press the SAUTE key of the Instant Pot. Put the coconut oil in the pot and melt.
4. In two batches, cook the spare ribs until all the sides are browned.
5. Transfer the browned meat into a plate.
6. While the ribs are cooking, put the tomatoes and the onion and blend until smooth.
7. When the ribs are browned, add the garlic into the pot and sauté for about 30 seconds or until fragrant.
8. Add the tomato and onion puree.
9. Add the salt, curry powder, 1 cup cilantro, and lemon juice. Bring to a boil. Return the browned ribs into the pot. Mix to coat the ribs with the sauce. Press the CANCEL key to stop the sauté function. Cover and lock the lid.
10. Press the MANUAL key, set the pressure to HIGH, and set the timer for 20 minutes.
11. When the Instant Pot timer beeps, release the pressure naturally for 10-15 minutes or until the valve drops. Turn the steam valve to VENTING to release remaining pressure. Unlock and carefully open the lid.
12. Scoop the grease off the top and discard. Taste and, if needed, adjust the seasoning.
13. Stir in the chopped cilantro and scallions.

Nutritional Info (per serving): Calories - 1211; Fat – 49.8; Fiber – 6.4; Carbs – 20.4; Protein – 163.2

Lamb and Feta Meatballs

(Prep + Cook Time: 15 minutes | Servings: 6)

Ingredients:

- 1 ½ pounds ground lamb
- 4 minced garlic cloves
- One, 28-ounce can of crushed tomatoes
- 6-ounce can of tomato sauce
- 1 beaten egg
- 1 chopped green bell pepper
- 1 chopped onion
- ½ cup crumbled feta cheese
- ½ cup breadcrumbs
- 2 tbsp chopped parsley
- 2 tbsp olive oil
- 1 tbsp chopped mint
- 1 tbsp water
- 1 tsp dried oregano
- ½ tsp salt
- ¼ tsp black pepper

Directions:

1. In a bowl, mix lamb, egg, breadcrumbs, mint, parsley, feta, water, half of the minced garlic, pepper, and salt.
2. With your hands, mold into 1-inch meatballs.
3. Turn your Instant Pot to SAUTE and add oil.
4. When hot, toss in the bell pepper and onion. Cook for 2 minutes before adding the rest of the garlic.
5. After another minute, mix in crushed tomatoes with their liquid, the tomato sauce, and oregano. Sprinkle in salt and pepper.
6. Put the meatballs in and ladle over the sauce before sealing the cooker lid.
7. Select MANUAL and adjust time to 8 minutes on HIGH pressure.
8. When time is up, hit CANCEL and carefully quick-release.
9. Serve meatballs with parsley and more cheese!

Nutritional Info (per serving): Calories - 384; Fat – 17; Fiber – 0; Carbs – 17; Protein – 38

Half-Hour Rosemary Lamb

(Prep + Cook Time: 35 minutes | Servings: 6)

Ingredients:

- 4 pounds cubed, boneless lamb
- 1 ½ cups veggie stock
- 1 cup sliced carrots
- 4 minced garlic cloves
- 4-6 rosemary sprigs
- 3 tbsp flour
- 2 tbsp olive oil
- Salt and pepper to taste

Directions:

1. Preheat your cooker with oil, using the SAUTE setting.
2. Season the lamb with salt and pepper. Put in the cooker along with minced garlic.
3. Cook until the lamb has browned all over.
4. Whisk the flour in quickly before slowly pouring in the stock.
5. Add rosemary and carrots. Seal the lid closed.
6. Select MANUAL and adjust time to 20 minutes on HIGH pressure.
7. When the timer beeps, hit CANCEL and quick-release the pressure.
8. Open up the lid and pick out the rosemary stems.
9. Serve lamb with plenty of sauce.

Nutritional Info (per serving): Calories - 921; Fat – 65; Fiber – 1; Carbs – 5; Protein – 72

Garlic Lamb Shanks with Port

(Prep + Cook Time: 1 hour 7 minutes | Servings: 4)

Ingredients:

- 4 pounds lamb shanks
- 1 cup chicken broth
- 1 cup port pine
- 20 peeled, whole garlic cloves
- 2 tbsp tomato paste
- 2 tbsp butter
- 2 tsp balsamic vinegar
- 1 tsp dried rosemary
- Salt and pepper to taste

Directions:

1. Trim any fat you don't want from the lamb and season generously with salt and pepper.
2. Heat oil in your Instant Pot on the SAUTE setting, and when hot, add the lamb. Brown all over.
3. When the lamb is golden, add garlic and stir until they've browned.
4. Pour in port and stock, and stir in tomato paste and rosemary.
5. When the tomato paste has dissolved, close and seal the lid.
6. Select MANUAL and cook on HIGH pressure for 32 minutes.
7. When time is up, hit CANCEL and wait 20 minutes for a natural pressure release. Carefully remove lamb.
8. Turn the pot back to SAUTE to boil the cooking liquid. Boil for 5 minutes to reduce it down and thicken.
9. Mix in butter, and then vinegar.
10. Serve with sauce poured over the lamb.

Nutritional Info (per serving): Calories - 640; Fat – 0; Fiber – 0; Carbs – 8.65; Protein – 62.35

Ginger-Spiced Lamb Shanks with Figs

(Prep + Cook Time: 1 hour 45 minutes | Servings: 6)

Ingredients:

- Four, 12-ounce lamb shanks
- 1½ cups bone broth
- 10 halved and stemmed dried figs
- 3 minced garlic cloves
- 1 sliced onion
- 2 tbsp coconut oil
- 2 tbsp coconut aminos
- 2 tbsp fresh, minced ginger
- 2 tbsp apple cider vinegar
- 2 tsp fish sauce
- Salt and pepper to taste

Directions:

1. Turn your Instant Pot to SAUTE and add 1 tablespoon of oil. When hot, brown the lamb all over. You'll probably have to do two at a time and add more coconut oil.
2. When all the shanks are browned, plate.
3. Add onion and ginger to the pot and stir for 3 minutes. Add vinegar, fish sauce, coconut aminos, and minced garlic.
4. Pour in the broth and figs, deglazing any stuck-on meat or onion.
5. Put the meat back into the pot. Close and seal the lid.
6. Hit MANUAL and cook on HIGH pressure for 60 minutes.
7. When time is up, hit CANCEL and wait for the pressure to come down on its own (30 minutes).
8. When safe, open the lid and move the shanks to clean plates.
9. With a tablespoon, skim off any excess fat from the sauce before tasting and seasoning with salt and pepper as needed.
10. Pour sauce over the lamb and serve!

Nutritional Info (per serving): Calories - 744; Fat – 42; Fiber – 4; Carbs – 35; Protein – 52

Quick Seafood Paella

(Prep + Cook Time: 55 minutes | Servings: 4)

Ingredients:

- For the fish stock:
- 6 cups water
- 4 white fish heads (I used cod)
- 2 carrots
- 1 celery
- 1 bay leaf
- Bunch parsley with stems
- For the paella:
- 1 ¾ cups seafood stock or vegetable stock
- 1 cup seafood mix (meaty white fish, squid, scallops)
- 2 cups mixed shellfish (clams, shrimp, and mussels)
- 2 cups rice, short-grain
- 1 green bell pepper, diced
- 1 red bell pepper, diced
- 1 yellow onion, medium-sized, diced
- 1/8 tsp ground turmeric
- 2 tsp sea salt
- 4 tbsp extra-virgin olive oil
- Large pinch saffron threads

Directions:

1. Put all the fish stock ingredients in the Instant Pot.
2. Press MANUAL and set the timer for 5 minutes.
3. When the timer beeps, let the pressure release naturally. Transfer the fish stock in a heatproof container and set aside.
4. Wash and dry the inner pot. Return to the housing. Press the SAUTE key.
5. Add the olive oil and heat. When the oil is hot, add the onions and peppers, and sauté for about 4 minutes or until the onions are soft.
6. Stir in the rice, saffron, seafood, and sauté for 2 minutes.
7. Add h stock, salt, and turmeric, and stir to mix.

8. Arrange the shellfish on top – do not mix. Lock the lid and close the steam valve. Cook on HIGH pressure for 6 minutes.
9. When the timer is up, let the pressure release naturally for 15 minutes.
10. Open the steam valve to release any remaining pressure. Carefully open the lid.
11. Mix the paella, close the lid, and let stand for 1 minute. Serve!

Notes: If you don't want to make your own fish stock, you can use vegetable stock instead. You can use avocado oil instead of olive oil to sauté the aromatic.

Nutritional Info (per serving): Calories - 665; Fat – 17.7; Fiber – 3.6; Carbs – 91.3; Protein – 33.3

Seafood Cranberries Plov
(Prep + Cook Time: 40 minutes | Servings: 4)

Ingredients:
- 1 package (16 ounces) frozen seafood blend, (I used Trader Joe's)
- 1 lemon, sliced
- 1 onion, large-sized, chopped
- 1 ½ cups basmati rice, organic
- 1 pepper, red or yellow, sliced
- ½ cup dried cranberries
- 2-3 tbsp butter
- 3 cups water
- 3-4 big shredded carrots
- Salt and pepper, to taste

Directions:
1. Press the SAUTE key of the Instant Pot and wait until the word HOT appears on the display.
2. Put the butter in the pot. Add the onion, carrots, pepper, and cook stirring for about 5-7 minutes.
3. Stir in the rice, seafood blend, and cranberries.
4. Season generously and add 3 cups water.
5. Press RICE and lock the lid.
6. Just before servings, squeeze fresh squeezed lemon juice over the dish.

Nutritional Info (per serving): Calories - 430; Fat – 7.3; Fiber – 3.3; Carbs – 66.6; Protein – 21.4

Shrimp Creole

(Prep + Cook Time: 20 minutes | Servings: 4)

Ingredients:

- 1 can (28 ounces) crushed tomatoes
- 1 pound jumbo shrimp, frozen, peeled and deveined
- 1 onion, medium-sized, chopped
- 1 tsp thyme
- ¼ tsp cayenne pepper, or to taste
- 2 cloves garlic, minced
- 2 stalks celery, diced
- 1 bay leaf
- 1 bell pepper, diced
- 1 tbsp tomato paste
- 1 tsp salt
- ½ tsp pepper
- 2 tsp olive oil

Directions:

1. Press the SAUTE key of the Instant Pot. Add the oil and heat.
2. When the oil is hot, add the vegetables and sauté for 3 minutes or until the veggies starts to soften.
3. Add the tomato paste. Stir and cook for 1 minute.
4. Add the crushed tomatoes, shrimp, seasoning, and stir to combine.
5. Press MANUAL, set the pressure to HIGH, and set the timer to 1 minute.
6. When the timer beeps, quick release the pressure.
7. Carefully open the lid. If the shrimp is not fully cooked, press the SAUTE key and cook the shrimp for 1 minute, constantly stirring.
8. Serve over rice.

Nutritional Info (per serving): Calories - 264; Fat – 4.5; Fiber – 7.9; Carbs – 24.4; Protein – 31.6 ☐

Grispy Skin Salmon Fillet
(Prep + Cook Time: 20 minutes | Servings: 2)

Ingredients:
- 2 salmon fillets, frozen (1-inch thickness)
- 1 cup tap water, running cold
- 2 tbsp olive oil
- Salt and pepper to taste

Directions:
1. Pour 1 cup water in the Instant Pot.
2. Set the steamer rack and put the salmon fillets in the rack. Lock the lid and close the steamer valve.
3. Press MANUAL, set the pressure on LOW, and set the timer for 1 minute.
4. When the timer beeps, turn off the pot and quick release the pressure.
5. Carefully open the lid. Remove the salmon fillets and pat them dry using paper towels.
6. Over medium-high heat, preheat a skillet.
7. Grease the salmon fillet skins with 1 tablespoon olive oil and generously season with black pepper and salt.
8. When the skillet is very hot, with the skin side down, put the salmon fillet in the skillet.
9. Cook for 1-2 minutes until the skins are crispy.
10. Transfer the salmon fillets into serving plates and serve with your favorite side dishes.
11. This dish is great with rice and salad.

Notes: You can use a nonstick skillet to make sure the skin does not stick to the skillet. If you do not like the skin on your salmon, you can remove it after pressure cooking. Increase the cooking time to 2 minutes.

Nutritional Info (per serving): Calories - 356; Fat – 25; Fiber – 0; Carbs – 0; Protein – 34.5

Dijon Salmon

(Prep + Cook Time: 10 minutes | Servings: 2)

Ingredients:

- 2 pieces firm fish fillets or steaks, such as salmon, scrod, cod, or halibut
- 1 cup water
- 1 tsp
- Dijon mustard per fish fillet
- Steamer basket or trivet

Directions:

1. On the fleshy portion of the fish fillets, spread 1 teaspoon of Dijon mustard over.
2. Pour 1 cup of water into the Instant Pot.
3. Set the steamer basket or trivet in the pot.
4. With the skin side faced down, put the fish fillets in the steamer basket/ trivet. Cover and lock the lid.
5. Press MANUAL and set the timer according to the thickest fish fillet.
6. When the timer beeps, turn the steam valve to quick release the pressure. Serve.

Nutritional Info (per serving): Calories - 191; Fat – 1.7; Fiber – 0; Carbs – 0.1; Protein – 41.2

Fast Salmon With Broccoli

(Prep + Cook Time: 4 minutes | Servings: 1)

Ingredients:

- 2.5 oz broccoli
- 2.5 oz salmon fillet
- 6 oz water
- Salt and pepper to taste

Directions:

1. Pour the water in the Instant Pot and set a steamer rack in the pot.
2. Chop the broccoli into florets. Season both the salmon and the broccoli with pepper and salt.
3. Put both on the steamer rack in the pot. Cover and lock the lid.
4. Press the STEAM key and set the timer for 2 minutes.
5. When the Instant Pot timer beeps, let the pressure release naturally for 10-15 minutes or until the valve drops. Eurn the steam valve to release remaining pressure.
6. Unlock and carefully open the lid. Serve.

Notes: This dish is good for a small lunch. If you are doubling this recipe, then add an additional 1 minute to the cooking time.

Nutritional Info (per serving): Calories - 119; Fat – 4.7; Fiber – 1.9; Carbs – 4.7; Protein – 15.9

Tuna and Pasta Casserole

(Prep + Cook Time: 10 minutes | Servings: 2)

Ingredients:

- 1 can cream of mushroom soup
- 1 cup cheddar cheese, shredded
- 1 cups frozen peas
- 2 cans tuna
- 2 ½ cups macaroni pasta
- ½ tsp salt
- ½ tsp pepper
- 3 cups water

Directions:

1. Mix the soup with the water in the Instant Pot. Except for the cheese, add the rest of the ingredients.
2. Stir to combine. Lock the lid and turn the steam valve to SEALING. Press MANUAL, set the pressure to HIGH, and set the timer for 4 minutes.

3. When the timer beeps, turn the steam valve to VENTING to quickly release the pressure. Unlock and open the lid.
4. Sprinkle the cheese on top. Close the lid and let sit for 5 minutes or until the cheese is melted and the sauce is thick.

Nutritional Info (per serving): Calories - 877; Fat – 30.7; Fiber – 7.9; Carbs – 95.9; Protein – 51.9

Tuna and Capers Tomato Pasta
(Prep + Cook Time: 20 minutes | Servings: 2)

Ingredients:
- 1 can (15 ounces) fire-roasted diced tomatoes
- 1 can (3.5 ounces) solid tuna packed in vegetable oil
- 2 cups pasta, your choice (I used Orecchiette)
- 2 garlic cloves, sliced
- 2 tbsp olive oil
- 2 tbsp capers
- Grated parmesan
- Red wine (just enough to fill ½ of the tomato can)
- Salt and pepper to taste
- Seasonings (I use oregano and dried chilies)

Directions:
1. Set the Instant Pot to SAUTE and wait until hot. Add the garlic and sauté until fragrant.
2. Add the pasta, seasonings, and tomatoes. Fill the empty can of tomatoes with red wine until 1/2 full and then pour enough water into the can until full.
3. Pour the wine mix in the Instant Pot. Lock the lid and turn the steam valve to SEALING.
4. Press the MANUAL key and set the timer for 6 minutes. When the timer beeps, turn the steam valve to quick release the pressure.
5. Carefully open the capers and tuna. Gently toss to combine.
6. Divide the pasta into serving bowls.

Nutritional Info (per serving): Calories - 672; Fat – 21.1; Fiber – 2.9; Carbs – 74.7; Protein – 28.3

Tuna and Buttery Crackers Casserole

(Prep + Cook Time: 25 minutes | Servings: 8)

Ingredients:

- 8 ounces fresh tuna
- 3 tbsp butter
- 3 tbsp all-purpose flour
- 3 ½ cups chicken stock
- 2 tsp salt
- 2 cups pasta (I used elbow mac)
- ¼ cup heavy cream
- 1 cup onion
- 1 cup frozen peas
- 1 cup cheddar, shredded
- 1 cup celery
- 1 cup buttery crackers, crushed
- Fresh ground black pepper to taste

Directions:

1. Press the SAUTE key of the Instant Pot to preheat it. When hot, put the celery and onion.
2. Sauté until the onion is translucent. Pour in the chicken stock and pasta, and season with salt and pepper.
3. Stir to combine for a bit. Put the fresh tuna on top of the pasta mix. Press CANCEL to stop the sauté function. Close and lock the lid.
4. Press MANUAL and set the timer for 5 minutes. Meanwhile, heat the sauté pan over medium-high.
5. Put the butter in the pan and melt. Stir in the flour and cook for 2 minutes. Remove the pan from the heat and set aside.
6. When the timer of the Instant Pot beeps, turn the steam valve to VENTING to quick release the pressure. Transfer the tuna onto a plate and set aside.
7. Pour the butter mix into the Instant Pot. Press the SAUTÉ key. Stir until the mixture is thick. Turn off the Instant Pot. Stir in the heavy cream, the peas, and the tuna.
8. Cover the mix with the crackers and then with the grated cheese.
9. Cover and let stand for 5 minutes. Serve.

Nutritional Info (per serving): Calories - 287; Fat – 12; Fiber – 1.8; Carbs – 27.8; Protein – 16.8

Cheesy Tuna Helper

(Prep + Cook Time: 15 minutes | Servings: 6)

Ingredients:

- 1 can (5 ounces) tuna, drained
- 1 cup frozen peas
- ¼ cup bread crumbs (optional)
- 16 ounces egg noodles
- 28 ounces canned cream mushroom soup
- 3 cups water
- 4 ounces cheddar cheese

Directions:

1. Put the noodles in the Instant Pot. Pour in the water to cover the noodles.
2. Add the frozen peas, tuna, and the soup on top of the pasta layer. Cover and lock the lid.
3. Press the MANUAL key, set the pressure to HIGH, and set the timer for 4 minutes. When the Instant Pot timer beeps, press the CANCEL key and unplug the Instant Pot. Turn the steam valve to quick release the pressure.
4. Unlock and carefully open the lid. Stir in the cheese.
5. If desired, you can pour the pasta mixture in a baking dish, sprinkle the top with bread crumbs, and broil for about 2 to 3 minutes. Serve.

Nutritional Info (per serving): Calories - 302; Fat – 13.6; Fiber – 2.4; Carbs – 27.7; Protein – 16.9

Fish in Orange Ginger Sauce

(Prep + Cook Time: 20 minutes | Servings: 4)

Ingredients:

- 4 pieces white fish fillets
- 3-4 spring onions
- 1 piece (thumb-sized) ginger, chopped
- 1 orange, zested and then juiced
- 1 cup white wine or fish stock
- Olive oil
- Salt and pepper

Directions:

1. Using a paper towel, pat the fish fillets dry. Rub the fillets with the olive oil and then season them lightly.

2. Add the white wine/ fish stock, orange zest, orange juice, ginger, and spring onion into the Instant Pot.
3. Set a steamer basket in the pot and then put the fish in the steamer basket. Close and lock the lid.
4. Press MANUAL and set the timer to 7 minutes.
5. Serve on top of an undressed garden salad.
6. The sauce will serve as the dressing.

Nutritional Info (per serving): Calories -268 ; Fat – 1.7; Fiber – 5.1; Carbs – 8.8; Protein – 41.9

Wild Alaskan Cod In The Pot
(Prep + Cook Time: 15 minutes | Servings: 2)

Ingredients:
- 1 large filet wild Alaskan cod (the big fillets can feed easily 2-3 people)
- 1 cup cherry tomatoes
- Salt and pepper, to taste
- Your choice of seasoning
- 2 tbsp butter
- Olive oil

Directions:
1. Choose an ovenproof dish that will fit your Instant Pot.
2. Put the tomatoes in the dish.
3. Cut the large fish fillet into 2-3 serving pieces. Lay them on top of the tomatoes.
4. Season the fish with salt, pepper, and your choice of seasoning.
5. Top each fillet with 1 tablespoon butter and drizzle with a bit of olive oil Put 1 cup water in the Instant Pot and set a trivet.
6. Place the dish on the trivet. Lock the lid and close the steam valve.
7. Press MANUAL and set the timer for 5 minutes if using thawed fish or for 9 minutes if using frozen fish.
8. When the timer beeps, let the pressure release naturally. Enjoy!

Nutritional Info (per serving): Calories - 832; Fat – 17.5; Fiber – 1.1; Carbs – 3.5; Protein – 156.2

Lemon-Dill Cod With Broccoli

(Prep + Cook Time: 5 minutes | Servings: 4)

Ingredients:
- One, 1 pound, 1-inch thick frozen cod fillet
- 2 cups of broccoli
- 1 cup water
- Dill weed
- Lemon pepper
- Dash of salt

Directions:
1. Cut the fish into four pieces.
2. Season with lemon pepper, salt, and dill weed.
3. Pour 1 cup of water into the Instant Pot and lower in the steamer basket.
4. Put the fish and broccoli florets in the basket. Close the cooker.
5. Select MANUAL and cook for 2 minutes on low pressure.
6. Quick-release the pressure after time is up, and you've turned off the cooker.
7. Serve right away.

Nutritional Info (per serving): Calories - 283; Fat – 8; Fiber – 2.4; Carbs – 6; Protein – 14

Cod Chowder

(Prep + Cook Time: 40 minutes | Servings: 6)

Ingredients:
- 2 pounds cod
- 4 cups potatoes, peeled and diced
- 4 cups chicken broth, organic
- 2 tbsp butter
- ½ mushrooms, sliced
- ½ cup flour
- 1 tsp old bay seasoning (or more)
- 1 cup onion, chopped
- 1 cup half-and-half OR heavy cream OR 1 can evaporated milk
- 1 cup clam juice
- 4-6 bacon slices, optional
- Salt and pepper, to taste

Directions:

1. Pour 1 cup water into the Instant Pot and set a trivet. Put the cod on the trivet. Close and lock the lid.
2. Press MANUAL, set the pressure to HIGH, and set the timer for 9 minutes.
3. Transfer the cod onto a large-sized plate. With a fork or a knife, cut the fish into large chunks. Set aside.
4. Remove the trivet and pour the liquid out from the inner pot. Return the inner pot into the housing.
5. Press the SAUTE key. Add the butter, onion, and mushrooms; sauté for 2 minutes or until soft.
6. Add the chicken broth and the potatoes.
7. Press the CANCEL key to stop the sauté function. Close and lock the lid.
8. Press the MANUAL key, set the pressure to HIGH, and set the timer for 8 minutes.
9. When the timer beeps, turn the steam valve to quick release the pressure.
10. Stir in the seasoning, pepper, salt, and fish. In a bowl, mix the clam juice with the flour until well blended.
11. Pour the mix into the pot. Turn off the Instant Pot.
12. Add the half-and-half and stir well until blended. Serve with fresh baked buttered rolls.

Notes: If you are using bacon, cook the bacon until crisp and then transfer into a paper towel lined plate. Add the onions and the mushrooms, cooking them in the bacon fat before adding the broth and potatoes.

Nutritional Info (per serving): Calories - 474; Fat – 16.3; Fiber – 3.3; Carbs – 32.4; Protein – 46.9

Cod Fillets with Almonds and Peas

(Prep + Cook Time: 10 minutes | Servings: 4)

Ingredients:

- 1 pound frozen cod fish fillet
- 2 halved garlic cloves
- 10-ounces frozen peas
- 1 cup chicken broth
- ½ cup packed parsley
- 2 tbsp fresh oregano
- 2 tbsp sliced almonds
- ½ tsp paprika

Directions:

1. Take the fish out of the freezer.
2. In a food processor, pulse together garlic, oregano, parsley, paprika, and 1 tablespoon almonds.
3. Turn your Instant Pot to SAUTE and heat a bit of olive oil.
4. When hot, toast the rest of the almonds until they are fragrant.
5. Take out the almonds and put on a paper towel.
6. Pour the broth in the cooker and toss in your herb mixture.
7. Cut the fish into 4 pieces and put in the steamer basket.
8. Lower into the cooker and close the lid.
9. Select MANUAL, and cook on high pressure for 3 minutes.
10. Hit CANCEL and quick-release the pressure.
11. The fish is done when it is solid, not translucent.
12. Add the frozen peas and close the lid again.
13. Cook on high pressure for 1 minute. Quick-release again.
14. Serve with the toasted almonds on top.

Notes: If you want a thicker sauce, remove the fish before mixing 1 tablespoon of cornstarch with 1 tablespoon of cold water, and pouring into the cooker. Turn the cooker to sauté and bring to a simmer until thickened.

Nutritional Info (per serving): Calories - 210; Fat – 26; Fiber – 3.6; Carbs – 6.3; Protein – 26

Tilapia bites

(Prep + Cook Time: 20 minutes | Servings: 8)

Ingredients:

- 3 eggs
- ½ cup half and half
- 1 tsp salt
- 1-pound tilapia fillets
- 1 tsp red pepper
- 1 tbsp lemon juice
- 3 tbsp olive oil
- 1 tsp coriander
- 1 tsp cinnamon
- ½ lemon

Directions:

1. Beat the eggs in the bowl and whisk them with the help of the hand whisker.
2. After this, add salt, red pepper, and half and half in the whisked eggs mixture. Stir it.
3. Grate the lemon and squeeze the juice from it.
4. Chop the tilapia fillets into the big cubes.
5. Sprinkle the fish with the coriander and cinnamon. Stir the mixture. Spray the Instant Pot with the olive oil inside.
6. Dip the tilapia cubes in the egg mixture. Then transfer the fish in the Instant Pot.
7. SAUTE the fish for 4 minutes on the each side or till you get golden brown color.
8. Then transfer the cooked tilapia bites in the paper towel and chill the dish.
9. Serve the dish!

Nutritional Info (per serving): Calories - 158; Fat – 9.9; Fiber – 0; Carbs – 2.31; Protein – 15

10 Minute Scampi Shrimp Paella

(Prep + Cook Time: 10 minutes | Servings: 4)

Ingredients:

- 1 ½ cups water or chicken broth
- 1 cup jasmine rice
- 1 lemon, medium-sized, juiced
- 1 pinch crushed red pepper, or to taste
- 1 pinch saffron
- 1 pound frozen shrimp, wild caught, shell and tail on
- 1 tsp sea salt (real salt)
- ¼ cup butter
- ¼ cup fresh Parsley, chopped
- ¼ tsp black pepper
- 4 cloves garlic, pressed or minced

Optional garnishes:

- Butter
- Hard parmesan cheese, asiago, or romano, grated
- Fresh Parsley, chopped
- Fresh squeezed lemon juice

Directions:

1. Except for the shrimp, combine the rest of the ingredients in the Instant Pot.
2. Layer the frozen shrimp on top of the rice layer. Lock the lid and close the steam valve.
3. Cook on HIGH pressure for 5 minutes.
4. When the timer beeps, quickly release the pressure. Garnish each serving with grate cheese, butter, and fresh parsley.

Notes: If you don't like shells on your shrimp, carefully remove the cooked shrimp from the top of the rice mix and peel the shells off. Return the peeled shrimp on the rice. Serve. Discard the shells.

Nutritional Info (per serving): Calories - 402; Fat – 13.7; Fiber – 3; Carbs – 42; Protein – 27

Spicy Lemony Salmon

(Prep + Cook Time: 10 minutes | Servings: 4)

Ingredients:

- 3-4 pieces (1-inch thick) salmon fillets, wild sockeye
- 1-2 tbsp assorted chili pepper (I used Nanami Togarashi)
- 1 lemon, sliced
- 1 lemon, juiced
- 1 cup water
- Salt and pepper to taste

Directions:

1. Season the salmon fillets with the lemon juice, salt, pepper, and Nanami Togarashi.
2. Pour 1 cup water in the Instant Pot and set the steam rack in the pot.
3. Place the salmon fillets on the rack, arranging them in a single layer, if possible, without overlapping.
4. Pour any leftover lemon juice and seasoning over the fillets. Lock the lid and close the steam valve.
5. Press MANUAL and set the timer for 5 minutes. Reduce the time by 1 minute for every 1/ 4-inch thinner fillets and 1 minute more for every 1/ 4-inch thicker fillet.
6. When the timer beeps, release the pressure quickly. Carefully open the lid and transfer the fillets into a serving plate. Enjoy!

Notes: You can find Nanami Togarashi in the Asian section of the grocery store. If you want a spicier dish, sprinkle a bit of red pepper flakes over the fillets before cooking.

Nutritional Info (per serving): Calories - 182; Fat – 8.1; Fiber – 1; Carbs – 3.1; Protein – 25.6

Spicy Sockeye Salmon

(Prep + Cook Time: 10 minutes | Servings: 4)

Ingredients:

- 4 wild sockeye salmon fillets
- 1 cup water
- 1 juiced lemon
- 1 sliced lemon
- 2 tbsp assorted chili pepper seasoning
- Salt and pepper to taste

Directions:

1. Prep your salmon by seasoning with chili pepper, salt, pepper, and lemon juice.
2. Put the steamer basket in your cooker with 1 cup of water.
3. Put the fish in the basket, trying not to overlap too much. Close and seal the lid.
4. Select MANUAL and adjust time to 5 minutes.
5. If the fillets are smaller, cut 1 minute off the time for every ¼-inch smaller than 1-inch, or add 1 minute for fillets ¼-inch bigger than 1-inch.
6. When time is up, hit CANCEL and quick-release the pressure.
7. Serve with fresh greens, rice pilaf, or another favorite side.

Nutritional Info (per serving): Calories - 194; Fat – 10; Fiber – 0; Carbs – 1; Protein – 24

Teriyaki Salmon

(Prep + Cook Time: 20 minutes | Servings: 4)

Ingredients:

- 1 ½ cups boiling water
- 5 salmon fillets
- 2-ounces dried mushrooms
- 4 washed and halved bok choy
- 3 sliced spring onions
- ¼ cup soy sauce
- 2 tbsp sweet rice wine
- 1 tbsp sesame oil
- 1 tbsp sugar

Directions:

1. Pour the boiling water over the mushrooms to rehydrate them.
2. Put the bok choy in your Instant Pot.

3. Add everything else (minus the salmon) and mushrooms/water on top. Put the salmon on top. Close and seal the lid.
4. Select MANUAL and cook for 4 minutes on HIGH pressure.
5. When time is up, press CANCEL and wait 10 minutes before quick-releasing. Serve!

Nutritional Info (per serving): Calories - 484; Fat – 34; Fiber – 3; Carbs – 17; Protein – 27

Herbed Garlic Salmon Fillet

(Prep + Cook Time: 30 minutes | Servings: 2)

Ingredients:

- 2 fresh salmon fillets
- ½ cup garlic and herb butter or homemade compound butter with garlic and herbs
- Salt and pepper, to taste
- 2 tbsp white wine
- ¼ cup cream
- 1 tsp lemon zest
- 2 cups water

Directions:

1. In the inner pot of the pressure cooker, add 2 cups of water and the trivet. Place the fish, skin side down on the trivet and season, to taste.
2. Close the lid completely and position the steam release handle to sealing position.
3. Press the MANUAL button and set the pressure cooking time to 5 minutes.
4. When the pressure cooking cycle is completed, slide the steam release handle to venting position to fully release the pressure.
5. Open the lid when the float valve has dropped down.
6. Remove the fish and cover to keep warm. Remove the trivet and drain the water.
7. Place the inner pot back in the pressure cooker and press the SAUTE button. Melt the garlic butter. Stir in the wine and cook until bubbling.
8. Stir in the cream and top with the lemon zest.
9. Mix well and cook until warm.
10. Transfer salmon to serving plates. Top with the creamy sauce and serve.

Steamed Asparagus and Shrimp

(Prep + Cook Time: 25 minutes | Servings: 4)

Ingredients:

- 1 pound shrimp, frozen or fresh, peeled and deveined
- 1 bunch asparagus (about 6 ounces)
- 1 tsp olive oil
- ½ tbsp Cajun seasoning (or your choice of seasoning.
- Lemon juice with salt and pepper would be delicious too)

Directions:

1. Pour 1 cup water in the Instant Pot.
2. Set the steam rack in the pot. In a single layer, put the asparagus on the rack.
3. Put the shrimp on top of the asparagus.
4. Drizzle the shrimp with olive oil and season with Cajun seasoning or your choice of seasoning. Lock the lid and close the steam valve.
5. Press STEAM, set the pressure to LOW, and set the timer for 2 minutes if using frozen shrimp or set to 1 minute if using fresh shrimp.
6. When the timer beeps, quickly release the pressure.
7. Carefully open the lid and enjoy!

Nutritional Info (per serving): Calories - 329; Fat – 6.4; Fiber – 4.2; Carbs – 11.1; Protein – 56.1

Shrimp Risotto

(Prep + Cook Time: 20 minutes | Servings: 4)

Ingredients:

- 4 ½ cups chicken broth
- 1 pound peeled and cleaned shrimp
- 1 ½ cups Arborio rice
- ¾ cup parmesan cheese
- ¼ cup fresh herbs
- 4 tbsp butter
- 1 chopped yellow onion
- 2 minced garlic cloves
- 2 tbsp dry white wine

Directions:

1. Melt the butter in your Instant Pot on SAUTE. Add garlic and onion and cook for 4 minutes.
2. Add the rice and stir to toast for 1 minute. Pour in the wine and cook until it evaporates.
3. Pour in 3 cups of broth and sprinkle in salt and pepper. Close and seal the lid.
4. Select MANUAL and cook on HIGH pressure for 9 minutes.
5. When time is up, click CANCEL and quick-release. Open the lid and add shrimp with the rest of the broth.
6. Turn the pot to SAUTE and cook for 3-5 minutes, or until the shrimp has become bright pink and solid.
7. Add cheese and the rest of the butter. Sprinkle on herbs and serve!

Nutritional Info (per serving): Calories - 479; Fat – 16; Fiber – 3; Carbs – 59; Protein – 28

Shrimp and Tomatillo Casserole

(Prep + Cook Time: 20 minutes | Servings: 4)

Ingredients:

- 1 ½ pounds peeled and cleaned shrimp
- 1 ½ pounds peeled and chopped tomatillos
- 1 stemmed, seeded, and minced jalapeno
- 1 cup shredded cheddar cheese
- 1 chopped yellow onion
- ½ cup clam juice
- ¼ cup chopped cilantro
- 2 tbsp lime juice
- 2 tbsp olive oil
- 2 tsp minced garlic

Directions:

1. Heat the oil in your Instant Pot on the SAUTE setting.
2. When shiny and hot, add the onion and stir until it becomes clear.
3. Add the garlic and jalapeno. Stir until aromatic; this should only take a minute or so.
4. Add tomatillos, lime juice, and clam juice.
5. Close and seal the lid. Select MANUAL and cook on high pressure for 9 minutes.
6. When the timer beeps, hit CANCEL and quick-release. Open the lid and hit the SAUTE button again.
7. Add cilantro and shrimp, and stir for 2 minutes. Stir in cheese and cover the lid, but don't bring to pressure.
8. Wait 2 minutes for the cheese to melt. Open the lid and stir before serving.

Nutritional Info (per serving): Calories - 300; Fat – 16; Fiber – 3; Carbs – 17; Protein – 22

Creamy Shrimp Pasta

(Prep + Cook Time: 15 minutes | Servings: 4)

Ingredients:

- 2 ½ cups chicken broth
- 8-ounces bowtie pasta
- 12-ounces cleaned frozen shrimp
- 1 cup Parmesan cheese
- ½ cup heavy cream
- 1 chopped yellow onion
- 1 tbsp olive oil
- 1 tbsp minced garlic
- 1 tsp all-purpose flour
- Salt and pepper to taste
- Handful of chopped parsley

Directions:

1. Heat the oil in your Instant Pot on the SAUTE setting. Cook onion until it becomes clear.
2. Add the pasta, broth, garlic, salt, pepper, and shrimp. Close and seal the lid.
3. Select MANUAL and cook for 7 minutes on HIGH pressure.
4. When time is up, hit CANCEL and quick-release the pressure.
5. With the lid off, turn the cooker back to SAUTE.
6. Pour in the cream, Parmesan, and flour.
7. Simmer until the sauce has thickened a little, which should take about 2 minutes.
8. Serve with chopped parsley on top!

Nutritional Info (per serving): Calories - 511; Fat – 22; Fiber – 1; Carbs – 47; Protein – 33

Green Chili Mahi-Mahi Fillets

(Prep + Cook Time: 10 minutes | Servings: 2)

Ingredients:

- ¼ cup green chili enchilada sauce, homemade or store-brought
- 2 Mahi-Mahi fillets, thawed
- 2 pats butter
- Salt and pepper to taste
- 1 cup water

Directions:

1. Pour 1 cup water into the Instant Pot and set a steamer rack.
2. Grease the bottom of each mahi-mahi fillet with 1 pat butter, spreading the pat from end to end – this will prevent the fish from sticking to the rack.
3. Put the fillets on the rack. Spread 1/ 4 cup enchilada sauce between each fillet using a pastry brush – cover them well.
4. Top with more enchilada sauce, if desired. Season fillets with salt and pepper. Lock the lid and close the steam valve. Press MANUAL, set the pressure to HIGH, and set the timer for 5 minutes.
5. When the timer beeps, quickly release the pressure and transfer the fillets into serving plates on a bed of greens.

Notes: The cooking time is sufficient to cook the fillets if they are thawed. Test the fish before taking out. If they are not done, close the lid and let cook with the residual heat of the pot for 1 minute.

Nutritional Info (per serving): Calories - 325; Fat – 22.9; Fiber – 1.7; Carbs – 18.6; Protein – 14

Lobster Tails

(Prep + Cook Time: 25 minutes | Servings: 4)

Ingredients:

- 4 lobster tails (1-pound each)
- 1 cup water
- ½ cup white wine
- ¼ cup melted butter

Directions:

1. Defrost your lobster tails in a bowl of cold water.
2. Cut the tails in half tip-to tip, so the meat is exposed.
3. Pour the wine and water in your Instant Pot, so the liquid reaches the halfway point.
4. Lower in the steamer attachment.
5. Put the lobster tails shell-side down in the steamer basket.
6. Select MANUAL and then steam on LOW pressure for 4 minutes.
7. When time is up, quick-release the pressure after turning off the cooker.
8. You know the meat is done when it is firm and white, not translucent.
9. Serve with melted butter.

Nutritional Info (per serving): Calories - 190; Fat – 12; Fiber – 0; Carbs – 0; Protein – 19

Trout-Farro Salad

(Prep + Cook Time: 55 minutes | Servings: 4)

Ingredients:

- 12-ounces skinned and chopped cooked trout
- 1 cup semi-pearled farro
- 1 large, shaved fennel bulb
- ½ cup low-fat mayonnaise
- ¼ cup low-fat sour cream
- 3 tbsp lemon juice
- 2 tbsp Dijon mustard
- 1 tsp white sugar
- 1 tsp ground black pepper
- Water as needed

Directions:

1. Put the farro in your Instant Pot and pour in just enough water so the grain is covered by two inches. Close and seal the lid.
2. Select MANUAL and cook on HIGH pressure for 17 minutes.
3. When time is up, hit CANCEL and quick-release the pressure.
4. Shave your fennel and put in a colander. Pour farro right on top of it, draining.
5. Toss fennel and farro together, and set aside for about 30 minutes.
6. When you're just about ready to serve, mix the mayo, sour cream, lemon juice, Dijon, white sugar, and pepper together.
7. Mix in the farro, fish, and fennel. Serve right away.

Nutritional Info (per serving): Calories - 460; Fat – 21; Fiber – 3; Carbs – 34; Protein – 30

Caramelized Haddock

(Prep + Cook Time: 55 minutes | Servings: 4)

Ingredients:

- 1 pound of haddock
- 3 garlic cloves Just under
- 1 cup of coconut water
- 1 minced red chili
- 1 minced spring onion
- ⅓ cup water
- ¼ cup white sugar
- 3 tbsp fish sauce
- 2 tsp black pepper

Directions:

1. Marinate the fish in garlic, fish sauce, and pepper for at least 30 minutes.
2. Put the sugar and regular water in the Instant Pot and heat on the lowest setting until the sugar has browned into a caramel.
3. Add fish and coconut water to the cooker. Close and seal lid.
4. Click on MANUAL and cook on HIGH pressure for 10 minutes.
5. When time is up, hit CANCEL and wait for the pressure to come down on its own. Serve with chili and onion.

Nutritional Info (per serving): Calories - 150; Fat – 1; Fiber – 1; Carbs – 18; Protein – 21

Oysters-in-the-Shell

(Prep + Cook Time: 15 minutes | Servings: 6)

Ingredients:
- 36 in-shell oysters
- 6 tbsp melted butter
- Salt and pepper to taste
- 1 cup water

Directions:
1. Clean the oysters.
2. Toss in the Instant Pot with 1 cup of water.
3. Select MANUAL and cook on HIGH pressure for 3 minutes.
4. When time is up, hit CANCEL and quick-release.
5. Serve right away with melted butter.

Nutritional Info (per serving): Calories - 142; Fat – 12; Fiber – 0; Carbs – 1; Protein – 7

Tender Octopus

(Prep + Cook Time: 20 minutes | Servings: 6)

Ingredients:
- 1 tsp salt
- 10 oz octopus
- 1 tsp cilantro
- 2 tbsp olive oil
- 1 tsp garlic powder
- 1 tsp lime juice
- 1 cup water

Directions:
1. Place the octopus in the Instant Pot. Sprinkle it with the cilantro, garlic powder, and salt. Stir it.
2. After this, pour the water in the Instant Pot and close the lid. Cook the dish at the HIGH pressure for 8 minutes.
3. Then remove the dish from the Instant Pot and put in the tray. Sprinkle the seafood with the olive oil.
4. Preheat the oven to 360 F and transfer the tray to the oven. Cook the dish for 7 minutes more.
5. When the octopus is cooked – remove it from the oven and sprinkle with the lemon juice.
6. Chill little and serve it. Enjoy!

Nutritional Info (per serving): Calories - 80; Fat – 5; Fiber – 0; Carbs – 1.5; Protein – 7

Tasty Cuttlefish

(Prep + Cook Time: 40 minutes | Servings: 6)

Ingredients:

- 1-pound squid
- 1 tbsp minced garlic
- 1 tsp onion powder
- 1 tbsp lemon juice
- 2 tbsp starch
- 1 tbsp chives
- 1 tsp salt
- 1 tsp white pepper
- 3 tbsp fish sauce
- 2 tbsp butter
- ¼ chili pepper

Directions:

1. Slice the squid.
2. Combine the minced garlic, onion powder, starch, chives, salt, and white pepper together. Stir the mixture.
3. Then chop the chili and add it to the spice mixture.
4. Then combine the sliced squid and spice mixture together. Stir it carefully.
5. After this, sprinkle the seafood mixture with the lemon juice and fish sauce. Stir it. Leave the mixture for 10 minutes.
6. Toss the butter in the Instant Pot and melt it.
7. Then place the sliced squid mixture in the Instant Pot and close the lid. Cook the dish for 13 minutes at the STEW mode.
8. When the dish is cooked – remove it from the Instant Pot.
9. Sprinkle the dish with the liquid from the cooked squid. Serve it!

Nutritional Info (per serving): Calories - 112; Fat – 4.9; Fiber – 0; Carbs – 3.92; Protein – 12

Red chili anchovy

(Prep + Cook Time: 25 minutes | Servings: 2)

Ingredients:

- 1 red chili pepper
- 10 oz anchovy
- 4 tbsp butter
- 1 tsp sea salt
- ½ tsp paprika
- 1 tsp chili flakes
- 1 tbsp basil
- 1 tsp dry dill
- 1 tsp rosemary
- 1/3 cup bread crumbs

Directions:

1. Remove the seeds from the chili pepper and slice it.
2. Combine the chili flakes, paprika, sea salt, basil, dry dill, and rosemary together in the shallow bowl. Stir the mixture.
3. Then sprinkle the anchovy with the spice mixture. Mix up it carefully with the help of the hands.
4. Add sliced chili pepper and leave the mixture for 10 minutes.
5. Meanwhile, toss the butter in the Instant Pot and melt it in the SAUTÉ mode.
6. Then dip the spiced anchovy in the bread crumbs and put the dipped fish in the melted butter.
7. Cook the anchovy for 4 minutes from the each side.
8. When the fish is cooked – remove it from the Instant Pot and put in the paper towel to avoid the excess oil.
9. Serve the anchovy immediately. Enjoy!

Nutritional Info (per serving): Calories - 356; Fat – 25; Fiber – 1; Carbs – 4.17; Protein – 28

Mackerel Salad

(Prep + Cook Time: 25 minutes | Servings: 6)

Ingredients:

- 1 cup lettuce
- 8 oz mackerel
- 1 tsp salt
- 1 tsp paprika
- 1 tbsp olive oil
- ½ tsp rosemary
- 1 garlic clove
- ½ cup fish stock
- 1 tsp oregano
- 7 oz tomatoes
- 1 big cucumbers
- 1 red onion

Directions:

1. Wash the lettuce and chop it. Rub the mackerel with the salt, paprika, and rosemary. Stir the fish carefully.
2. Place the spiced mackerel in the Instant Pot.
3. Add the fish stock and close the lid. Cook the dish at the pressure mode for 10 minutes.
4. Peel the garlic clove and slice it. Peel the red onion and slice it.
5. Combine the sliced red onion with the chopped lettuce. Slice the cucumber and chop tomatoes.
6. Add the vegetables to the lettuce mixture.
7. When the mackerel is cooked – remove it from the Instant Pot and chill it little. Chop the fish roughly.
8. Add the chopped fish in the lettuce mixture.
9. Sprinkle the salad with the olive oil and stir it carefully with the help of the fork to not damage the fish.
10. Serve the cooked salad immediately. Enjoy!

Nutritional Info (per serving): Calories - 123; Fat – 6.5; Fiber – 1; Carbs – 5.29; Protein – 11

Fish Pho

(Prep + Cook Time: 40 minutes | Servings: 6)

Ingredients:

- 4 oz salmon
- 7 oz squid
- 5 cup water
- 1 garlic clove
- ½ cup fresh dill
- 1 tbsp salt
- ¼ cup soy sauce
- 1 tsp ground black pepper
- ½ tbsp coriander
- ¼ tsp thyme
- 1 jalapeno pepper
- 8 oz rice noodles
- 5 oz bok choy
- 1 tsp chili flakes

Directions:

1. Place the water, salt, fresh dill, soy sauce, ground black pepper, coriander, thyme, and chili flakes in the Instant Pot. Stir the mixture and SAUTE it for 15 minutes.
2. Meanwhile, chop the salmon and squid. Peel the garlic clove and slice it.
3. When the time is over – open the Instant Pot lid and remove all the ingredients from the Instant Pot except the liquid.
4. Put the chopped salmon and squid. Add sliced garlic clove. Stir the mixture gently and add more salt if desired.
5. Then close the Instant Pot and cook the dish at the PRESSURE for 10 minutes more.
6. Then open the Instant Pot lid and ladle the seafood Pho in the serving bowls.
7. Serve the dish immediately. Enjoy!

Nutritional Info (per serving): Calories - 140; Fat – 4; Fiber – 1; Carbs – 14.5; Protein – 11

Mediterranean Style Fish
(Prep + Cook Time: 25 minutes | Servings: 2-4)

Ingredients:
- 4 white fish fillets (any white fish, I used cod)
- 1 lb cherry tomatoes, halced
- 1 cup Black salt-cured Olives (Taggiesche, French or Kalamata)
- 2 tbsp Pickled Capers
- 1 bunch of fresh Thyme
- Olive oil
- 1 clove of garlic, pressed
- Salt and pepper to taste
- 1½ - 2 cups water

Directions:
1. Prepare the base of the pressure cooker with 1½ to 2 cups of water and trivet or steamer basket.
2. Line the bottom of the heat-proof bowl with cherry tomato halves (to keep the fish filet from sticking), add Thyme (reserve a few springs for garnish).
3. Place the fish fillets over the cherry tomatoes, sprinkle with remaining tomatoes, crushed garlic, a dash of olive oil and a pinch of salt.
4. Insert the dish in the Instant Pot. Set 7-8 minutes cooking time at LOW pressure (or 4-5 at HIGH). When time is up, release pressure using the natural method.
5. Distribute fish into individual plates, top with cherry tomatoes, and sprinkle with olives, capers, fresh Thyme, a crackle of pepper and a little swirl of fresh olive oil.

Catfish With Herbs

(Prep + Cook Time: 20 minutes | Servings: 6)

Ingredients:

- 1 tsp fresh parsley
- 1 tsp dill
- 1 tbsp olive oil
- 14 oz catfish
- ¼ cup fresh thyme
- 3 garlic cloves
- ¼ cup water
- 2 tbsp soy sauce
- 1 tbsp salt

Directions:

1. Wash the fresh parsley and fresh thyme. Chop the greens.
2. Combine the chopped greens with the dill and salt. Stir the mixture.
3. After this, peel the garlic cloves and slice them. Pour the olive oil in the Instant Pot.
4. Add the sliced garlic and SAUTE it for 1 minute.
5. Then combine the catfish with the green mixture. Add soy sauce and water.
6. Stir the mixture and transfer it to the Instant Pot.
7. SAUTE the dish for 4 minutes on the each side.
8. When the dish is cooked – you will get the light golden brown color of the fish.
9. Serve the dish hot! Enjoy!

Nutritional Info (per serving): Calories - 103; Fat – 5.2; Fiber – 0; Carbs – 2.42; Protein – 11

Almond Milk Cod

(Prep + Cook Time: 45 minutes | Servings: 4)

Ingredients:

- 3 tbsp almond flakes
- ½ cup almond milk
- 8 oz cod
- ¼ cup fish sauce
- 3 tbsp soy sauce
- 1 tbsp lime zest
- 1 tsp minced garlic
- 1 tbsp butter

Directions:

1. Choo the roughly and transfer it to the mixing bowl.
2. Add fish sauce and soy sauce. Stir the mixture.
3. Ager this, sprinkle the fish with the lime zest and minced garlic. Stir it.

4. Then add almond milk and leave the fish for 10 minutes to marinate.
5. Then toss the butter in the Instant Pot and melt it.
6. Then add the almond milk cod in the Instant Pot. Close the lid and cook the dish at the SAUTE mode for 10 minutes.
7. When the time is over – open the Instant Pot lid and add almond flakes.
8. Stir the dish gently and cook it for 3 minutes.
9. Then remove the dish from the Instant Pot.
10. Serve it immediately. Enjoy!

Nutritional Info (per serving): Calories - 128; Fat – 6.1; Fiber – 1; Carbs – 7.19; Protein – 11

Crab Legs with Garlic-Butter Sauce
(Prep + Cook Time: 10 minutes | Servings: 2)

Ingredients:
- 1 cup water
- 2 pounds frozen or fresh crab legs
- 1 minced garlic clove
- 4 tbsp salted butter
- 1 halved lemon
- 1 tsp olive oil

Directions:
1. Pour water in your Instant Pot and lower in the steamer basket. Add the crab legs.
2. Choose the "steam" option adjust time to 3 minutes for fresh, and 4 for frozen. In the meantime, heat the oil in a skillet.
3. Cook garlic for just 1 minute, stirring so it doesn't burn.
4. Add the butter and stir to melt. Squeeze the halved lemon in the butter.
5. By now, the crab will be done, so hit "cancel" and quick-release the pressure.
6. Serve crabs with the garlic butter on the side.

Nutritional Info (per serving): Calories - 346; Fat – 7; Fiber – 0; Carbs – 2; Protein – 44

Simple Chicken Soup

(Prep + Cook Time: 50 minutes | Servings: 4)

Ingredients:

- 16-ounces water
- 16-ounces chicken stock
- 2 frozen, boneless chicken breasts
- 4 medium-sized potatoes
- Three peeled carrots
- ½ big diced onion
- Salt and pepper to taste

Directions:

1. Put everything into the pressure cooker, including salt and pepper.
2. Turn on your Instant Pot by selecting MANUAL, and then 35 minutes on HIGH pressure.
3. When time is up, turn off the cooker and wait 15 minutes for the pressure to come down by itself.
4. Carefully open the cooker, stir, and serve!

Nutritional Info (per serving): Calories - 72; Fiber – 0; Carbs – 7; Protein – 5

Chicken Tortilla Soup

(Prep + Cook Time: 30 minutes | Servings: 4)

Ingredients:

- 2, 6-inch corn tortillas cut into 1-inch squares
- 3-4 cups chicken broth
- 3 chicken breasts
- 1 big, chopped tomato
- 1 chopped onion
- 2 minced garlic cloves
- 15 ounces of black beans
- 1 cup frozen corn
- 2 tbsp chopped cilantro
- 1 bay leaf
- 1 tbsp olive oil
- 2 tsp chili powder
- 1 tsp ground cumin
- ¼ tsp ground cayenne pepper

Directions:

1. Turn on the Instant Pot to SAUTE.
2. Pour in the olive oil and cook the onion while stirring until soft.
3. Add the cilantro, garlic, and tortillas.
4. Stir and wait 1 minute.
5. Add the black beans, corn, tomato, 3 cups of broth, chicken, and spices.
6. Turn off the SAUTE function and close the lid.
7. Switch over to SOUP mode and adjust the time to just 4 minutes.
8. When time is up, quick-release the pressure.
9. Carefully take out the chicken and shred before returning back to the pot. Stir everything well.
10. Serve with cilantro, cheese, lime juice, and any other toppings you enjoy.

Nutritional Info (per serving): Calories - 200; Fat – 9; Fiber – 2; Carbs – 24; Protein – 7

Bean Soup

(Prep + Cook Time: 65 minutes | Servings: 6)

Ingredients:

- 1 cup cannellini beans
- 7 cups water
- 1 cup dill
- 4 tbsp salsa
- 1 jalapeno pepper
- 1/3 cup cream
- 2 tsp salt
- 1 tsp white pepper
- 1 white onions
- 1 sweet red pepper
- 1-pound chicken fillet
- 1 tsp soy sauce

Directions:

1. Place the cannellini beans in the Instant Pot.
2. Chop the chicken fillet and add it in the Instant Pot too.
3. Add water and cook the beans at the PRESSURE mode for 35 minutes.
4. Meanwhile, chop the dill and jalapeno peppers. Slice the onions and chop the sweet red peppers.
5. Add the vegetables to bean mixture and close the lid. Set the Instant Pot mode SOUP and cook the dish for 15 minutes more.
6. Then sprinkle the soup with the cream, salsa, white pepper, and soy sauce. Stir the soup carefully and cook it for 5 minutes more.
7. Remove the soup from the Instant Pot and let it chill little.
8. Ladle the soup into the serving bowls. Enjoy!

Nutritional Info (per serving): Calories - 188; Fat – 10.3; Fiber – 2; Carbs – 17.25; Protein – 7

Lentil, Potato and Carrot Soup (veg)

(Prep + Cook Time: 25 minutes | Servings: 6)

Ingredients:

For the sauté:
- 1 clove garlic, minced
- 1 onion, small-sized, minced
- 1 tbsp olive oil (or dry sauté with no added oil)

For the soup:
- 1 cup lentil blend (autumn blend, or mix of red lentils, yellow split peas, brown lentil and Beluga lentils)
- 2 carrots, medium-sized, cubed
- 1 potato, medium-sized, peeled and cubed
- 1 sweet potato, small-sized, peeled and cubed
- 1 tsp marjoram
- 1 tsp thyme
- ½ tsp smoked paprika
- ¼ tsp rosemary powder (OR 1 teaspoon dried whole rosemary)
- 5 cups water
- 1 bay leaf

After cooking:
- ¼ cup nutritional yeast
- Salt and pepper to taste

Directions:

1. Press the SAUTE key of the Instant Pot. Add the olive oil and heat. Add the onion and sauté until translucent.
2. Add the garlic and sauté for 1-2 minutes. Press the CANCEL key to turn off the sauté function.
3. Add all the soup ingredients in the pot.
4. Lock the lid and close the steam valve. Press MANUAL and set the timer to 10 minutes.
5. When the timer beeps, let the pressure release naturally. Open the steam valve to release any remaining pressure.
6. Carefully open the lid, stir to mix, and ladle into bowls.
7. Serve with crusty bread.

Nutritional Info (per serving): Calories - 214; Fat – 3.2; Fiber – 13.8; Carbs – 35.5; Protein – 12.7

Minestrone Soup

(Prep + Cook Time: 25 minutes | Servings: 4)

Ingredients:

- 2 tbsp lard OR olive oil
- 2 stalks celery, diced
- 1 large onion, diced
- 1 large carrot, diced
- 3 cloves garlic, minced
- 1 tsp dried oregano
- 1 tsp dried basil
- Sea salt and pepper, to taste
- 1 can (28 ounces) San Marzano tomatoes, diced in a food processor or a blender
- 1 can (15 ounces) white or cannellini beans, (or about 2 cups freshly cooked and drained)
- 4 cups bone broth or vegetable broth
- 1 bay leaf
- ½ cup fresh spinach OR kale (without the rib) torn into shreds
- 1 cup elbow pasta, gluten-free
- 1/3 cup parmesan cheese, finely grated (omit for vegan option)
- 1-2 tbsp fresh pesto, optional

Directions:

1. Press the SAUTE button of the Instant Pot. Put in the olive oil, carrot, garlic, onion, and celery. Sauté until softened.
2. Add the oregano, basil, salt, and pepper. Add the tomatoes, broth, bay leaves, kale, and pasta. Press CANCEL. Close and lock the lid.
3. Press MANUAL, set the pressure to HIGH, and set the timer for 6 minutes.
4. When the timer beeps, let it sit for about 1-2 minutes then do a quick release. Carefully open the lid.
5. Add the white kidney beans. Ladle into bowls.
6. Garnish each serving with parmesan cheese and a dollop of pesto.

Nutritional Info (per serving): Calories - 567; Fat – 11; Fiber – 20.2; Carbs – 84.9; Protein – 35.8

Spiced-Carrot Chilled Soup (veg)

(Prep + Cook Time: 1 hour 40 minutes | Servings: 4)

Ingredients:

- 2 pounds trimmed, peeled, and chopped carrots
- 3 tbsp olive oil
- Salt to taste
- Dukkah to taste
- Water as needed

Directions:

1. Put carrots in your Instant Pot with ½ cup of water.
2. Seal the lid. Hit MANUAL and adjust time to 30 minutes.
3. When time is up, hit CANCEL and quick-release the pressure.
4. Remove carrots and blend with olive oil until smooth.
5. Pour soup through a sieve to get a really smooth texture.
6. Add water if necessary to get the right consistency.
7. Add salt to taste before storing in the fridge until chill.
8. Before serving, whisk and sprinkle on dukkah.

Note: Dukkah is a spice blend made from sesame seeds, cumin, salt, pepper, coriander, and hazelnuts. You can find it online, or at Trader Joe's and Whole Foods.

Nutritional Info (per serving): Calories - 159; Fat – 12; Fiber – 4; Carbs – 15; Protein – 2

Potato Soup With Leek and Cheddar
(Prep + Cook Time: 25 minutes | Servings: 8)

Ingredients:
- 4 medium gold potatoes, peeled and diced, I used Yukon
- 1 ½ cups cream or half and half
- 1/3 cup cheddar cheese, grated
- 3 tbsp leeks, cleaned and thinly sliced, white and light green (reserve 2 for serving)
- 1 ½ tsp dried oregano
- 1 tsp kosher salt
- 2 bay leaves
- 2 tbsp unsalted butter
- ¾ cup white wine
- 4 cloves garlic, crushed
- 4 sprigs fresh thyme
- 5 cups vegetable broth
- Leeks, and cheese, for topping

Directions:
1. Set the Instant Pot to SAUTE.
2. Put the butter in the pot and melt. When melted, add the leek and season with salt and sauté until soft.
3. Add the garlic and sauté for 30 seconds. Press CANCEL. Reserve a few portion of the leek and set aside for serving.
4. Add the thyme, bay leaves, oregano, broth, white wine, and potatoes into the pot. Stir to mix.
5. Close and lock the lid. Set the pressure to HIGH and set the timer to 10 minutes.
6. When the timer beeps, quick release the pressure. Carefully open the pot.
7. Add the cream and with an immersion blender, puree the soup until desired consistency. Press the WARM button and heat the soup through.
8. When the soup is hot, sprinkle with the sautéed leeks, and sprinkle with cheese.

Nutritional Info (per serving): Calories - 198; Fat – 8.1; Fiber – 3.3; Carbs – 21.3; Protein – 6.7

Cheddar Broccoli and Potato Soup

(Prep + Cook Time: 25 minutes | Servings: 4)

Ingredients:

- 1 broccoli head, medium-sized, broken into large florets
- 1 cup cheddar cheese, shredded
- 1 cup half and half
- 2 cloves garlic, crushed
- 2 pounds Yukon Gold Potatoes, peeled and then cut into small chunks
- 2 tbsp butter
- 4 cups vegetable broth
- Chives or green onion, chopped, for garnish
- Salt and pepper to taste

Directions:

1. Press the SAUTE key. When the pot is hot, add the butter and the garlic, and sauté for 1 minute or until the garlic starts to brown.
2. Add the potatoes, broccoli, broth, and season with a bit of salt and pepper. Lock the lid and close the steam valve. Cook for 5 minutes on HIGH.
3. When the timer beeps, press CANCEL and let the pressure release naturally for 10 minutes. Open the steam valve to release remaining pressure.
4. Add the half-and-half and ½ cup cheddar cheese. Using an immersion blender, blend until smooth.
5. Alternatively, you can blend in batches in a large-sized blender. If you want a thinner soup, just add more broth.
6. Season with salt and pepper to taste.
7. Serve hot with remaining cheddar.

Nutritional Info (per serving): Calories - 522; Fat – 35.7; Fiber – 2.7; Carbs – 23.8; Protein – 27.7

Split Pea Soup (veg)

(Prep + Cook Time: 55 minutes | Servings: 6)

Ingredients:

- 1 bay leaf
- 1 pound split peas
- 1 yellow onion, diced
- ½ tbsp smoked paprika
- ¼ tsp thyme
- 2 cloves garlic, minced
- 2 tbsp coconut oil (butter or your choice of oil)
- 3 carrots, sliced
- 3 stalks celery, sliced
- 6 cups vegetable broth
- Fresh ground pepper

Directions:

1. Put the onion, celery, carrots, and garlic in the pot. Add the rest of the ingredients.
2. Lock the lid and close the steam valve. Press MANUAL and set the timer to 15 minutes.
3. When the timer beeps, let the pressure release naturally. Open the steam valve to release any remaining pressure in the pot and carefully open the lid.
4. Stir the soup, taste, and adjust seasoning as needed.
5. Serve hot with crusty bread.

Nutritional Info (per serving): Calories - 360; Fat – 6.9; Fiber – 20.9; Carbs – 52.3; Protein – 24.1

Lentil Soup (veg)

(Prep + Cook Time: 20 minutes | Servings: 6)

Ingredients:

- 1 pound waxy potatoes, such as Red Bliss or Yukon Gold (I used a blend that included purple potatoes)
- 1 bunch Rainbow Chard OR similar greens, such as spinach, chopped
- 1 cup green or brown lentils, sorted and rinsed
- 1 cup red lentils, sorted and rinsed
- 1 ½ tsp smoked paprika
- 1 medium onion, chopped
- 1 tsp salt
- 2 carrots, sliced into ¼ inch pieces
- 2 celery stalks, diced (optional)
- 2 tsp cumin
- 3 cloves garlic, minced
- 8 cups water
- Salt and pepper to taste

Directions:

1. Set the Instant Pot to SAUTE. Add the garlic, onions, celery, carrots, potatoes, and spices. Sauté for 3-5 minutes until the onions are soft.
2. Stir in the lentils and add the water. Press CANCEL. Close and lock the lid. Set the pressure to HIGH and set the timer to 3 minutes.
3. When the timer beeps, quick release the pressure. Carefully open the lid.
4. Stir in the chard and season with salt and pepper to taste. Serve.

Nutritional Info (per serving): Calories - 302; Fat – 1.1; Fiber – 22.7; Carbs – 55.6; Protein – 18.6

Sweet Potato Soup (veg)

(Prep + Cook Time: 35 minutes | Servings: 4)

Ingredients:

- 6 carrots, peeled and diced
- 3-4 large red sweet potatoes, peeled and diced
- 1 whole onion, chopped
- 3-4 cloves garlic, chopped
- 2 tbsp butter
- ½ tsp thyme
- ½ tsp ground sage
- 1 quart vegetarian broth
- Salt and pepper to taste

Directions:

1. Set the Instant Pot to SAUTE. Put the butter in and then add the garlic, onion, and carrots. Sauté until the onions are translucent.
2. Add the sweet potatoes, broth, and seasonings.
3. Press CANCEL. Close and lock the lid. Press MANUAL. Set the pressure to HIGH and set the timer for 20 minutes.
4. When the timer beeps, quick release the pressure. Carefully open the lid and stir the soup to blend.
5. With an immersion blender, blend until soft and serve.

Nutritional Info (per serving): Calories - 230; Fat – 7.4; Fiber – 6.2; Carbs – 33.5; Protein – 8.1

Turmeric Sweet Potato Soup (veg)

(Prep + Cook Time: 45 minutes | Servings: 8)

Ingredients:

- 6 carrots, peeled and sliced
- 4 cups vegetable broth
- 4 cloves garlic, coarsely chopped
- 3-4 sweet potatoes, large-sized, peeled and diced
- 2 tsp ground turmeric
- 2 tbsp coconut, OR vegetable oil
- 1 tsp paprika
- 1 onion, large-sized, chopped
- Salt and pepper to taste

Directions:

1. Press the SAUTÉ key of the Instant Pot. Put the oil in the pot. Add the garlic, onion, and carrots and sauté until the onion is transparent.
2. Add the sweet potatoes, paprika, turmeric, pepper, salt, and pour in the broth.
3. Press the CANCEL key to stop the sauté function. Cover and lock the lid. Press the MANUAL key, set the pressure to HIGH, and set the timer for 20 minutes.
4. When the Instant Pot timer beeps, press the CANCEL key and unplug the Instant Pot.
5. Quick release the pressure. Unlock and carefully open the lid.
6. When the ingredients are cooked, puree right in the pot using an immersion blender.
7. Alternatively, you can puree in batches in a blender on HIGH speed.
8. Serve garnished with spiced pumpkin seeds or crispy fried shallots.

Nutritional Info (per serving): Calories - 117; Fat – 4.2; Fiber – 3.1; Carbs – 16.1; Protein – 4

Dried Beans Vegetarian Soup (veg)
(Prep + Cook Time: 45 minutes | Servings: 6)

Ingredients:

- 1 bag (20 oz) 15 bean soup blend of Hurst Beans (save a seasoning packet for another use)
- 1 can (14.5 oz) Red Gold petite diced tomatoes, undrained
- 1 dried bay leaf
- 1 lemon, fresh squeezed juice
- 1 red bell pepper, seeded and chopped
- 1 sweet onion, small-sized, chopped
- 1 tbsp olive oil
- ½ tsp ground red pepper
- 2 carrots, peeled and chopped
- 2 stalks celery, chopped with tops
- 2-3 sprigs fresh thyme
- 3 cloves garlic, chopped
- 8 cups vegetable stock, OR 4 cups water plus 4 cups stock
- Kosher salt and fresh black pepper to taste

Directions:

1. Sort the beans, rinse, and drain.
2. Except for the lemon juice and tomatoes, put all of the ingredients into a 6-quart Instant Pot, ending with the olive oil. Cover and lock the lid. Press the MANUAL key, set the pressure to HIGH, and set the timer for 45 minutes.
3. When the Instant Pot timer beeps, press the CANCEL key. Let the pressure release naturally for 10-15 minutes or until the valve drops.
4. Using an oven mitt or a long handled spoon, turn the steam valve to release remaining pressure.
5. Unlock and carefully open the lid. Taste, and if needed, adjust seasoning. Stir in the lemon juice and tomatoes. If desired, slightly mash a couple of beans. Serve.

Notes: If desired, you can cook the dish a bit longer on SAUTE mode after adding the lemon, tomato, and seasoning to meld the new added ingredients.

Nutritional Info (per serving): Calories - 142; Fat – 4.6; Fiber – 5.7; Carbs – 17.3; Protein – 9.6

Instant Pot Vegetable Soup (veg)
(Prep + Cook Time: 30 minutes | Servings: 6)

Ingredients:
- 1 can (14 oz) petite diced tomatoes
- 1 yellow onion, chopped
- ½ tsp ground pepper
- ½ tsp salt
- ¼ cup flat-leaf parsley, chopped
- 12 oz Green Beans (Simple Truth Frozen Organic)
- 12 oz Mixed Vegetables (Simple Truth Frozen Organic)
- 2 ¾ cups vegetable broth
- 2 tsp olive oil
- ¾ tsp dried oregano
- ¾ tsp dried thyme
- 4 garlic cloves, minced
- Salt and pepper to taste

Directions:
1. Press the SAUTE key of the Instant Pot. Put the olive oil in the pot and let heat for 1 minute.
2. Add the onion, cook, occasionally stirring for about 5 minutes until or softened.
3. Stir in the garlic, thyme, and oregano; cook for 1 minute.
4. Add the mixed frozen veggies, green beans, tomatoes, salt and pepper to taste, and pour in the broth. Stir until combined.
5. Press the CANCEL key to stop the sauté function. Cover and lock the lid. Press the MANUAL key, set the pressure to HIGH, and set the timer for 4 minutes.
6. When the Instant Pot timer beeps, press the CANCEL key. Let the pressure release naturally for 5 minutes.
7. Using an oven mitt or a long handled spoon, turn the steam valve to release remaining pressure. Unlock and carefully open the lid.
8. Stir in the parsley and season to taste. Serve.

Nutritional Info (per serving): Calories - 94; Fat – 2.6; Fiber – 5.7; Carbs – 13.9; Protein – 5.1

Quinoa Soup (veg)

(Prep + Cook Time: 40 minutes | Servings: 6)

Ingredients:

- 3 cups boiling water
- 2 bags of frozen mixed veggies (12 oz)
- 1 15 oz can of white beans
- 1 15 oz can of fire-roasted diced tomatoes
- 1 15 oz can of pinto beans
- ¼ cup rinsed quinoa
- 1 tbsp dried basil
- 1 tbsp minced garlic
- 1 tbsp hot sauce
- ½ tbsp dried oregano
- Dash of salt
- Dash of black pepper

Directions:

1. Put everything in the Instant Pot and stir. Close and seal the lid.
2. Select MANUAL and set time to 2 minutes on HIGH pressure.
3. When time is up, hit CANCEL and quick-release the pressure.
4. When all the pressure is gone, open the cooker and season to taste. Serve.

Note: The reason the time range is so wide is because it can take between 15-20 minutes for the Instant Pot to reach pressure if you're using frozen veggies. Using boiling water helps with that, and if you use fresh veggies, it takes very little time to get to pressure)

Nutritional Info (per serving): Calories - 201; Fat – 1.1; Fiber – 11; Carbs – 37; Protein – 11

Mushroom Barley Soup

(Prep + Cook Time: 35 minutes | Servings: 8)

Ingredients:

- 1 onion, medium-sized, diced
- 1 pound baby Bella mushrooms, sliced
- 1 sage sprig
- 1 tsp salt
- ¼ tsp freshly ground pepper
- ¼ tsp garlic powder
- 2 carrots, diced
- 2 stalks celery, diced
- ¾ cup pearl barley (do not use instant)
- 4 garlic cloves, chopped
- 4 thyme sprigs
- 8 cups beef broth or stock

Directions:

1. Pour all of the ingredients in the Instant Pot and stir to mix. Cover and lock the lid.
2. Press the MANUAL key, set the pressure to HIGH, and set the timer for 20 minutes.
3. When the Instant Pot timer beeps, press the CANCEL key and unplug the Instant Pot. Let the pressure release naturally for 10 minutes. Turn the steam valve to release remaining pressure.
4. Unlock and carefully open the lid. Serve and enjoy!

Nutritional Info (per serving): Calories - 136; Fat – 1.8; Fiber – 4.8; Carbs – 22.3; Protein – 8.6

Turkish Soup (veg)

(Prep + Cook Time: 15 minutes | Servings: 2)

Ingredients:

- 2 ½ cups water
- 1 cup red lentils
- 1 chopped carrot
- 1 chopped potato
- 1 chopped onion
- ½ cup celery
- 3 minced garlic cloves
- ½ tbsp rice
- 3 tsp olive oil
- ½ tsp paprika
- ½ tsp coriander
- Salt to taste

Directions:

1. Turn your Instant Pot to SAUTE and add oil.
2. While that heats up, prep your veggies.
3. When oil is hot, cook the garlic for a few minutes until fragrant. Rinse off the rice and lentils, and put them in the Instant Pot.
4. Add 2 ½ cups of water, paprika, salt, and veggies. Close and seal the lid.
5. Select MANUAL and cook on HIGH pressure for 10 minutes.
6. When time is up, hit CANCEL and quick-release.
7. Let the mixture cool for a little while before pureeing in a blender. Serve.

Nutritional Info (per serving): Calories - 531; Fat – 9; Fiber – 10; Carbs – 73; Protein – 29

Italian Soup

(Prep + Cook Time: 25 minutes | Servings: 6)

Ingredients:

- 3 large potatoes (Russet or red), unpeeled and sliced into ¼-inch thick pieces
- 2 cups fresh kale, chiffonade (sliced into ribbons)
- 1 pound hot Italian sausage, casing removed
- 4 slices bacon, rough chopped
- 1 cup heavy cream OR half & half
- 1 ½ quarts chicken broth or stock
- 1 onion, chopped
- ¼ cup water
- 4 garlic cloves, minced

Directions:

1. Set the Instant Pot to SAUTE mode and let heat. When hot, add the bacon and cook until crisp.
2. Transfer the bacon into a plate line with paper towel to drain most of the grease. Put the onions in the pot, sauté for 3 minutes.
3. Add the sausage, sauté for about 5 minutes, breaking them into pieces.
4. Add the garlic and sauté for 1 minute. If needed, turn off the pot and drain excess grease.
5. Add the potatoes, water, and broth. Lock the lid and close the steam valve. Press MANUAL, set the pressure to high, and set the timer to 5 minutes.
6. When the timer beeps, let the pressure release naturally for 10 minutes. Open the steam valve to release any remaining pressure.
7. Add the kale and stir until wilted. Add the cream and stir to combine.
8. Ladle into serving bowls and top each serving with crisp bacon.

Notes: You can substitute hot sausage with mild sausage, then add hot pepper flakes to add heat.

Nutritional Info (per serving): Calories - 581; Fat – 35.7; Fiber – 5.2; Carbs – 35.3; Protein – 28.7

Fresh Garden Soup (veg)

(Prep + Cook Time: 20 minutes | Servings: 4)

Ingredients:

- 4 cups vegetable broth
- 4 cups baby spinach
- Two, 15-ounce cans white beans, drained
- Two, 15-ounce cans of red beans, drained
- One, 14-ounce can of diced tomatoes
- 3 cups water
- 1 cup chopped onion
- ½ stalk celery, chopped
- ½ cup chopped zucchini
- ½ cup green beans
- ½ cup shredded carrots
- 4 minced garlic cloves
- 3 tbsp olive oil
- 2 tbsp minced parsley
- 1 ½ tsp salt
- 1 ½ tsp dried oregano
- ½ tsp dried basil
- ½ tsp black pepper
- ¼ tsp dried thyme

Directions:

1. Turn your cooker to the SAUTE setting and heat oil.
2. When hot, cook celery, garlic, green beans, and onions until the onion begins to turn clear.
3. Pour in the broth, (drained) tomatoes, red beans, water, carrots, and spices. Stir before sealing the lid.
4. Press SOUP and adjust time to 3 minutes.
5. When time is up, hit CANCEL and quick-release. Add white beans and spinach. Put the lid back on, but do not bring to pressure.
6. Let the soup sit for 10 minutes. Taste and season as needed before serving.

Nutritional Info (per serving): Calories - 319; Fat – 11; Fiber – 6; Carbs – 47; Protein – 15

Green Soup (veg)
(Prep + Cook Time: 55 minutes | Servings: 4)

Ingredients:
- ½ cup split peas, rinsed
- 8 ounces mushrooms, halved
- 3 medium-sized carrots, peeled and cubed
- 1 medium-sized sweet potato, peeled and cubed
- 1 pound chopped kale
- 1 pound chopped spinach leaves
- 1 medium-sized white onion, peeled and chopped
- 2 tsp minced garlic
- 1 ½ tsp salt
- ½ tsp ground black pepper
- 1 tsp thyme
- 2 tbsp dried basil
- 2 tsp oregano
- 3 tbsp nutritional yeast
- 1 tbsp cashew butter
- 1 tbsp lemon juice
- 48 fluid ounce water

Directions:
1. Plug in and switch the Instant Pot, and place peas, sweet potatoes, carrots, onion, garlic, and water.
2. Secure pot with lid, then position pressure indicator, select MANUAL option and adjust cooking time on timer pad to 8 minutes and let cook.
3. Instant Pot will take 10 minutes to build pressure before cooking timer starts.
4. When the timer beeps, switch off the Instant Pot and let pressure release naturally for 10 minutes and then do quick pressure release.
5. Then uncover pot and puree mixture using an immersion blender.
6. Add mushrooms, kale, spinach, salt, black pepper, thyme and oregano and stir until well combined.
7. Pour in 1 cup water and secure pot with lid. Switch on Instant Pot, select MANUAL option, set the pressure to HIGH and adjust cooking time on timer pad to 5 minutes and let cook.

8. When the timer beeps, switch off the Instant Pot and let pressure release naturally for 10 minutes and then do quick pressure release.
9. Then uncover pot and puree mixture using an immersion blender. Stir in yeast, basil, butter and lemon juice and serve immediately.

Nutritional Info (per serving): Calories - 128; Fat –7.4

Chicken and White Bean Chili With Tomatoes

(Prep + Cook Time: 35 minutes | Servings: 8)

Ingredients:

- 4 ounces canned mild green chilies, diced,
- 3 cups canned great northern beans, drain and rinse
- 3 ¾ cups chicken, boneless breasts, diced
- 2 cups chicken broth or stock, reduced fat
- 14 ounces canned tomatoes, diced
- ¼ tsp cayenne pepper
- ½ tsp paprika
- ½ tsp garlic powder
- 1 tbsp cumin
- 1 ¼ cups onion, diced

Directions:

1. Combine all of the ingredients in the Instant Pot. Lock the lid and close the steam valve.
2. Press the SOUP key and adjust the time for 10 minutes.
3. When the timer beeps, release the pressure quickly and enjoy.

Nutritional Info (per serving): Calories - 188; Fat – 3.5; Fiber – 6.6; Carbs – 17.2; Protein – 23.3

Chicken Cream Chesse

(Prep + Cook Time: 35 minutes | Servings: 6)

Ingredients:

- 1 can black beans, drained and rinsed (15 ounces)
- 1 can corn, undrained (15.25 ounces)
- 1 can rotel, undrained (10 ounces)
- 1 pound chicken breasts, boneless skinless
- 1 package dry ranch seasoning (1 ounce)
- 2 tsp cumin, or to taste
- 2 tsp chili powder, or to taste

Directions:

1. Put all the ingredients in the Instant Pot. Lock the lid and close the steam valve.
2. Set the PRESSURE to HIGH and set the timer for 20 minutes.
3. When the timer beeps, let the pressure release for 10-15 minutes.
4. Open the steam valve to release any remaining pressure from the pot. Carefully open the lid.
5. Remove the chicken and shred.
6. Break up the cream cheese and stir into the pot. Cover and let the cheese melt.
7. When the cheese is melted, open the lid and return the shredded meat in the pot. Stir everything to mix.

Notes: Serve with tortilla chips or rice.

Nutritional Info (per serving): Calories - 619; Fat – 7.1; Fiber – 22.5; Carbs – 120.5; Protein – 32.8

Fennel Chicken Soup

(Prep + Cook Time: 55 minutes | Servings: 6)

Ingredients:

- 4 green onions, chopped
- 4 cups water, filtered
- 3 cloves garlic, peeled and chopped
- 2 cups chicken bone broth
- 1/8 tsp salt
- ½ onion, chopped
- 1 tbsp dried oregano
- 1 pound chicken thighs or/ and breast, boneless, skinless, cut into chunks
- 1 cup spinach or kale, chopped
- 1 bulb fennel, large-sized, chopped
- 1 bay leaf

Directions:

1. Put all of the ingredients into the Instant Pot. Cover and lock the lid.
2. Press the SOUP key and set the timer for 30 minutes.
3. When the Instant Pot timer beeps, press the CANCEL key and unplug the Instant Pot. Let the pressure release naturally for 10 minutes. Turn the steam valve to release remaining pressure.
4. Unlock and carefully open the lid.
5. Divide between serving bowls and serve.

Notes: This soup can be frozen and reheated.

Nutritional Info (per serving): Calories - 181; Fat – 6.3; Fiber – 2.2; Carbs – 6; Protein – 24.6

Turkey Chili

(Prep + Cook Time: 60 minutes | Servings: 4)

Ingredients:

- 1 can (15-ounce) fire-roasted diced tomatoes
- 1 can (15-ounce) kidney beans, including their liquid
- 1 pound ground turkey
- 1 tbsp olive oil
- 1 tsp ground cumin
- 1 yellow onion, medium-sized, diced
- ½ tsp dried oregano leaves
- ¼ cup your favorite hot sauce
- 2 fresh cayenne peppers, chopped (seeds included)
- 2 green bell peppers, seeded and diced
- 4 cloves garlic, chopped

To serve:

- ¼ cup cilantro, chopped
- 1 cup Monterey Jack cheese, grated

Directions:

1. Set the Instant Pot to SAUTE. Put the oil in the pot. Add the garlic, onion, and peppers.
2. Sauté for about 10 minutes until the onions are soft and start to brown.
3. Add the oregano and cumin; sauté for 2 minutes or until fragrant. Add the turkey.
4. With a spatula or a spoon, break the meat. Sauté for 5 minutes or until cooked through and opaque.
5. Add the beans, tomatoes, and hot sauce. Stir to combine. Close and lock the lid.
6. Press BEAN/ CHILI. When the timer beeps, release the pressure naturally or do a quick release. Carefully open the lid. Ladle the chili into bowls.
7. Serve hot. If desired, top with grated cheese and cilantro. Serve with cornbread or rice.

Notes: If you have no fresh cayenne chili peppers, use jalapeno, serrano, or canned chipotle for a smoky heat.

Nutritional Info (per serving): Calories - 781; Fat – 26.7; Fiber – 19.8; Carbs – 79.6; Protein – 64.4

Smoked Turkey Soup

(Prep + Cook Time: 1 hour 20 minutes | Servings: 8)

Ingredients:

- 11-ounces smoked turkey drumstick
- 6 cups water
- 2 cups dried black beans
- 2 bay leaves
- 1 chopped onion
- 1 chopped celery stalk
- 1 chopped carrot
- 3 pressed garlic cloves
- ½ cup chopped parsley
- ½ tbsp olive oil
- 1 ¼ tsp salt
- ¼ tsp black pepper

Directions:

1. Put oil in your Instant Pot and heat. Add carrots, celery, onions, and parsley.
2. Cook and stir for 8-10 minutes, until the veggies have softened. Toss in garlic and cook for another minute.
3. Pour in water, and add beans, turkey, black pepper, and bay leaves.
4. When boiling, close and seal the lid. Hit MANUAL and cook on HIGH pressure for 45 minutes.
5. When the timer beeps, turn off cooker and wait for a natural pressure release.
6. When safe, open the lid and pick out the bay leaves.
7. Take out the turkey and pick off the meat, and plate for now.
8. Blend the soup to your desired texture and add meat. Season to taste.

Nutritional Info (per serving): Calories - 133; Fat – 2; Fiber – 16; Carbs – 26; Protein – 19

Buffalo Chicken Soup

(Prep + Cook Time: 20 minutes | Servings: 4)

Ingredients:

- 3 cups chicken bone-broth
- 2 tbsp ghee, OR butter
- 2 cups cheddar cheese, shredded
- 2 chicken breasts, boneless, skinless, frozen or fresh
- ¼ cup diced onion
- 1/3 cup hot sauce
- ½ cup celery, diced
- 1 tbsp ranch dressing mix
- 1 cup heavy cream
- 1 clove garlic, chopped

Directions:

1. Except for the cheddar cheese and heavy cream, put the rest of the ingredients into the Instant Pot. Cover and lock the lid.
2. Press the MANUAL key, set the pressure to HIGH, and set the timer for 10 minutes.
3. When the Instant Pot timer beeps, press the CANCEL key and unplug the Instant Pot. Turn the steam valve to quick release the pressure. Unlock and carefully open the lid.
4. Carefully remove the chicken, shred the meat, and then return the shredded meat into the soup.
5. Add the cheese and cream and stir to combine. Ladle into bowls and serve.

Nutritional Info (per serving): Calories - 528; Fat – 40.9; Fiber – 0; Carbs – 4.1; Protein – 35.2

Enchilada Soup

(Prep + Cook Time: 35 minutes | Servings: 6)

Ingredients:

- 1 ½ pounds chicken thighs, boneless, skinless
- 1 bell pepper, thinly sliced
- 1 can (14.5 ounces) fire-roasted crushed tomatoes
- 1 onion, thinly sliced
- 1 tbsp chili powder
- 1 tbsp cumin
- 1 tsp oregano
- ½ cup water
- ½ tsp ground pepper
- ½ tsp sea salt
- ½ tsp smoked paprika
- 2 cups bone broth
- 3 cloves garlic, minced

For garnish:

- Fresh cilantro
- 1 avocado

Directions:

1. Except for the garnish ingredients, put all of the ingredients in the pot in the following order: chicken, tomatoes, bell pepper, onion, garlic, broth, water, cumin, chili powder, oregano, paprika, sea salt, pepper. Cover and lock the lid.
2. Press the MANUAL key, set the pressure to HIGH, and set the timer for 20minutes.
3. When the Instant Pot timer beeps, press the CANCEL key and unplug the Instant Pot. Turn the steam valve to quick release the pressure.
4. Unlock and carefully open the lid. Using 2 forks, shred the chicken right in the Instant Pot.
5. Ladle into servings bowls and top each serving with fresh cilantro and avocado.

Nutritional Info (per serving): Calories - 347; Fat – 16; Fiber – 4.7; Carbs – 13.4; Protein – 36

Bacon-y Potato Chowder

(Prep + Cook Time: 15 minutes | Servings: 8)

Ingredients:
- 5 pounds russet potatoes, peeled and cubed
- 1 pound bacon, fried crisp and rough chopped
- 1 cup heavy cream
- ¼ cup butter
- ½ cup whole milk
- 4 cups chicken stock
- 3 stalks celery, sliced thin
- 1 tsp ground black pepper
- 1 tbsp seasoning salt (I used Country Bob's)
- 1 large onion, small diced
- 1 clove garlic, minced
- Shredded cheddar cheese, sour cream, and diced green onion for garnish

Directions:
1. Put the potato chunks in the pot.
2. Add the garlic, onion, celery, seasoning salt, pepper, and butter. Stir to mix.
3. Add the chicken stock and the bacon. Close and lock the lid. Press MANUAL and set the timer to 5 minutes.
4. When the timer beeps, quick release the pressure. Carefully open the lid.
5. With a potato masher, crush the veggies until the mixture is a semi-smooth mash. If you want, you can leave a few big chunks of potato for texture.
6. Add the whole milk and the cream. Stir to mix. Ladle into bowls.
7. Top each serving with sour cream, shredded cheddar cheese, and sliced green onion.

Nutritional Info (per serving): Calories - 629; Fat – 15.3; Fiber – 7.4; Carbs – 49.1; Protein – 27.3

Cheese Tortellini and Chicken Soup

(Prep + Cook Time: 35 minutes | Servings: 6)

Ingredients:

- 2 whole chicken breast, skinless and boneless
- 2 small bags frozen cheese tortellini
- 2 cups baby carrots, chopped
- ½ white onion, chopped
- 1 cup celery, chopped
- 2 cartons (32 ounces each) chicken broth

Your choice of spices for chicken (I used the following):

- 1 tbsp garlic, minced
- 1 tbsp paprika
- 1 tbsp parsley
- 1 tsp pepper
- 1 tsp salt

Directions:

1. Pour 1 cup of the chicken broth in the Instant Pot. Add the chicken breast. Sprinkle the top of the chicken with the spices. Lock the pot and close the steam valve.
2. Press the MANUAL key, set the pressure to HIGH, and set the timer to 15 minutes.
3. Meanwhile, prepare the vegetables.
4. When the timer beeps, open the steam valve to quick release the pressure.
5. Remove the chicken from the pot and shred using two forks. Return the shredded meat into the pot.
6. Add the vegetables and the tortellini.
7. Add one container of the chicken broth and add 1/ 2 of the other container in the pot.
8. If desired, add more parsley or spices. Lock the lead and close the steam valve. Press MANUAL, set the pressure to HIGH and set the timer for 3 minutes.
9. When the timer beeps, let the pressure release quickly.
10. Ladle into bowls and enjoy!

Nutritional Info (per serving): Calories - 597; Fat – 12.2; Fiber – 1.7; Carbs – 75.4; Protein – 44.6

Navy Bean, Spinach, and Bacon Soup

(Prep + Cook Time: 45 minutes | Servings: 6)

Ingredients:

- 4 slices bacon, center cut, chopped
- 4 cups chicken broth, reduced sodium
- 3 cups baby spinach
- 3 cans (15 ounces each) navy beans, rinsed and drained
- 2 tbsp tomato paste
- 2 bay leaves
- 1 sprig fresh rosemary (I used a bouquet garni for tosing)
- 1 onion, medium-sized, chopped
- 1 celery stalk, large-sized, chopped
- 1 carrot, large-sized, chopped

Directions:

1. Put 1 can beans and 1 cup water in blender, and blend. Press the SAUTÉ key of the Instant Pot.
2. Put the bacon in the pot and cook until crisp. Remove and transfer into a plate lined with paper towel.
3. Add the onion, celery, and carrots into the pot, and sauté for about 5 minutes or until soft. Stir in the tomato paste.
4. Add the beans, pureed beans, bay leaves, rosemary, and broth. Lock the lid and close the steam valve. Cook for 15 minutes on HIGH pressure.
5. When the timer beeps, release the pressure quickly or naturally. Carefully open the lid.
6. Remove the bay leaves and the rosemary. Pour 2 cups of the soup in a blender and blend. Return into the soup.
7. Add the spinach and stir until wilted. Ladle between 6 bowls ad top each serving with bacon.

Nutritional Info (per serving): Calories - 437; Fat – 9.5; Fiber – 53.2; Carbs – 134.5; Protein – 56.4

Cream Of Asparagus Soup

(Prep + Cook Time: 25 minutes | Servings: 4)

Ingredients:

- 8 ounces organic sour cream
- 5 cups bone broth, homemade or store-bought
- 3 tbsp ghee, grass-fed butter or healthy fat of choice
- 2 pounds fresh asparagus, woody ends removed and then cut into 1-inch pieces
- 2 garlic cloves, smashed or chopped
- ½ tsp dried thyme
- 1 yellow onion, chopped
- 1 tsp Celtic sea salt, to taste
- 1 lemon, organic, zested and juiced

Directions:

1. Press the SAUTE key of the Instant Pot. Add your healthy fat of choice.
2. When the fat is melted, add the garlic and onion, and cook for 5 minutes, occasionally stirring, just until the garlic and onions are fragrant and start to caramelize.
3. Add the dried thyme and cook, stirring, for 1 minute. Add the broth.
4. With a wooden spoon, scrape any caramelized bits in the bottom of the pot.
5. Add the asparagus, lemon juice, lemon zest, and salt. Press the CANCEL key to stop the sauté function. Lock the lid and close the steam valve.
6. Press the MANUAL, set the pressure to HIGH, and set the timer to 5 minutes.
7. When the timer beeps, press CANCEL and unplug the pot. Let the pressure release naturally. Open the steam valve and carefully open the lid.
8. With an immersion blender, puree the soup or blend in small batches using a blender until soft.
9. Add the sour cream during blending. Return into the Instant Pot, if using a blender and reheat if needed.
10. Alternatively, you can reheat in a stockpot. Season to taste, as needed.

11. Top each serving with extra sur cream, extra-virgin olive oil, or lemon juice. Notes: If you want a dairy-free soup, use plain or full-fat coconut milk instead of sour cream.
12. This will change the taste of the soup a bit. You can also use bacon fat or avocado oil instead of ghee.
13. You can store this soup in the refrigerator for 2 days.

Nutritional Info (per serving): Calories - 317; Fat – 23.5; Fiber – 5.8; Carbs – 16.9; Protein – 13.4

Butternutsquash-Apple Soup
(Prep + Cook Time: 25 minutes | Servings: 6)

Ingredients:
- 1 apple, peeled and then cut up
- 1 whole butternut squash, peeled and then cut up into small cubes
- 4 cups chicken broth or vegetable broth
- Ginger powder or pureed ginger (I like the ginger that comes in the tube from the supermarket)
- Olive oil to taste

Directions:
1. Press the SAUTÉ key of the Instant Pot.
2. When the pot is hot, add the oil and some butternut squash cubes.
3. Cook for about 5 minutes or until the squash are slightly brown.
4. Add the rest of the squash cubes and the rest of the ingredients. Lock the lid and close the steam valve.
5. Press MANUAL, set the pressure to HIGH, and set the time to 10 minutes.
6. When the timer beeps, press CANCEL and release the pressure quickly.
7. With an immersion blender, puree the soup in the pot.
8. Alternatively, puree the soup in a high-powered blender.

Nutritional Info (per serving): Calories - 171; Fat – 1.9; Fiber – 5.9; Carbs – 35.1; Protein – 7.3

Butternut Squash Sweet Potato Soup

(Prep + Cook Time: 40 minutes | Servings: 4)

Ingredients:

- 3 cups bone broth or vegetable broth or chicken broth
- 2 tbsp coconut oil
- 2 cups sweet potatoes, peeled and cubed
- 2 cups butternut squash, peeled, seeded, and cubed
- 2 cloves garlic, crushed
- ½ tsp turmeric
- ½ tsp ground nutmeg
- 1 tsp walnuts, chopped, for garnish, optional
- 1 tsp or pinch Himalayan pink salt
- 1 tsp fresh parsley, for garnish, optional
- 1 tsp dried tarragon
- 1 tsp cinnamon
- 1 onion, small-medium, cubed
- 1 inch ginger, peeled
- 1 ½ tsp curry powder

Directions:

1. Press the SAUTE key of the Instant Pot.
2. When the pot is hot, add the coconut oil, ginger, garlic, onions, and pinch of salt. Sauté until the onion is slightly soft.
3. Add the rest of the ingredients and stir to mix. Lock the lid and close the steam valve. Press MANUAL and set the timer for 10 minutes.
4. When the timer beeps, let the pressure release naturally. Carefully open the lid.
5. With an immersion blender, puree the soup right in the pot.
6. Alternatively, transfer the soup in a blender of a food processor, and puree in batches if needed.
7. Be careful because the soup will be hot.
8. Serve immediately and garnish.

Nutritional Info (per serving): Calories - 236; Fat – 8.8; Fiber – 6; Carbs – 35.2; Protein – 6.4

Easy Weeknight Stew

(Prep + Cook Time: 65 minutes | Servings: 4)

Ingredients:
- 1 can (14 ounces) diced fire-roasted tomatoes (you can use regular tomatoes)
- 1 can (14 ounces) full-fat coconut milk
- 1 handful cilantro, fresh chopped, to garnish
- 1 onion, diced
- 1 pound string beans, cut into
- 1 inch pieces
- 1 tbsp salt
- 1 tbsp cumin
- 1 tsp fresh ginger, minced
- 2 cloves garlic, minced
- 2 cups broth (chicken or you can use pork)
- 3 medium-sized bulbs celeriac, peeled and then chopped (you can use 6 stalks celery, chopped)
- 3 pounds pork shoulder or country style ribs, cut into 1-2 inch squares
- 3 tbsp curry powder
- 6 carrots, peeled and chopped
- Sea salt and pepper to taste

Directions:
1. In a large-sized bowl, combine the cubed meat with the ginger, curry powder, salt, and cumin, and mix well.
2. Except for the cilantro, pepper, and salt, put all the ingredients into the Instant Pot. Lock the lid and close the steam valve.
3. Turn on the pot and press the STEW key.
4. When the timer beeps, turn off the pot, and let the pressure release quickly or naturally.
5. Carefully open the lid, if needed, season with salt and pepper, and then garnish with cilantro.
6. If you want a thicker stew, stir in some arrowroot starch.

Notes: Beef and lamb would also work great for this stew. Choose cuts with more connective tissue and not lean steaks. You can use butternut squash instead of the carrots and you can add freshly chopped spinach once the stew has cooled so the leaves are still bright green with a crunch.

Nutritional Info (per serving): Calories - 745; Fat – 30.2; Fiber – 9.9; Carbs – 27.6; Protein – 79.1

Rainbow Soup (veg)
(Prep + Cook Time: 25 minutes | Servings: 8)

Ingredients:
- 5 cups veggie broth
- 3 minced garlic cloves
- 3 cups cooked black beans
- 2 diced carrots
- 15-ounce can diced tomatoes
- 1 chopped small red cabbage
- 1 chopped onion
- 1 diced jalapeno chile
- 1 chopped yellow bell pepper
- 6-ounces quartered mushrooms
- 2 tbsp tomato paste
- 1 tbsp oregano
- 1 tbsp chili powder
- 1 tsp cumin
- Salt to taste

Directions:
1. Mix everything in your pressure cooker, minus the salt.
2. Close the lid, select MANUAL, and cook on high pressure for 6 minutes.
3. When time is up, turn off the cooker and wait 15 minutes.
4. Release any remaining pressure.
5. Salt and serve!

Nutritional Info (per serving): Calories - 169; Fat – 1; Fiber – 11; Carbs – 32; Protein – 11

Speedy Chili Texas Trail

(Prep + Cook Time: 20 minutes | Servings: 8)

Ingredients:

- 2 tbsp canola oil
- 1 large onion, peeled, chopped
- 1½ pounds ground beef, turkey or chicken
- 2 cups of your favorite Bloody Mary (spicy preferred)
- 2 cans (14 ounces each) diced tomatoes with green chilies (or 28-ounce can diced tomatoes with juice)
- 2 cans (14 ounces each) kidney beans, drained and rinsed well
- 4 tbsp of your favorite chili powder, divided, or more if desired
- 1½ cups water

For serving, optional:

- Corn chips Cheese,
- Shredded Green onions,
- Sliced Sour cream

Directions:

1. Press the SAUTE key of the Instant Pot. Add the oil and heat.
2. Add the onion and sauté until golden brown, about 8 minutes.
3. Add the meat and cook until browned, breaking them while cooking.
4. Stir in the Bloody Mary mix and press the MORE sauté mode to increase heat. Stir and scrape any browned bits from the pot.
5. Add the beans, tomatoes, 2 tablespoons chili powder, and stir well.
6. Bring to just boiling, then add the water. Lock the lid and close the steam valve. Cook for 5 minutes on HIGH pressure.
7. When the timer beeps, quick release the pressure. Carefully open the lid. Just before serving, stir in chili pepper to desired spiciness.
8. Let stand for 5 minutes and ladle into bowls.
9. Garnish each serving as desired. Serve!

Nutritional Info (per serving): Calories - 508; Fat – 8.9; Fiber – 18; Carbs – 68.5; Protein – 41.1

Cauliflower Butternut Soup

(Prep + Cook Time: 35 minutes | Servings: 6)

Ingredients:

- 1 pound cauliflower, frozen
- 1 pound butternut squash, cubed, frozen
- ½ cup half-and-half, cream, or milk
- 1 onion, diced 1 tsp paprika
- ½-1 tsp dried thyme
- ¼ tsp sea salt
- ¼- ½ tsp red pepper flakes, optional
- 1-2 tsp oil, for sautéing
- 2 cups vegetable broth
- 2-3 cloves garlic, minced

Optional toppings:

- Bacon, crumbled (regular, veggie, or turkey)
- Cheddar cheese
- Croutons Green onions, chopped
- Hot sauce or sriracha
- Mozzarella and parmesan cheese
- Pesto Pumpkin seeds
- Sour cream, chives, and cheddar
- Sunflower seeds

Directions:

1. Press the SAUTE key of the Instant Pot. Add the oil and heat.
2. Add the onion and sauté until golden and tender.
3. Add the garlic and sauté for a couple of seconds or until fragrant.
4. Add the butternut squash, cauliflower, spices, and vegetable broth. Lock the lid and close the steam valve. Press the CANCEL to stop the sauté function.
5. Press MANUAL, set the pressure to HIGH, and the timer for 5 minutes.
6. When the timer beeps, turn the pot off, and open the steam valve to quick release the pressure.
7. Add half-and-half or your choice or dairy. With an immersion blender, puree until smooth.
8. Alternatively, let cool for a bit, and blend in a food processor or a blender. Top each serve with desired toppings.

Nutritional Info (per serving): Calories - 93; Fat – 1.9; Fiber – 4; Carbs – 16.5; Protein – 4.9

Texas-Style Big Chili

(Prep + Cook Time: 55 minutes | Servings: 4)

Ingredients:
- 1 pound beef, grass-fed, organic
- 1 onion, large-sized, diced
- 1 green bell pepper, seeds removed and diced
- 1 tbsp fresh parsley, chopped
- 1 tbsp Worcestershire sauce
- 1 tsp garlic powder
- 1 tsp onion powder
- 1 tsp paprika
- 1 tsp sea salt
- ½ tsp ground black pepper
- 26 ounces tomatoes, finely chopped
- 4 carrots, large-sized, chopped into small pieces
- 4 tsp chili powder
- Pinch cumin

For serving, optional
- Jalapenos, sliced
- Onions, diced
- Sour cream, dairy-free

Directions:
1. Press the SAUTÉ key.
2. Add the ground beef into the Instant Pot and cook until browned.
3. Add the remaining ingredients and mix well to combine. Lock the lid and close the steam valve.
4. Press CANCEL to stop the sauté function.
5. Press MEAT/ STEW key.
6. When the timer beeps, let the pressure release naturally.
7. Enjoy!

Nutritional Info (per serving): Calories - 308; Fat – 8.1; Fiber – 6; Carbs – 21.7; Protein – 37.8

An English Fish Stew

(Prep + Cook Time: 20 minutes | Servings: 6)

Ingredients:

- 2 tbsp of butter
- 1 giant onion peeled up and diced
- 2 celery stalks diced up
- 4 massive carrots and peeled up and dice
- 4 medium sized potatoes peeled and reduced to half
- 1 pound of firm flesh white fish fillets reduce to half size
- 2 cups of fish broth
- 1 cup of chilly water
- 1 piece of bay leaf
- Half a teaspoon of dried thyme
- 1 cup of heavy cream
- 1 cup of fresh thawed frozen corn kernels
- Salt and freshly ground white or black pepper
- Fresh parsley

Directions:

1. Put your Instant Pot to SAUTE mode and toss in the butter and let it melt down.
2. Toss in the onions and Saute them for three minutes.
3. Stir in the celery, carrot, potatoes and Saute for another minute.
4. Toss the fish, bay leaf, thyme, and pour the fish stock Lock up the lid of your cooker and let it cook at HIGH pressure for 4 minutes.
5. Once done, release your pressure quickly and discard the bay leaf.
6. Stir in some cream to make the mix a bit heavy alongside corn.
7. Season with some pepper and salt Simmer until the corn is fully cooked and the chowder is scorching.
8. Serve by garnishing with parsley.

Nutritional Info (per serving): Calories - 165; Carbs – 6; Protein – 24

Wintery Stew (veg)
(Prep + Cook Time: 25 minutes | Servings: 4)

Ingredients:
- 2 tbsp olive oil
- 3 cloves garlic, crushed and minced
- 1 cup yellow onion, diced
- 1 cup green bell pepper, chopped
- 2 cups carrots, chopped
- 2 cups parsnips, chopped
- 2 cups red potatoes, cubed
- 1 cup beets, cubed
- 2 cups tomatoes, chopped
- 1 tbsp fresh tarragon, chopped
- 1 tbsp fresh dill, chopped
- 1 tsp salt
- 1 tsp black pepper
- 1 tbsp molasses
- 4 cups vegetable stock

Directions:
1. Place the olive oil in a pressure cooker and turn on the SAUTE or brown setting.
2. Add in the garlic and onion. Sauté for 2 minutes.
3. Next add in the green bell pepper, carrots, parsnips, red potatoes, beets and tomatoes.
4. Season with tarragon, dill, salt, black pepper and molasses. Mix well.
5. Add in the vegetable stock.
6. Cover and seal the pressure cooker. Set the pressure to HIGH and cook for 7 minutes.
7. Use the natural release method to release the steam before serving.

Sweet Peanut Stew (veg)

(Prep + Cook Time: 35 minutes | Servings: 4)

Ingredients:

- 1 cup brown rice
- 2 tbsp olive oil
- 2 tbsp shallots, diced
- 2 cloves garlic, crushed and minced
- 1 tsp salt
- 1 tsp black pepper
- 2 tsp crushed red pepper flakes
- 4 cups vegetable stock
- ½ cup chunky natural peanut butter
- 2 cups fresh pineapple, chunked
- 3 cups fresh spinach, torn
- ½ cup peanuts, chopped
- ½ cup fresh cilantro, chopped

Directions:

1. Place the olive oil in a pressure cooker and turn on the SAUTE or brown setting.
2. Add in the shallots, garlic, salt, black pepper and crushed red pepper flakes. Sauté for 2 minutes.
3. Add in the rice, vegetable stock and peanut butter.
4. Cover and seal the pressure cooker. Cook on HIGH for 15 minutes.
5. Using the quick release, open the pressure cooker and release the steam.
6. Add in the pineapple and spinach. Cover and bring the pressure back up to low. Continue to cook for 2 minutes.
7. Use the natural release method to release the steam.
8. Serve garnished with chopped peanuts and fresh cilantro.

Breakfast Potato Hash (veg)

(Prep + Cook Time: 20 minutes | Servings: 6)

Ingredients:

- 1 large sweet potato, diced larger than the potatoes since they cook faster (about 1 cup)
- 1 large potato, diced to about ½-inch cubes (about 1 cup)
- 1 cup bell pepper, chopped (about 2 peppers)
- 1 clove garlic, minced
- 1 tbsp olive oil
- 1 tsp cumin
- 1 tsp paprika
- ½ tsp black pepper
- ½ tsp kosher salt
- ½ cup water
- Pinch cayenne

Directions:

1. Toss the veggies with the oil and the spices.
2. Add the mix into the Instant Pot and then add the 1/2 cup water in the pot.
3. Set the pressure to HIGH and the timer to 0 minutes.
4. When the timer beeps, turn the valve to release pressure naturally.
5. Open the pot and press the SAUTE button. Sauté for about 5 to 6 minutes or until the potato cubes begin to brown.
6. Serve.

Nutritional Info (per serving): Calories - 393; Fat – 7.9; Fiber – 8.7; Carbs – 55.6; Protein – 6.5

Baked Potatoes (veg)

(Prep + Cook Time: 15 minutes | Servings: 8)

Ingredients:

- 5 pounds potatoes, peeled, if desired, chopped into roughly the same size
- 1½ cups water

Directions:

1. Pour the water into the Instant Pot container and then insert a steam rack.
2. Put the potatoes in the rack.
3. Close and lock the lid and make sure that the steam release valve is sealed. Press MANUAL and set the timer to 10 minutes.
4. When the timer beeps at the end of the cooking cycle, let the pressure release naturally for about 20 minutes.
5. Open the steam release valve to release any pressure remaining in the pot.
6. Serve and enjoy.

Nutritional Info (per serving): Calories - 156; Fat – 0.2; Fiber – 5.4; Carbs – 35.6; Protein – 3.8

Sweet Potatoes (veg)

(Prep + Cook Time: 25 minutes | Servings: 6)

Ingredients:

- 6 sweet potatoes, medium-sized (about 150 grams each)
- 2 cups water

Directions:

1. Wash the sweet potatoes clean and prick.
2. Pour 2 cups of water into the Instant Pot and put the steamer rack.
3. Layer the sweet potatoes on the rack.
4. Close and lock the lid. Press the MANUAL, set the pressure to HIGH, and the timer to 10 minutes.
5. When the timer beeps, turn the valve to VENTING for quick pressure release.
6. Let the sweet potatoes cool and serve or store in an airtight container for up to 5 days.

Notes: If you are using large-sized sweet potatoes, set the timer to 12-15 minutes.

Nutritional Info (per serving): Calories - 177; Fat – 0.3; Fiber – 6.2; Carbs – 41.8; Protein – 2.3

Sweet Potato Spinach Curry with Chickpeas

(Prep + Cook Time: 20 minutes | Servings: 2)

Ingredients:

- 1 small can of drained chickpeas
- 1 ½ cups chopped sweet potatoes
- 3 chopped garlic cloves
- 2 cups chopped fresh spinach
- 1 ½ cups water
- 2 chopped tomatoes
- ½ chopped red onion
- ½-inch thumb of ginger, chopped
- 1 tsp olive oil
- 1 tsp coriander powder
- ½ tsp garam masala
- ¼ tsp cinnamon
- Salt and pepper to taste
- Squeeze of lemon

Directions:

1. Pour oil in your Instant Pot and heat on SAUTE.
2. When the oil is hot, add the ginger, onion, and garlic.
3. When the onions are clear, add the spices and mix. After 30 seconds, add tomatoes and mix to coat everything.
4. Add sweet potatoes, chickpeas, 1 ½ cups water, and a dash of salt. Close and seal the lid. Select MANUAL and cook on high pressure for 8-10 minutes.
5. When time is up, hit CANCEL and do a natural pressure release.
6. Add the fresh spinach and stir so the heat wilts the leaves.
7. Taste and season more if necessary. Serve with a squirt of fresh lemon.

Nutritional Info (per serving): Calories – 166.5; Fat – 21; Fiber – 7; Carbs – 32; Protein – 6.8

Sweet Potato Chili (veg)

(Prep + Cook Time: 35 minutes | Servings: 4)

Ingredients:

- 2 cups veggie broth
- 1 medium-sized peeled and chopped sweet potato
- One 28 oz can of diced tomatoes with liquid
- 1 15 oz can rinsed and drained kidney beans
- 1 15 oz can rinsed and drained black beans
- 4 minced garlic cloves
- 1 chopped green bell pepper
- 1 chopped red bell pepper
- 1 chopped red onion
- 1 tbsp olive oil
- 1 tbsp chili powder
- 2 tsp unsweetened cocoa powder
- 1 tsp ground cumin
- 1 tsp cayenne pepper
- ¼ tsp ground cinnamon
- Sea salt and pepper to taste

Directions:

1. Turn your pot to SAUTE and add oil.
2. When shiny, add bell peppers, sweet potato, and onion.
3. Cook while stirring until the onions begin to turn clear.
4. Add all the spices and beans, broth, and tomatoes. Stir.
5. Close and seal the lid. Select MANUAL and cook on HIGH pressure for 10 minutes.
6. When time is up, hit CANCEL and wait for a natural pressure release.
7. When the pressure is gone, open the cooker. The potatoes should be fork-tender.
8. Taste and season more if necessary before serving.

Nutritional Info (per serving): Calories - 297; Fat – 4; Fiber – 35; Carbs – 53; Protein – 16

Garlicky Mashed Potatoes (veg)

(Prep + Cook Time: 20 minutes | Servings: 4)

Ingredients:

- 4 medium russet, yellow finn or yukon gold potatoes
- ¼ cup parsley, chopped
- ½ cup milk, non-dairy
- 1 cup vegetable broth
- 6 cloves garlic, peeled and cut in half
- Salt to taste

Directions:

1. Cut each potato into 8-12 chunks. Put into the Instant Pot.
2. Add the broth and the garlic.
3. Close and lock the lid. Press manual and set the timer to 4 minutes.
4. When the timer beeps, turn the valve to quick release the pressure.
5. With a hand blender or a masher, mash the potatoes.
6. Depending on the consistency you want, add all the soymilk or just the amount you need.
7. Add salt taste and then add the parsley, stir to combine. If desired, add pepper.
8. Serve hot.

Nutritional Info (per serving): Calories - 234; Fat – 7.8; Fiber – 6; Carbs – 37.1; Protein – 5.9

Scalloped Potatoes

(Prep + Cook Time: 15 minutes | Servings: 6)

Ingredients:

- 6 peeled and thinly-sliced potatoes
- 1 cup chicken broth
- ⅓ cup milk
- ⅓ cup sour cream
- 2 tbsp potato starch
- 1 tbsp chopped chives
- 1 tsp salt
- Dash of pepper
- Dash of paprika

Directions:

1. Pour the broth into your Instant Pot. Add chives, potatoes, salt, and pepper. Close and seal the lid.
2. Select MANUAL and adjust time to 5 minutes on HIGH pressure.
3. When time is up, turn off the cooker and quick-release.
4. Move the potatoes to a broiler-safe dish. Pour milk, sour cream, and potato starch into the liquid in your Instant Pot.
5. Turn back to SAUTE and whisk for 1 minute.
6. Pour everything over the potatoes and mix.
7. Add paprika and cook under the broiler for a few minutes, until the top is brown.

Nutritional Info (per serving): Calories - 168; Fat – 3; Fiber – 3; Carbs – 31; Protein – 4

Coconut Butter Garlic New Potatoes (veg)
(Prep + Cook Time: 10 minutes | Servings: 2)

Ingredients:

- 1.1 lb potatoes
- 3 tbsp coconut butter
- Handful fresh herbs
- Salt and pepper to taste
- 2/3 cup water

Directions:

1. Pour the water in the Instant Pot and set a steamer dish in the pot. Put the new potatoes in the steamer dish.
2. Add the fresh herbs, garlic, coconut butter, and a generous sprinkle of pepper and salt. Cover and lock the lid.
3. Press the MANUAL key, set the pressure to HIGH, and set the timer for 4 minutes. When the Instant Pot timer beeps, keep warm for 5 minutes.
4. Quick release the pressure.
5. When the potatoes are cool enough, transfer into a serving bowl and discard the excess coconut butter mixture.
6. Serve with additional fresh herbs, such as rosemary, parsley, chives, or whatever you have on hand.

Nutritional Info (per serving): Calories - 279; Fat – 21; Fiber – 9.4; Carbs – 44.4; Protein – 5.4

Fingerling Potatoes

(Prep + Cook Time: 35 minutes | Servings: 4)

Ingredients:

- 1 ½ pounds
- 1-inch thick (or less) fingerling potatoes
- ½ cup chicken broth
- 2 tbsp butter
- Leaves from 1 rosemary sprig
- Salt and pepper to taste

Directions:

1. Prick the potatoes, so they don't explode in the cooker.
2. Turn the Instant Pot to SAUTE and add butter.
3. When melted, add the potatoes and stir. Cook for the next 10 minutes, stirring once and awhile.
4. When the skins are crispy and the butter smells rich and nutty, pour in the broth. Close and seal the lid.
5. Press MANUAL and adjust time to 7 minutes on HIGH pressure.
6. When time is up, hit CANCEL and wait 10 minutes before quick-releasing.
7. Season well with salt, pepper, and rosemary before serving.

Nutritional Info (per serving): Calories - 175; Fat – 4; Fiber – 3; Carbs – 27; Protein – 4

Coconut Tofu Curry (veg)

(Prep + Cook Time: 35 minutes | Servings: 4)

Ingredients:

- 10 fluid oz coconut milk, full-fat
- 1 tbsp curry powder
- 2 tbsp peanut butter
- 1 tbsp garam masala
- 2 cups cubed green bell pepper
- 2 tsp salt
- 8 oz tomato paste
- 1 cup cubed onion
- 2 tsp mince garlic
- 1 cup diced tofu, firm

Directions:

1. In a food processor or blender place all the ingredients except tofu and pulse until smooth.
2. Place tofu in a 6 quarts Instant Pot and then top with prepared sauce.

3. Plug in and switch on Instant Pot, secure with lid and position pressure indicator.
4. Select MAUAL option, adjust cooking time on timer pad to 4 minutes and let cook. Instant Pot will take 10 minutes to build pressure before cooking timer starts.
5. When the timer beeps, switch off the Instant Pot and then do quick pressure release.
6. Uncover pot and stir and serve immediately.

Nutritional Info (per serving): Calories - 297; Fat – 23; Fiber – 6; Carbs – 25; Protein – 16.4

Steamed Broccoli (veg)
(Prep + Cook Time: 10 minutes | Servings: 2)

Ingredients:
- 2-3 cups broccoli florets
- ¼ cup water
- A bowl with ice and cold water

Directions:
1. Pour the water into the Instant Pot container.
2. Put the steamer insert in the pot. Place the broccoli in the steamer.
3. Press MANUAL, set the pressure to HIGH, and the timer to 0 minutes.
4. Carefully watch the pot. Ready the bowl with iced water.
5. One the timer beeps after the end of the cooking cycle, immediately open the valve to quick pressure release.
6. Remove the steamer insert and then put the broccoli in the ice bath to stop cooking and helps keep the broccoli's bright green color.

Nutritional Info (per serving): Calories - 31; Fat – 0.3; Fiber – 2.4; Carbs – 6; Protein – 2.5

Garlicky Broccoli (veg)

(Prep + Cook Time: 20 minutes | Servings: 4)

Ingredients:

- 1-2 heads broccoli (about 0.8 pound), cut into 2-4 cups florets
- ½ cup water
- 6 garlic cloves, minced
- 1 tbsp peanut oil
- Fine sea salt, roughly 1/8-1/4 tsp, to taste
- 1 tbsp rice wine, optional
- Bowl with ice and cold water

Directions:

1. Pour 1/2 cup water into the Instant Pot and put the steamer rack in the pot.
2. Put the broccoli florets into the steamer rack. Close and lock the lid. Set the pressure to LOW and the timer to 0 minutes.
3. When the timer beeps, turn the steamer valve to VENTING. Carefully open the lid.
4. Immediately put the broccoli florets in the ice bath or put them under running cold water to stop cooking.
5. Drain and set aside to air dry. Pour out the hot water from the pot and dry.
6. Press the SAUTE button and wait until the pot is as hot as it can get. Add 1 tablespoon peanut oil, coating the whole bottom of the pot.
7. Add the minced garlic and sauté for about 25 to 30 seconds; do not let the garlic burn.
8. Add the broccoli florets and, if using, the rice wine; stir for 30 seconds.
9. Season with salt to taste and stir for 30 seconds more.
10. Serve.

Nutritional Info (per serving): Calories - 134; Fat – 7.4; Fiber – 4.9; Carbs – 14.9; Protein – 5.6

Breakfast Kale (veg)

(Prep + Cook Time: 10 minutes | Servings: 4)

Ingredients:

- 10 oz kale
- 2 tsp vinegar, your favorite flavored

For the faux parmesan cheese:

- 1 cup raw cashews
- ½ cup nutritional yeast
- 1 tbsp salt-free seasoning (I used Benson's)
- ½ cup water

Directions:

1. Fill the Instant Pot container with washed and chopped kale.
2. Pour in the water. Close the lid and lock, and, make sure the valve is closed. Plug the pot and then set to MANUAL, set to pressure, and the timer to 4 minutes.
3. Meanwhile, put all the faux Parmesan ingredients into a food processor. Process until the mixture is powdery. If you prefer it chunkier, process less.
4. When the timer beeps at the end of the cooking cycle, turn the steam to quick release pressure and carefully open the lid. Transfer the kale in a serving plate.
5. Pout about 2 teaspoons of your favorite flavored vinegar.
6. Top with the faux parmesan. Serve over cooked brown rice or with a small potato.

Nutritional Info (per serving): Calories - 303; Fat – 17; Fiber – 7.1; Carbs – 27.8; Protein – 16.6

Steamed Carrot Flowers (veg)
(Prep + Cook Time: 15 minutes | Servings: 4)

Ingredients:
- 1 pound thick carrots, peeled
- 1 cup water

Directions:
1. With a sharp knife, cut 4-5 long groves along the carrot body; reserve what comes off to use in a sauce or stock.
2. Cut the carrots into coins, which now makes them into flowers. Put the carrot flowers in the steaming basket.
3. Pour 1 cup water into the Instant Pot, then put the steamer basket in the pot.
4. Close and lock the lid. Set the pressure to LOW and the timer to 4 minutes. When the timer beeps, quick release the pressure.
5. Carefully remove the steamer basket from the pot to stop cooking.
6. Transfer the carrot flowers into a serving dish.
7. Serve naked or without seasoning or dressing or at least taste them before drizzling with a bit of olive oil and pinch of salt.

Nutritional Info (per serving): Calories - 46; Fat – 0; Fiber – 2.8; Carbs – 11.2; Protein – 0.9

Maple Glazed Carrots
(Prep + Cook Time: 40 minutes | Servings: 8)

Ingredients:
- 2 pounds carrots, peeled and then diagonally sliced into thick pieces
- ½ cup water
- ¼ cup raisins
- 1 tbsp maple syrup
- 1 tbsp butter
- Pepper to taste

Directions:
1. Wash the carrots. Peel them and then slice into thick diagonal pieces. Put the carrots into the Instant Pot.
2. Add the raisins and the water. Close and lock the lid. Set the pressure to LOW and the timer to 3 or 4 minutes.

3. When the timer beeps, turn the valve to VENTING to quick release the pressure.
4. Remove the carrots from the pot and strain. In the still warm Instant Pot bowl, melt the butter and the maple syrup.
5. Add the carrots and gently stir to coat. Sprinkle with pepper and serve.

Nutritional Info (per serving): Calories - 79; Fat – 1.5; Fiber – 3; Carbs – 16.4; Protein – 1.1

Pumpkin Puree (veg)
(Prep + Cook Time: 30 minutes | Servings: 6)

Ingredients:
- 2 pounds small-sized sugar pumpkin or pie pumpkin, halved and seeds scooped out
- ½ cup water

Directions:
1. Pour the water into the Instant Pot and set the steamer rack.
2. Put the pumpkin halves on the rack. Set the pressure to HIGH and the timer to 13 or 15 minutes.
3. When the timer beeps, turn the valve to quick release the pressure. Let the pumpkin cool.
4. When cool enough to handle scoop out the flesh into a bowl.
5. Puree using an immersion blender or puree in a blender.

Notes: You can stir pumpkin into your oatmeal, use it to make a dessert, stir some with an applesauce for instant pumpkin applesauce, mix with softened butter with some sugar and spices like cinnamon, nutmeg, or cloves to make a compound butter for biscuits, blend it to make a creamy soup, and much more.

Nutritional Info (per serving): Calories - 51; Fat – 0.4; Fiber – 4.4; Carbs – 12.2; Protein – 1.7

Maple Mustard Brussels Sprouts

(Prep + Cook Time: 25 minutes | Servings: 8)

Ingredients:

- 16 Brussels sprouts, medium or large-sized (about 1-2 inch diameter), cut into halves or into quarters to make 3 cups total
- 1 ½-2 tbsp Dijon mustard
- ½ cup onion, diced
- ½ cup vegetable stock OR water
- ½-1 tbsp maple syrup
- 2 tsp pure sesame OR sunflower oil, optional
- Salt and freshly ground black pepper

Directions:

1. Set the Instant Pot to SAUTE. If using, pour the oil in the pot.
2. Add onion and sauté, or if not using oil, dry sauté, for about 1-2 minutes or until starting to soften.
3. In a glass jar or in a jar, whisk the stock with the mustard. Set aside.
4. Add the Brussels sprouts and then the stock mix in the pot.
5. Stir to coat and then drizzle the maple syrup over the veggies without stirring. Close and lock the lid. Turn the steam valve to SEALING and cook on LOW pressure for 3 minutes.
6. If your Instant Pot does not have a pressure option, cook for 2 minutes since the standard pressure for pots without pressure option is HIGH.
7. When the timer beeps, turn the steam valve to VENTING for quick pressure release. Carefully unlock and open the lid.
8. Transfer the sprouts into a bowl.
9. If desired, season to taste with salt and pepper.

Notes: If you are using small sprouts, do not cut them into halves. The cooking time indicated for this recipe cooks the sprouts al dente. If you want then softer, cook them for 1-2 minutes more.

Nutritional Info (per serving): Calories - 46; Fat – 0.5; Fiber – 3.1; Carbs – 9.6; Protein – 0

Steamed Artichokes (veg)

(Prep + Cook Time: 45 minutes | Servings: 4)

Ingredients:

- 2 medium-sized whole artichokes (about 5 ½ oz each)
- 1 lemon wedge
- 1 cup water

Directions:

1. Rinse the artichokes clean and remove any damaged outer leaves.
2. With a sharp knife, trim off the stem and top third of each artichoke carefully. Rub the cut top with a lemon wedge to prevent browning.
3. Pour 1 cup water into the Instant Pot and set the steamer basket or rack. Pout the artichokes on the steamer/ rack.
4. Press MANUAL and set the timer to 20 minutes.
5. When the timer beeps, press CANCEL to turn off the warming function. Let the pressure release naturally for 10 minutes.
6. Open the lid and with tongs, remove the artichokes from the pot.
7. Serve warm with your dipping sauce of choice, such as garlic butter, something mayonnaise-y, champagne vinaigrette with a flair of Dijon mustard, chimichurri or green goddess dressing.

Notes: If cooking larger artichokes, set the timer to 25 minutes and if cooking smaller artichokes, set the timer to 15 minutes.

Nutritional Info (per serving): Calories - 77; Fat – 0.2; Fiber – 8.8; Carbs – 17.4; Protein – 5.3

Zucchini and Mushrooms (veg)

(Prep + Cook Time: 20 minutes | Servings: 6)

Ingredients:

- 8-12 oz mushrooms, sliced or separated depending on type of mushroom
- 4 medium zucchini, cut into
- ½-inch slices (about 8 cups)
- 1 can (15 ounce) crushed or diced tomatoes with juice
- 1 large sprig fresh basil, sliced
- 1 tbsp extra-virgin olive oil
- ½ tsp black pepper, or to taste
- ½ tsp salt, or to taste
- 2 cloves garlic, minced
- 1 ½ cup onions, diced

Directions:

1. Press the SAUTE button of the Instant Pot. Add the olive oil and heat.
2. Add the garlic, onions, and mushrooms; cook, frequently stirring, until the onions are soft and the mushrooms lose their moisture.
3. Add the basil and sprinkle with the salt and pepper. Sauté for 5 minutes until the mushrooms are soft.
4. Add the zucchini, stir. Add the tomatoes with the juices over the zucchini; do not stir.
5. Close and lock the lid. Press the MANUAL button. Set the pressure to LOW and the timer to 1 minute.
6. When the timer beeps, turn the steam valve to quick release the pressure. Carefully remove the cover.
7. If the zucchini are still a little undercooked, just cover the pot and let rest for 1 minutes to allow the zucchinis to soften.
8. Serve over pasta, rice, baked potatoes, or polenta. If desired, you can stir a can of white beans.

Nutritional Info (per serving): Calories - 96; Fat – 2.8; Fiber – 5; Carbs – 15.2; Protein – 5.6

Brussels Sprouts (veg)

(Prep + Cook Time: 5 minutes | Servings: 4)

Ingredients:

- 1 pound Brussels sprouts
- ¼ cup pine nuts
- Salt and pepper to taste
- Olive oil
- 1 cup water

Directions:

1. Pour the water into the Instant Pot. Set the steamer basket.
2. Put the Brussels sprouts into the steamer basket.
3. Close and lock the lid. Press the MANUAL button. Set the pressure to HIGH and set the time to 3 minutes.
4. When the timer beeps, turn the valve to VENTING to quick release the pressure.
5. Transfer the Brussel sprouts into a serving plate, season with olive oil, salt, pepper, and sprinkle with the pine nuts.

Notes: To prepare the Brussels sprouts, wash them and remove the outer leaves. If some of them are quite large, cut those in half for uniformity - so that they will cook evenly. You will also have to wash the silicone ring of your Instant Pot well after cooking this dish since they can get rather smelly. Soak the ring in dish soap with baking soda and then dry on the counter.

Nutritional Info (per serving): Calories - 106; Fat – 6.2; Fiber – 4.6; Carbs – 11.4; Protein – 5

Broccoli Salad

(Prep + Cook Time: 25 minutes | Servings:6)

Ingredients:

- 1 white onion
- 1-pound broccoli
- ½ cup chicken stock
- 1 tbsp salt
- 1 tsp olive oil
- 1 tsp garlic powder
- 3 tbsp raisins
- 2 tbsp walnuts, crushed
- 1 tsp oregano
- 1 tbsp lemon juice

Directions:

1. Wash the broccoli carefully and separate it into the small florets.
2. Place the broccoli florets in the Instant Pot and sprinkle them with the salt.
3. Close the lid and cook the vegetables at the PRESSURE mode for 10 minutes.
4. Then toss the broccoli into the ice water immediately to save the bright color.
5. Transfer the chilled broccoli in the serving bowl.
6. Peel the onion and slice it.
7. Add the sliced onion in the broccoli.
8. Sprinkle the mixture with the garlic powder, oregano, crushed walnuts, raisins, and lemon juice.
9. Add olive oil and stir the mixture gently to not damage the ingredients of the salad. Serve it!

Nutritional Info (per serving): Calories - 68; Fat – 3; Fiber – 3; Carbs – 4.1; Protein – 4

Sweet and Sour Spicy Savoy (veg)

(Prep + Cook Time: 15 minutes | Servings: 4)

Ingredients:

- 2 tbsp peanut oil
- 1 tbsp shallots, diced
- ½ cup leeks, sliced
- 2 cloves garlic, crushed and minced
- 1 tbsp fresh grated ginger
- 2 tsp crushed red pepper flakes
- 1 head savoy cabbage, sliced
- 1 cup vegetable stock
- ¼ cup rice vinegar
- ¼ cup brown sugar
- 1 tbsp soy sauce
- 1 tbsp garlic chili paste

Directions:

1. Place the peanut oil in a pressure cooker and turn on the SAUTE or brown setting.
2. Add in the shallots, leeks, garlic, ginger and crushed red pepper flakes.
3. Sauté for 2 minutes before adding in the cabbage.
4. Combine the vegetable stock, rice vinegar, brown sugar, soy sauce and garlic chili paste.
5. Mix well and pour into the pressure cooker.
6. Cover and seal the pressure cooker and set to high. Cook for 3 minutes.
7. Use the natural release method to release the steam from the pressure cooker before serving.

Kale With Lemon and Garlic (veg)

(Prep + Cook Time: 15 minutes | Servings: 4)

Ingredients:

- 1 pound kale, cleaned and then stems trimmed
- 1 tbsp olive oil
- ½ cup water
- ½ lemon, juiced
- ½ tsp kosher salt
- 3 cloves garlic, slivered
- Freshly ground black pepper

Directions:

1. Set the Instant Pot to SAUTE. Pour in the oil and stir in the garlic.
2. Heat the oil for about 2 minutes or until the garlic is just fragrant.
3. Stir a big handful of kale into the oil and garlic and then start packing the remaining kale into the pot. The pot will be filled. Don't worry because the kale will quickly wilt – just pack the kale enough to close the pot lid. Sprinkle with salt and then pour water over the top of everything.
4. Close and lock the lid. Set the pressure to HIGH and cook for 5 minutes.
5. When the timer beeps, turn the steam release valve to quick release the pressure. Carefully remove the lid.
6. While still in the pot, squeeze the lemon juice over the kale and stir in the freshly ground pepper.
7. With a tong or a slotted spoon, scoop out the kale from the pot, leaving as much liquid as possible in the pot. Serve.

Nutritional Info (per serving): Calories - 90; Fat – 3.5; Fiber – 1.8; Carbs – 12.7; Protein – 3.5

Citrus Cauliflower Salad (veg)

(Prep + Cook Time: 20 minutes | Servings: 4)

Ingredients:

- Florets from 1 small cauliflower
- Florets from 1 small Romanesco cauliflower
- 1 pound broccoli
- 2 peeled and sliced seedless oranges
- 1 zested and squeezed orange
- 1 sliced hot pepper
- 4 tbsp olive oil
- 1 tbsp capers (not rinsed)
- Salt to taste
- Pepper to taste

Directions:

1. Pour 1 cup of water into your Instant Pot. Add florets into your steamer basket and lower in the cooker.
2. Close and seal. Hit STEAM and cook for 6 minutes.
3. While that cooks, make your vinaigrette. Mix the orange juice, zest, hot pepper, capers, olive oil, salt, and pepper. Peel your oranges and slice very thin.
4. When the timer beeps, hit CANCEL and quick-release.
5. Mix florets with oranges and dress with the vinaigrette.

Nutritional Info (per serving): Calories - 241; Fat – 15; Fiber – 8; Carbs – 22; Protein – 3

Eggplant with Carrots, Tomatoes, and Bell Peppers (veg)

(Prep + Cook Time: 30 minutes | Servings: 4)

Ingredients:

- 1 eggplant, chopped
- 1 onion, chopped
- 2 bell peppers,
- 1 green,
- 1 red, deseeded and chopped
- 1-2 tomatoes, chopped
- 2 carrots, peeled and chopped
- 1-2 fresh garlic cloves
- Salt and pepper to taste
- Olive oil, for sautéing

Directions:

1. Prepare all the vegetables and chop them. You can use a vegetable chopper to do this.
2. Set the Instant Pot to SAUTE. Grease the bottom of the inner pot with olive oil. Add the onions, carrots, and tomatoes.
3. Sauté until slightly browned. Add the remaining ingredients, except for the garlic cloves.
4. Add the tomato sauce and then the spices.
5. Set the pot to MANUAL and the timer for 10 minutes.
6. When the timer beeps, quick release the pressure or release the pressure naturally.
7. Serve and enjoy.

Nutritional Info (per serving): Calories - 78; Fat – 0.5; Fiber – 6.6; Carbs – 18.3; Protein – 2.6

Eggplant Chili (veg)

(Prep + Cook Time: 35 minutes | Servings: 6)

Ingredients:

- 1 large eggplant, cubed
- 1 medium onion, peeled and finely chopped
- 4 tsp minced garlic
- 1 medium-sized green bell pepper, seeded and diced
- 1 medium-sized red bell pepper, seeded and diced
- 1 medium-sized yellow bell pepper, seeded and diced
- 1 medium-sized carrot, peeled and diced
- 16 oz chopped tomatoes
- 30 oz cooked kidney beans
- 6 oz tomato paste
- 2 tsp olive oil and more as needed
- 8 fluid oz vegetable stock
- 1 tsp salt and more as needed
- 1 tbsp Mexican chili spice mix
- 1 tbsp sweet paprika
- ¼ tsp ground coriander

Directions:

1. Cut eggplant into bite-sized pieces, drizzle with 1 teaspoon oil and sprinkle with 1/8 teaspoon salt, toss to coat and set aside until required.
2. Plug in and switch on a 6-quarts Instant Pot, select SAUTE option and let heat.
3. Then add oil, onion, garlic and bell peppers and cook for 3 minutes or until vegetables begin to tenderize.
4. When the vegetables are tender, stir in all the spices, add remaining vegetables and toss to coat. Continue cooking for another minute.
5. Then stir in tomato juice and vegetable stock.
6. Press CANCEL, select STEW option and secure pot with lid. Then position pressure indicator and adjust cooking time on timer pad to 4 minutes and let cook.
7. When the timer beeps, switch off the Instant Pot and do a quick pressure release.
8. Then uncover the pot and stir chili. To reduce chili to desired thickness, switch on Instant Pot and simmer chili by selecting SAUTE option. Adjust seasoning and serve warm.

Nutritional Info (per serving): Calories - 262; Fat – 5.3; Fiber – 12; Carbs – 44; Protein – 10.9

Stuffed Eggplant (veg)

(Prep + Cook Time: 20 minutes | Servings: 4)

Ingredients:
- 2 eggplants
- 6 tbsp lentils, cooked
- 8-10 cherry tomatoes, softened
- ½ white onion, diced
- ½ tsp salt
- 1 tbsp paprika
- 1 green pepper
- 1 green chili
- Few sprigs mint and parsley
- 1 cup water

Directions:
1. Pour 1 cup water and set a trivet in the inner pot of the Instant Pot.
2. Put the eggplant and the green pepper in the trivet.
3. Close and lock the lid, turn the steam release valve to SEALING, and set the timer for 4 minutes on HIGH pressure.
4. Meanwhile, dice the onions and sauté until soft. If you have caramelized onions on hand, then feel free to use it instead.
5. Mix in the onions with the lentils. Set aside.
6. When the timer beeps, quick release the pressure. Carefully open the pot and take out the eggplants and the green peppers.
7. Carefully slice the eggplant lengthwise into halves. Scoop out the meat, leasing a 1-cm border. Cut the eggplant meat into smaller pieces.
8. Cut the green peppers, cherry tomatoes, green chili into smaller pieces.
9. Mix the eggplant with the green peppers and season with salt and paprika. Into the hollowed out eggplants, scoop the lentils, dividing equally between the 4 halves.
10. Add the eggplant mix on top of the lentil layer.
11. Top with the herbs, softened cherry tomatoes, and, is using, feta cheese. Serve.

Nutritional Info (per serving): Calories - 199; Fat – 2; Fiber – 19.6; Carbs – 40.3; Protein – 10.5

Five Spice Eggplant (veg)
(Prep + Cook Time: 15 minutes | Servings: 4)

Ingredients:

- 2 tbsp coconut oil
- 4 cups eggplant, peeled and cubed
- 2 cups fresh spinach, torn
- 1 tsp salt
- 1 tsp black pepper
- 1 tbsp five spice powder
- 1 cup vegetable stock
- ½ cup coconut milk
- Fresh scallions for garnish

Directions:

1. Place the coconut oil in a pressure cooker and set to the SAUTE setting. Add the eggplant and sauté for 1-2 minutes.
2. Add in the spinach and season with salt, black pepper and five spice powder.
3. Pour in the vegetable stock and coconut milk. Mix well.
4. Cover and seal the pressure cooker. Set to HIGH and cook for 4 minutes.
5. Use the natural release method to release the steam from the pressure cooker.
6. Garnish with fresh scallions before serving.

Spaghetti Squash (veg)
(Prep + Cook Time: 20 minutes | Servings: 4)

Ingredients:

- 1 whole winter squash
- 8 fluid oz water, chilled

Directions:

1. Cut squash in half lengthwise and remove and discard seeds using a spoon.
2. In the Instant Pot pour water and then insert a steamer basket.
3. Place squash halves in the steamer and secure pot with lid. Then position pressure indicator and adjust cooking time on timer pad to 6 minutes and let cook until done.
4. When the timer beeps, switch off the Instant Pot and do a quick pressure release.
5. Then uncover the pot, transfer squash from the pot and gently pull of the flesh from the skin as strands using a fork.
6. Serve squash spaghetti immediately.

Nutritional Info (per serving): Calories - 178; Fat – 3.3; Fiber – 1.2; Carbs – 39.7; Protein – 1

Caramelized Onion (veg)

(Prep + Cook Time: 50 minutes | Cup: 1)

Ingredients:

- 3 tbsp unsalted butter
- 3 large onions, halved and then sliced into 1/8-innch pieces
- ½ tsp kosher salt
- ¼ cup water

Directions:

1. Press the SAUTE button of the Instant Pot.
2. Add the butter and melt.
3. Add the onions and while sautéing, sprinkle with the salt. Occasionally stirring, sauté for 8 minutes or until the onions are soft and slightly browned.
4. Add the water and close the lid. Press the MANUAL button. Set the pressure to HIGH and set the timer to 20 minutes.
5. When the timer beeps, open the valve to quick pressure release. Reset to SAUTE and constantly stir the onions for about 5-8 minutes to reduce any liquid.
6. Let cool completely and store in an airtight container. Keep in the fridge for up to 1 week.

Notes: Caramelized onions add great flavor and texture in salads, burgers, deli-style sandwiches, pizza, tart, pasta dishes, dips, quiche, or frittatas, and base for French onion soup.

Nutritional Info (per serving): Calories - 27; Fat – 1.9; Fiber – 0.5; Carbs – 2.3; Protein – 0.3

Wheat Berry Balsamic Basil Salad (veg)

(Prep + Cook Time: 45 minutes | Servings: 6)

Ingredients:

For the wheat berries:

- 1 ½ cups wheat berries (hard red winter wheat kernels)
- 1 pinch salt
- 4 cups water
- 1 tbsp olive oil

For the salad:

- 1 cup grape tomatoes, halved
- 1 large handful fresh basil, chopped
- 1 large handful fresh parsley, chopped
- 1 tbsp balsamic vinegar
- 1 tbsp olive oil
- ½ cup Kalamata olives, chopped
- 1-2 green onions, chopped
- 1-2 oz feta cheese

Directions:

1. Set the Instant Pot to SAUTE. Pour in the olive oil and heat.
2. When the oil is hot, add the wheat berries and cook for about 5 minutes on medium sauté, stirring frequently until the wheat berries are fragrant.
3. Pour in the water and add the salt. Press CANCEL. Close and lock the lid. Press the MANUAL button. Set the pressure to HIGH and the timer to 30 minutes.
4. When the timer beeps, let the pressure release naturally for 10 minutes. Turn the steam valve to release any remaining pressure. Open the lid.
5. Drain the wheat berries in a colander. Rinse under running cold water to cool and transfer in a large-sized bowl.
6. Toss the wheat berries with the remaining ingredients and season with to taste with salt and pepper.

Nutritional Info (per serving): Calories - 130; Fat – 7.4; Fiber – 1.5; Carbs – 14.5; Protein – 3.5

Sweet and Sour Red Cabbage (veg)

(Prep + Cook Time: 35 minutes | Servings: 4)

Ingredients:

For the sauté ingredients:

- 4 cloves garlic, minced
- ½ cup onion, minced
- 1 tbsp mild oil, OR use broth for oil-free

For the Instant Pot:

- 1 cup water
- 1 cup applesauce
- 1 tbsp apple cider vinegar
- 6 cups cabbage, chopped
- Salt and pepper to taste

Directions:

1. Press the SAUTE key of the Instant Pot and select the NORMAL option for medium heat.
2. Add the oil/ broth into the pot. Add the onion and sauté until they become transparent. Add the garlic and sauté 1 minute.
3. Add the Instant Pot ingredients. Press the CANCEL key to stop the sauté function. Cover and lock the lid. Press the MANUAL key, set the pressure to HIGH, and set the timer for 10 minutes.
4. When the Instant Pot timer beeps, press the CANCEL key. Using an oven mitt or a long handled spoon, turn the steam valve to quick release the pressure.
5. Unlock and carefully open the lid. Serve.

Nutritional Info (per serving): Calories - 104; Fat – 3.7; Fiber – 4.6; Carbs – 17.5; Protein – 2.2

Ratatouille (veg)

(Prep + Cook Time: 30 minutes | Servings: 8)

Ingredients:

- 4 small zucchini, sliced thin
- 2 small eggplants, peeled and then sliced thin
- 1 can (28 oz) crushed tomatoes
- 1 jar (12 oz) roasted red peppers, drained and sliced
- 1 medium onion, sliced thin
- 1 tbsp olive oil
- 1 tsp salt
- 2 cloves garlic, crushed
- ½ cup water

Directions:

1. With the slicing disk of a food processor, prepare the zucchini, eggplant, and onion.
2. Alternatively, you can slice them thin by hand. Press the SAUTE button of the Instant Pot.
3. Put the olive oil in and heat until shimmering.
4. Add the vegetables and sauté for 3 minutes or until they start to soften.
5. Season with the salt and then add the crushed tomatoes and the water; stir to combine.
6. Close and lock the lid. Press the MANUAL button of the pot. Set the pressure to HIGH and set the timer to 4 minutes.
7. When the timer beeps, turn the steam valve to quick release the pressure.
8. Serve immediately. If there are any leftovers, you can store in the refrigerator for up to 5 days.

Nutritional Info (per serving): Calories - 116; Fat – 2.2; Fiber – 9.5; Carbs – 22.1; Protein – 2.2

Boiled Peanuts (veg)

(Prep + Cook Time: 1 hour 20 minutes | Servings: 4)

Ingredients:

- 1 pound large raw peanuts
- 1/8 cup sea salt
- Water as needed

Optional:

- 2 tsp Cajun seasoning with garlic, jalapeno peppers, etc.
- 1 tbsp BBQ seasoning
- 1 tsp sugar

Directions:

1. Rinse the peanuts under running cool water.
2. Remove any roots, twigs, or material that does not belong. Put into the Instant Pot. Add the salt and add enough water to cover.
3. Put a trivet on to hold the peanuts down. Close and lock the lid.
4. Set the pressure to HIGH and set the time to 70 minutes.
5. When the timer beeps, let the pressure release naturally and let sit for 30 minutes.
6. If the peanuts are still too hard for your liking, just cook more.

Notes: You can slow cook thee peanuts for 10 hours. Depending on your preference, peanuts are cooked at about 60-80 minutes. You can actually start at 60 minutes then cook more in increments until desired tenderness is achieved.

Nutritional Info (per serving): Calories - 643; Fat – 55.8; Fiber – 9.6; Carbs – 18.3; Protein – 29.3

Spinach Potato Taco Filling

(Prep + Cook Time: 25 minutes | Servings: 6)

Ingredients:

- 2 Yukon gold potatoes, large-sized, cut into small dice
- 1 package (8 oz) frozen spinach
- 1 medium onion, diced
- ½ cup diced chipotles tomatoes, plus
- ½ cup tomato juice from can
- 2 tsp garlic granules
- 2 tsp ground cumin
- ½ cup nondairy milk, unsweetened, unflavored
- 3 tbsp nutritional yeast
- Sea salt and freshly ground black pepper
- 12 corn tortillas, for serving
- 1/3 cup water

Directions:

1. Put the potatoes, 1/2 bag frozen spinach, cilantro, 1/2 can chipotle tomatoes with 1/2 of its juice, spices, and season with salt and pepper to taste.
2. Add 1/3 cup water. Turn the pressure release valve to sealing. Press MANUAL and set the timer to 2 minutes.
3. When the timer beeps, turn the steam release valve to quick release pressure.
4. There will be excess liquid in the pot. Press SAUTE mode and cook the excess liquid off.
5. Add the milk and yeast. Cook until thick.
6. Serve with corn tortillas or tortilla chips or nachos.

Nutritional Info (per serving): Calories - 117; Fat – 3.4; Fiber – 3.5; Carbs – 19.6; Protein – 4.1

Tofu, Kale, and Sweet Potato (veg)

(Prep + Cook Time: 15 minutes | Servings: 4)

Ingredients:

- 1 peeled and cut sweet potato
- 2 cups sliced kale leaves (stems and ribs removed)
- 8 oz cubed tofu
- 1 chopped onion
- 2 minced garlic cloves
- ¼-½ cup veggie broth
- 1-3 tsp tamari
- 1 tsp ground ginger
- ½ tsp ground cayenne
- 1 tsp olive oil Squeeze of lemon juice

Directions:

1. After prepping your ingredients, turn your Instant Pot to SAUTE and add oil.
2. When hot, sauté the tofu for a minute. Mix in the tamari with a few tablespoons of broth. Stir for a minute.
3. Add sweet potatoes, onion, garlic, and the rest of the broth. Select MANUAL and cook on high pressure for 2 minutes.
4. When time is up, hit CANCEL and quick-release the pressure.
5. Throw in the kale and seal back up for another 1 minute on HIGH pressure. Quick-release.
6. Divide up the meal and serve with a squirt of fresh lemon.

Nutritional Info (per serving): Calories - 133; Fat – 5; Fiber – 2.25; Carbs – 13; Protein – 11

Easy Seitan Roast Serves (veg)

(Prep + Cook Time: 30 minutes | Servings: 4)

Ingredients:

- 1 ½ cups vital wheat gluten
- 1 cup veggie broth
- ⅓ cup tapioca flour
- 3 tbsp nutritional yeast
- 2 tbsp coconut aminos
- 1 tbsp olive oil
- 1 tbsp vegan Worcestershire sauce
- 1 tsp garlic powder
- ½ tsp dried thyme
- ½ tsp dried rosemary
- ¼ tsp black pepper
- ¼ tsp sea salt
- 3 cups veggie broth
- 2 cups water
- ¼ cup coconut aminos
- 2 tbsp vegan Worcestershire
- 1 tsp onion powder

Directions:

1. Let's start with the first list of ingredients. Whisk all the dry ingredients together.
2. In a separate bowl, mix the wet ones. Pour the wet into the dry. Fold first with a spoon, and then knead by hand for a few minutes.
3. Form into a round shape, pulling at the top, and then rolling under so it's smooth. Shape into a more oblong loaf and roll tightly in cheesecloth, tying off the ends.
4. Put the roast in your Instant Pot. Pour in all the ingredients in the second ingredient list. Lock and seal the lid.
5. Select MANUAL and cook on HIGH pressure for 25 minutes.
6. When time is up, hit CANCEL and wait 10 minutes before quick-releasing the pressure.
7. Slice and serve!

Notes: When you slice seitan, it should have a meaty texture - not too soft, and not too chewy.

Nutritional Info (per serving): Calories - 451; Fat – 4; Fiber – 0; Carbs – 51; Protein – 42

Polenta with Fresh Herbs (veg)

(Prep + Cook Time: 20 minutes | Servings: 6)

Ingredients:

- 4 cups veggie broth
- 1 cup coarse-ground polenta
- ½ cup minced onion
- 1 bay leaf
- 3 tbsp fresh, chopped basil
- 2 tbsp fresh, chopped Italian parsley
- 2 tsp fresh, chopped oregano
- 2 tsp minced garlic
- 1 tsp fresh, chopped rosemary
- 1 tsp salt

Directions:

1. Preheat your cooker and dry-sauté the onion for about a minute.
2. Add the minced garlic and cook for one more minute.
3. Pour in the broth, along with the oregano, rosemary, bay leaf, salt, half the basil, and half the parsley. Stir.
4. Sprinkle the polenta in the pot, but don't stir it in. Close and seal the lid.
5. Select MANUAL and cook on high pressure for 5 minutes.
6. When the timer beeps, hit CANCEL and wait 10 minutes.
7. Pick out the bay leaf. Using a whisk, stir the polenta to smooth it.
8. If it's thin, simmer on the SAUTE setting until it reaches the consistency you like.
9. Season to taste with salt and pepper before serving.

Nutritional Info (per serving): Calories - 103; Fiber – 2; Carbs – 3; Protein – 0

Polenta with Honey and Pine Nuts

(Prep + Cook Time: 25 minutes | Servings: 6)

Ingredients:

- 5 cups water
- 1 cup polenta
- ½ cup heavy cream
- ½ cup honey
- ¼ cup pine nuts
- Salt to taste

Directions:

1. Mix pine nuts and honey with water in your Instant Pot.
2. Turn on the SAUTE function and bring to a boil while stirring.
3. Mix in polenta. Close and seal lid. Select MANUAL and adjust time to 12 minutes.
4. When time is up, hit CANCEL and quick-release.
5. Mix in cream and wait 1 minute before serving with a sprinkle of salt.

Nutritional Info (per serving): Calories - 282; Fat – 11; Fiber – 1.5; Carbs – 25; Protein – 1

Steamed Asparagus (veg)

(Prep + Cook Time: 25 minutes | Servings: 4)

Ingredients:

- 1 pound asparagus, cleaned and 1-inch snapped from the woody, tough stalk
- 1 cup water
- 1 tbsp onion, diced
- 2 tbsp olive oil
- Mediterranean sea salt, freshly milled Pepper, for sprinkling

Directions:

1. Pour the water into the Instant Pot and then put the steamer rack. Put the asparagus on the rack.
2. Drizzle with the olive oil and sprinkle with the onion. Close and lock the lid.
3. Press STEAM and set the timer to 2 minutes.
4. When the timer beeps, turn the valve to quick release the pressure.
5. Transfer the asparagus into a serving plate.
6. Sprinkle with salt and pepper.

Nutritional Info (per serving): Calories - 84; Fat – 7.1; Fiber – 2.4; Carbs – 4.6; Protein – 2.5

Steamed Artichokes (veg)

(Prep + Cook Time: 35 minutes | Servings: 6)

Ingredients:

- 6 long, narrow artichokes
- 3 smashed garlic cloves
- 2 cups water
- 1-2 cups of olive oil Juice of
- 1 lemon
- 1 sliced lemon
- 1 tbsp whole peppercorns

Directions:

1. Pour 2 cups of water, lemon juice, lemon slices, and peppercorns in your Instant Pot.
2. Prep artichokes by tearing off the tough leaves on the outside, peeling the stem, cutting off the end of the stem, and cutting the top half off of the leaves horizontally, so you end up with what looks like a hat.
3. Pry open the leaves and take out the hairy, hard part to access the heart, leaving the dotty part where the hairy part was attached.
4. Open the leaves up a bit more and dip in the pressure cooker, head down, and swirl around before putting in the steamer basket.
5. Put basket with artichokes in the pressure cooker. Close and seal lid. Select MANUAL and cook on high pressure for 5 minutes.
6. When time is up, quick-release the pressure after hitting CANCEL.
7. Shake the artichokes and put in a strainer for 15 minutes to dry out.
8. In a pan, heat up about 2 centimeters of oil and just fry the artichokes head down until their edges start to turn golden.
9. Plate and dab with a paper towel to remove excess oil before serving.

Nutritional Info (per serving): Calories - 40; Fat – 2; Fiber – 9; Carbs – 3; Protein – 1

BBQ Tofu (veg)

(Prep + Cook Time: 15 minutes | Servings: 6)

Ingredients:

- Two, 14 oz packages of extra-firm tofu
- One, 12 oz bottle of your favorite BBQ sauce
- 4 peeled and minced garlic cloves
- 1 chopped onion
- 1 cored, seeded, and chopped red bell pepper
- 1 cored, seeded, and chopped green bell pepper
- 1 diced celery stalk
- 2 tbsp olive oil
- Pinch of curry powder

Directions:

1. Turn your Instant Pot on to the SAUTE function and add oil.
2. Add garlic, bell peppers, celery, and onion.
3. Sprinkle on the curry powder and salt. Cook for just 2 minutes.
4. Add tofu and stir for 5 minutes. Pour in the BBQ sauce.
5. Close and seal the lid. Hit MANUAL and adjust time to 2 minutes on HIGH pressure.
6. When time is up, hit CANCEL and quick-release the pressure.
7. Serve tofu with rice or another side.

Nutritional Info (per serving): Calories - 283; Fat – 16; Fiber – 1; Carbs – 25; Protein – 13

Mushroom Gravy (veg)

(Prep + Cook Time: 45 minutes | Servings: 4)

Ingredients:

- 2 tbsp olive oil
- 8 oz sliced white mushrooms
- 4 tbsp all-purpose flour
- 4 tbsp vegan butter
- 2 fluid ounce vegetable broth
- 2 fluid ounce almond milk
- 22 fluid ounce water

Directions:

1. Plug in and switch on the Instant Pot, select SAUTE option, add oil and let heat.
2. Then add mushrooms and cook for 5-7 minutes or until nicely golden brown.
3. Pour in broth and continue cooking until mushrooms turn into dark color.
4. Press CANCEL, then pour in water and stir until just mixed. Secure pot with lid, then position pressure indicator, select MANUAL option and adjust cooking time on timer pad to 5 minutes and let cook.
5. Instant Pot will take 10 minutes to build pressure before cooking timer starts.
6. When the timer beeps, switch off the Instant Pot and let pressure release naturally for 10 minutes and then do quick pressure release.
7. Then uncover the pot and drain mushrooms and return to the pot, reserve broth.
8. Place a medium-sized saucepan over medium heat, add butter and let heat until melt completely.
9. Then gradually stir in flour and then slowly whisk in reserved broth until combined.
10. Pour in milk, stir in mushrooms and bring the mixture to simmer, whisk occasionally.
11. Simmer mixture for 8 minutes until gravy reaches desired thickness and then ladle into serving platters. Serve immediately.

Nutritional Info (per serving): Calories -64 ; Fat – 0.79; Fiber – 1; Carbs – 12.7; Protein – 2

Carrot Puree (veg)

(Prep + Cook Time: 25 minutes | Servings: 4)

Ingredients:

- 1 ½ pounds carrots, peeled and roughly chopped
- 1 tbsp soy butter, softened
- 1 tbsp honey
- ½ tsp salt
- 8 fluid oz water
- Brown Sugar as needed for more sweetness

Directions:

1. Rinse peeled carrots, pat dry and then chop roughly into small pieces. In the Instant Pot, pour water and then insert a steamer basket.
2. Place chopped carrots into the basket and secure pot with lid.
3. Then position pressure indicator and adjust cooking time on timer pad to 4 minutes and let cook.
4. When the timer beeps, switch off the Instant Pot and do a quick pressure release.
5. Then uncover the pot and transfer carrots to a food processor or blender.
6. Pulse until smooth and transfer puree to a bowl. Stir in honey, salt, and butter.
7. For more sweetness stir in brown sugar to taste and serve immediately.

Nutritional Info (per serving): Calories - 45; Fat – 0; Fiber – 3; Carbs – 11; Protein – 1

Carrots with Pancetta, Butter, and Leeks
(Prep + Cook Time: 20 minutes | Servings: 4)

Ingredients:

- 1 pound baby carrots
- 4-ounces diced pancetta
- 1 sliced leek
- 2 cups water
- ¼ cup sweet white wine
- 2 tbsp chopped butter
- Black pepper to taste

Directions:

1. On the cooker's SAUTE setting, cook pancetta until crisp.
2. Add the white and green parts of the leek and wait for 1 minute. Pour in the wine and deglaze the pot.
3. Add carrots and a dash of pepper before stirring.
4. Pour pot contents into a 1-quart baking dish. Nestle in pats of butter.
5. Put a piece of parchment paper on top of the dish followed by foil, which you should seal over the dish.
6. Carefully wipe out the cooker and add 2 cups of water. Lower in a trivet and then put the dish on top. Seal the lid.
7. Select MANUAL and adjust time to 7 minutes.
8. When time is up, quick-release the pressure.
9. Carefully take out the dish and stir before serving.

Nutritional Info (per serving): Calories - 201; Fat – 14; Fiber – 3; Carbs – 14; Protein – 6

Maple-Glazed Carrots (veg)
(Prep + Cook Time: 40 minutes | Servings: 8)

Ingredients:

- 2 pounds carrots, peeled and then diagonally sliced into thick pieces
- ¼ cup raisins
- ½ cup water
- 1 tbsp maple syrup
- 1 tbsp butter
- Pepper to taste

Directions:

1. Wash the carrots. Peel them and then slice into thick diagonal pieces. Put the carrots into the Instant Pot.

2. Add the raisins and the water.
3. Close and lock the lid. Turn the steam valve to SEALING. Set the pressure to LOW and the timer to 3 or 4 minutes.
4. When the timer beeps, turn the valve to quick release the pressure.
5. Remove the carrots from the pot and strain. In the still warm Instant Pot bowl, melt the butter and the maple syrup.
6. Add the carrots and gently stir to coat. Sprinkle with pepper and serve.

Nutritional Info (per serving): Calories - 79; Fat – 1.5; Fiber – 3; Carbs – 16.4; Protein – 1.1

Corn Cob (veg)
(Prep + Cook Time: 15 minutes | Servings: 6)

Ingredients:
- 6 ears corn
- 1 cup water

Directions:
1. Shuck the corn and then cut off the pointy ends. Pour the water into the Instant Pot and then put the steamer insert.
2. Layer up to 6 ears, arranging them in a crisscross pattern in the steamer insert. Close and lock the lid.
3. Press manual, set the pressure to HIGH, and set the timer to 3 minutes.
4. When the timer beeps at the end of the cooking cycle, open the valve to quick pressure release.
5. Remove the corn from the steamer basket.
6. Top your corn with salt, butter, or your choice of toppings.

Nutritional Info (per serving): Calories - 59; Fat – 0.5; Fiber – 1.7 ; Carbs – 14.1; Protein – 1.9

Wrapped Carrot With Bacon

(Prep + Cook Time: 25 minutes | Servings: 8)

Ingredients:

- 1-pound carrot
- 9 oz bacon
- 1 tsp salt
- ½ tsp ground black pepper
- 1 tsp ground white pepper
- 1 tsp paprika
- ¼ cup chicken stock
- 1 tbsp olive oil
- ¼ tsp marjoram

Directions:

1. Wash the carrot carefully and peel it. Sprinkle the carrot with the ground black pepper.
2. Combine the salt, ground white pepper, paprika, and marjoram together. Stir the mixture.
3. Slice the bacon. Then combine the sliced bacon and spice mixture together. Stir it carefully.
4. Then wrap the carrot in the sliced bacon.
5. Pour the olive oil in the Instant Pot and add wrapped carrot. Close the lid and SAUTE the carrot for 10 minutes.
6. Then add the chicken stock and cook the dish at the pressure mode for 8 minutes more.
7. When the time is over – release the remaining pressure and open the lid. Chill the carrot little.
8. Enjoy!

Nutritional Info (per serving): Calories - 141; Fat – 11.4; Fiber – 3; Carbs – 7.91; Protein – 4

Beets With Blue Cheese

(Prep + Cook Time: 35 minutes | Servings: 6)

Ingredients:

- 6 beets (about 1 ½ pounds)
- ¼ cup crumbled blue cheese
- ½ tsp kosher salt
- ½ tsp fresh ground black pepper
- 1 cup water

Directions:

1. Trim the leaves from the beats, making sure not to cut the root off or into the beet. Rinse and remove any dirt.
2. Pour the water into the inner pot and set a rack. Put the beets on the rack. Close and lock the lid.
3. Press PRESSURE, set the pressure to HIGH, and set the time for 20 minutes.
4. When the timer beeps at the end of the cooking cycle, turn the valve for quick pressure release. If you have time, you can let the pressure go down naturally.
5. Carefully open the lid and transfer the beets onto a cutting board.
6. Let them cool down for 1-2 minutes. Using a paper towel, peel off the skin and then pull off the roots.
7. Trim the stems and then cut the beets into halves, then into quarters.
8. Sprinkle them with salt and pepper, then transfer into a serving bowl. Top with the crumbled cheese and serve.

Nutritional Info (per serving): Calories - 64; Fat – 1.8; Fiber – 2; Carbs – 10.2; Protein – 2.9

Kale With Lemon And Garlic (veg)

(Prep + Cook Time: 15 minutes | Servings: 6)

Ingredients:

- 1 pound kale, cleaned and then stems trimmed
- 1 tbsp olive oil
- ½ cup water
- ½ lemon, juiced
- ½ tsp kosher salt
- 3 cloves garlic, slivered
- Freshly ground black pepper

Directions:

1. Set the Instant Pot to SAUTE. Pour in the oil and stir in the garlic. Heat the oil for about 2 minutes or until the garlic is just fragrant.
2. Stir a big handful of kale into the oil and garlic and then start packing the remaining kale into the pot.
3. The pot will be filled. Don't worry because the kale will quickly wilt – just pack the kale enough to close the pot lid.
4. Sprinkle with salt and then pour water over the top of everything.
5. Close and lock the lid. Set the pressure to HIGH and cook for 5 minutes. When the timer beeps, turn the steam release valve to VENTING to quick release the pressure. Carefully remove the lid.
6. While still in the pot, squeeze the lemon juice over the kale and stir in the freshly ground pepper.
7. With a tong or a slotted spoon, scoop out the kale from the pot, leaving as much liquid as possible in the pot. Serve.

Nutritional Info (per serving): Calories - 90; Fat – 3.5; Fiber – 1.8; Carbs – 12.7; Protein – 3.5

Pepper Jack Mac 'n Cheese

(Prep + Cook Time: 10 minutes | Servings: 4)

Ingredients:

- 2 ½ cups elbow macaroni
- 2 cups chicken stock
- 1 ½ cups shredded pepper jack cheese
- 1 ½ cups mozzarella cheese
- 1 cup heavy cream
- ½ cup whole milk
- 1 tbsp butter
- 1 tsp salt
- 1 tsp black pepper

Directions:

1. Pour chicken stock and cream into the Instant Pot. Add macaroni, salt, and pepper. Seal and close the lid.
2. Select MANUAL and adjust to 7 minutes on HIGH pressure.
3. When time is up, hit CANCEL and carefully quick-release. Mix in butter, milk, and cheese.
4. Stir well and serve!

Nutritional Info (per serving): Calories - 702; Fat – 49; Fiber – 3; Carbs – 48; Protein – 30

Sesame Bok Choy

(Prep + Cook Time: 5 minutes | Servings: 4)

Ingredients:

- 1 medium head of bok choy (with leaves separated)
- 1 cup water
- 2 tsp sesame seeds
- 1 tsp soy sauce
- ½ tsp sesame oil
- Salt and pepper to taste

Directions:

1. Pour water into the cooker and lower in the steamer basket. Stack leaves, with the thickest leaves on the bottom. Close and seal the lid.
2. Press MANUAL and adjust time to 4 minutes,
3. When time is up, turn off cooker and quick-release.
4. Move the bok choy to a bowl and dress with the sesame oil, sesame seeds, and soy sauce.
5. Season to taste with salt and pepper.

Nutritional Info (per serving): Calories - 54; Fat – 0; Fiber – 2; Carbs – 5; Protein – 3

Mushroom-Stuffed Eggplant Boats

(Prep + Cook Time: 50 minutes | Servings: 8)

Ingredients:

- 4 medium-sized eggplants
- 1 pound oyster mushrooms
- 2 cups diced tomatoes
- 1 cup vegan cheddar cheese + ½ cup
- 1 cup diced celery
- 1 onion
- 1 tbsp olive oil
- 1 tbsp dried basil
- 1 tbsp dried oregano
- 1 tsp salt
- 1 cup water
- 1 tsp ground black pepper

Directions:

1. Prep the eggplants by cutting in half lengthwise and scooping out the flesh.
2. There should be about ½-inch of eggplant flesh left, so the shell doesn't fall apart.
3. Save the scooped out part. Put them in the pressure cooker basket. Pour 1 cup of water in the cooker. Close and seal the lid.
4. Cook on HIGH pressure for 5 minutes.
5. While that cooks, chop up the eggplant you scooped out along with the celery and onion.
6. When the Instant Pot beeps, hit CANCEL and quick-release.
7. Take out the basket and shells.
8. Put all the ingredients (except cheese) in the cooking liquid, and seal the lid again. Cook for 10 minutes on HIGH pressure.
9. When time is up, hit CANCEL and quick-release again.
10. Divide up the filling between your eggplant shells and sprinkle on cheeses.
11. Bake in a 350-degree oven for 25 minutes to cook all the flavors together.

Nutritional Info (per serving): Calories - 174; Fat – 7; Fiber – 6; Carbs – 26; Protein – 6

Vegetable Pasta Salad

(Prep + Cook Time: 25 minutes | Servings: 10)

Ingredients:

- 8 oz pasta
- 3 cups vegetable stock
- 1 cup bread crumbs
- ½ cup cream cheese
- 3 medium cucumbers
- 1 tsp oregano
- ½ cup spinach
- 2 tomatoes
- 1 red onion
- 1 tsp paprika

Directions:

1. Put the pasta in the Instant Pot and add vegetable stock. Close the lid and cook the pasta on the MANUAL mode for 10 minutes.
2. Then rinse the pasta with the hot water. Place the cooked pasta in the mixing bowl.
3. Peel the red onion and slice it. Wash the spinach carefully and chop it. Chop the tomatoes and cucumbers.
4. Add the sliced onion, chopped spinach, tomatoes, and cucumbers in the pasta bowl.
5. Sprinkle the salad with the oregano and paprika.
6. Add cream cheese. Mix up the mixture until you get homogenous mass.
7. Then add bread crumbs and stir the salad.
8. Serve it immediately.

Nutritional Info (per serving): Calories - 654; Fat – 69.3; Fiber – 2; Carbs – 12; Protein – 3

Potato Mini Cakes

(Prep + Cook Time: 30 minutes | Servings: 6)

Ingredients:

- 9 oz mashed potato
- 2 eggs
- 1 tbsp starch
- 1 onion
- 1 tbsp sour cream
- 1 tsp salt
- 4 oz scallions
- 1 tbsp olive oil
- 1/3 cup flour
- 1 tsp onion powder

Directions:

1. Place the mashed potato in the blender and add eggs. Blend the mixture until you get a smooth texture.
2. Transfer the potato mixture to the mixing bowl.
3. Chop the scallions and them in the mixture.
4. Then add flour, onion powder, salt, starch, and sour cream. Peel the onion and grate it.
5. Add the grated onion on the potato mixture.
6. Mix up the mixture and knead the soft non-sticky dough.
7. Make the medium balls from the potato mixture and flatten them well.
8. After this, pour the olive oil in the Instant Pot.
9. Add the potato mini cakes in the Instant Pot and SAUTE them for 3 minutes from the each side.
10. When all the potato mini cakes are cooked – let them chill little and cut the dish into the strips.
11. Serve the dish immediately. Enjoy!

Nutritional Info (per serving): Calories - 138; Fat – 5.8; Fiber – 2; Carbs – 16.6; Protein – 5

Vegan Italian Tofu Scramble (veg)

(Prep + Cook Time: 5 minutes | Servings: 4)

Ingredients:

- 1 block of extra firm tofu
- 1 can Italian-style diced tomatoes
- ¼ cup veggie broth
- 2 tbsp jarred banana pepper rings
- 1 tbsp Italian seasoning

Directions:
1. Crumble the tofu in your Instant Pot, and pour over broth, banana peppers, can of diced tomatoes, and Italian seasoning.
2. Mix well and seal the lid.
3. Hit MANUAL and adjust cook time to 4 minutes.
4. When the timer beeps, hit CANCEL and quick-release the pressure.
5. Stir and serve!

Nutritional Info (per serving): Calories - 137; Fat – 6; Fiber – 3.7; Carbs – 9; Protein – 11

Southern Style Boiled Peanuts (veg)
(Prep + Cook Time: 75 minutes | Servings: 4)

Ingredients:
- 1 pound large raw peanuts
- 1/4 cup sea salt
- Water as needed

Optional:
- 2 tsp Cajun seasoning with garlic, jalapeno peppers, etc.
- 1 tbsp BBQ seasoning
- 1 tsp sugar

Directions:
1. Rinse the peanuts under running cool water. Remove any roots, twigs, or material that does not belong. Put into the Instant Pot.
2. Add the salt and add enough water to cover. Put a trivet on to hold the peanuts down. Close and lock the lid.
3. Set the pressure to HIGH and set the time to 70 minutes.
4. When the timer beeps, let the pressure release naturally and let sit for 30 minutes.
5. If the peanuts are still too hard for your liking, just cook more.

Notes: You can slow cook thee peanuts for 10 hours. Depending on your preference, peanuts are cooked at about 60-80 minutes. You can actually start at 60 minutes then cook more in increments until desired tenderness is achieved.

Nutritional Info (per serving): Calories - 643; Fat – 55.8; Fiber – 9.6; Carbs – 18.3; Protein – 29.3

Potato Stew Mixed With Chard

(Prep + Cook Time: 10 minutes | Servings: 2)

Ingredients:

- 2 tbsp of olive oil
- 1 tsp of cumin seed
- 1 medium sized diced up onion
- 1 jalapeno pepper
- ½ a tsp of turmeric
- 1 tbsp of peeled minced fresh ginger
- 1 tsp of salt
- 2 medium sized sweet potatoes peeled up and cut into ½ a inch cubes
- 1 tsp of ground coriander
- ¾ cup of water
- 1 bunch of Swiss chard
- 1 can of unsweetened coconut milk
- ¼ cup of finely chopped up fresh cilantro
- Lime wedges for serve

Directions:

1. Put your Instant Pot to SAUTE mode and pour some oil over medium heat.
2. Toss in the cumin seeds and wait until they are dancing in the oil.
3. After 3 minutes, add the jalapeno, ginger, turmeric, salt, sweet potatoes and cook it for another 3 minutes while stirring it.
4. Toss in the coriander now and keep stirring it until it has a nice fragrance.
5. Pour in some water and a bit salt followed by the coconut milk, chard.
6. Close up the lid and lock it up. Let it cook for 3 minutes at HIGH pressure keeping the heat at high.
7. Once done, wait for a while and quickly release the pressure.
8. Take it out from the pot and serve with some cilantro, while dashing it with some lime.

Nutritional Info (per serving): Calories - 398; Fat – 25; Carbs – 33; Protein – 13

Border Corn with Squash and Zucchini (veg)

(Prep + Cook Time: 20 minutes | Servings: 4)

Ingredients:

- 2 tbsp olive oil
- 1 cup red onion, diced
- 1 tbsp jalapeno pepper, diced
- 4 cups fresh corn kernels
- 1 cup red bell pepper diced
- 1 cup summer squash, cubed
- 1 cup zucchini, cubed
- 2 cups tomatoes, diced
- 1 tsp salt
- 1 tsp black pepper
- 1 tsp cumin
- ¼ cup fresh cilantro, chopped
- 1 ½ cup vegetable stock

Directions:

1. Place the olive oil in the Instant Pot and turn on the SAUTE or brown setting.
2. Add in the red onion and jalapeno pepper. Sauté for 2 minutes.
3. Add in the corn kernels, red bell pepper, summer squash, zucchini and tomatoes.
4. Mix well and then season with salt, black pepper, cumin and cilantro.
5. Pour in the vegetable stock.
6. Cover and seal the pressure cooker. Set the Instant Pot to LOW and cook for 5 minutes.
7. Use the natural release method to release the steam from the pressure cooker.

Chicken Stock
(Prep + Cook Time: 120 minutes | Liters: 4)

Ingredients:
- 1 chicken carcass
- 1 onion, cut into quarters
- 10-15 whole pieces peppercorns
- 2 bay leaves
- 2 tbsp apple cider vinegar
- Veggie scraps, optional
- Water as needed

Equipment: 4-5 mason jars

Directions:
1. Put the chicken carcass in the Instant Pot. If desired, feel free to add the skin.
2. Add the vegetable scraps, onion, apple cider vinegar, peppercorns, and bay leaves.
3. Fill the pot with water to 1/2-inch below the max line. Cover and lock the lid. Press the SOUP key and set the timer for 120 minutes.
4. When the Instant Pot timer beeps, press the CANCEL key and unplug the Instant Pot. Let the pressure release naturally for 10-15 minutes or until the valve drops – do not turn the steam valve for at least 30 minutes. Turn the steam to release remaining pressure.
5. Unlock and carefully open the lid. Strain out everything else from the stock and discard.
6. Put a funnel over a mason jar. Pour the stock into the mason jar – do not overfill. If you are planning to freeze your stock, use 5 mason jars.
7. Let the stock cool and then store in the fridge or freeze within 3 days.

Notes: Let the jars cool completely before putting them in the fridge or freezing them. If not freezing, be sure to use in 3 days. If not using within 3 days, then freeze.

Nutritional Info (per serving): Calories - 162; Fat – 5.8; Fiber – 0; Carbs – 3.9; Protein – 20.5

Vegetable Stock (veg)

(Prep + Cook Time: 30 minutes | Cups: 8)

Ingredients:

- 2 green onions, sliced
- 2 tsp minced garlic
- 4 medium-sized carrots, peeled and chopped
- 4 celery stalks, chopped
- 6 parsley sprigs
- 4 thyme sprigs
- 1,8 liters water
- 2 bay leaves
- 8 black peppercorns
- 1½ tsp salt

Directions:

1. Prepare vegetables. In a 6-quarts Instant Pot, pour in water and add all the ingredients except salt.
2. Plug in and switch on the Instant Pot, and secure pot with lid.
3. Then position pressure indicator, press SOUP option, and adjust cooking time to 30 minutes and let cook. Instant Pot will take 10 minutes to build pressure before cooking timer starts.
4. When the timer beeps, switch off the Instant Pot and let pressure release naturally for 10 minutes and then do quick pressure release.
5. Then uncover the pot and pass the mixture through a strainer placed over a large bowl to collect stock and vegetables on the strainer.
6. Stir salt into the stock and let cool completely before storing or use it later for cooking.

Tomato Sauce (veg)
(Prep + Cook Time: 50 minutes | Cups: 8)

Ingredients:
- 4.2 pounds tomatoes, cut into halves or quarters, less or more to fill the Instant Pot to the max level
- 1 onion, minced
- 1 tbsp oregano
- 1 tbsp salt
- 1 tbsp sugar
- 2 bay leaves
- 2 tbsp basil, chopped
- 2-3 tbsp parsley, chopped
- Lemon juice (1 tbsp per jar)

Directions:
1. Put all of the ingredients in the Instant Pot. Cover and lock the lid. Press the MANUAL key, set the pressure to HIGH, and set the timer for 30-40 minutes.
2. While the sauce is cooking, sterilize the mason and new lids in a pot of boiling water for 15 minutes.
3. Drain the sterilized jars and lids on a paper towel.
4. When the Instant Pot timer beeps, press the CANCEL key and unplug the Instant Pot. Let the pressure release naturally for 10-15 minutes or until the valve drops.
5. Unlock and carefully open the lid. Set a food mill over another pot.
6. Scoop out the tomatoes into the food mill. The tomatoes will mush up quickly and go through the pot, leaving the seeds and the skins behind.
7. Put 1 tablespoon lemon juice or 1/4 teaspoon citric acid on each mason jar and immediately fill the mason jars with the hot sauce.
8. Wipe the rims to ensure that the lids will seal. Put the lids on and screw them down.
9. Put the jars in the boiling water where you sterilized the jars and rims. Sterilize for 30 minutes.
10. Remove the jars and let them cool – make sure that each lid pops and is concave.

Nutritional Info (per serving): Calories - 60; Fat – 0.7; Fiber – 3.5; Carbs – 12.9; Protein – 2.5

Beef Bone Broth

(Prep + Cook Time: 90 minutes | Servings: 8)

Ingredients:

- 5 ounces carrots
- 4-5 sprigs thyme
- 4 cloves garlic
- 3 pounds beef bones (oxtail or neck bones preferred)
- 3 bay leaves
- 1 onion, roughly chopped
- Half head celery, chopped
- Water, filtered
- Pepper to taste
- Salt to taste

Directions:

1. Cut the celery and onion. Add into the Instant Pot.
2. Add the rest of the ingredients into the pot.
3. Fill the pot with water up to the line before the max line of the Instant Pot.
4. Cover and lock the lid. Turn the steam valve to SEALING. Press the MANUAL key, set the pressure to HIGH, and set the timer for 90 minutes.
5. When the Instant Pot timer beeps, press the CANCEL key and unplug the Instant Pot. Turn the steam valve to quick release the pressure.
6. Unlock and carefully open the lid. Strain the broth and store in freezer.

Nutritional Info (per serving): Calories -18 ; Fat – 0.6; Fiber – 0; Carbs – 0.1; Protein – 2.9

Bone Broth

(Prep + Cook Time: 1 hour 40 minutes | Servings: 8)

Ingredients:

- 1 tsp unrefined sea salt
- 1-2 tbsp apple cider vinegar
- 2-3 pounds bones (2-3 pounds lamb, beef, pork, or non-oily fish, or 1 carcass of whole chicken)
- Assorted veggies (1/2 onion, a couple carrots, a couple stalks celery, and fresh herbs, if you have them on hand)
- Water, filtered

Directions:

1. Put the bones in the Instant Pot. Top with the veggies. Add the salt and apple cider vinegar.
2. Pour in enough water to fill the pot 2/3 full.
3. If you have enough time, let the pot sit for 30 minutes to allow the vinegar to start pulling the minerals out of the bones.
4. Cover and lock the lid. Press the SOUP key, set the pressure to LOW, and set the timer for 120 minutes.
5. When the Instant Pot timer beeps, press the CANCEL key and unplug the Instant Pot. Let the pressure release naturally for 10-15 minutes or until the valve drops.
6. Unlock and carefully open the lid. Strain the broth.
7. Discard the veggies and bones. Pour the broth into jars. Store in the refrigerator or freeze.
8. Note: If you are using pork, lamb, or beef bones, roast them in a preheated 350F oven for 30 minutes. This step is optional, but it does wonders to the flavors of the broth.

Nutritional Info (per serving): Calories - 9; Fat – 0.3; Fiber – 0; Carbs – 0.1; Protein – 1.4

Meat Sauce

(Prep + Cook Time: 15 minutes | Servings: 4)

Ingredients:
- 1 can Hunts traditional pasta sauce
- 1 pound extra-lean ground beef
- ¼ cup fresh parsley, chopped
- 3-4 cloves garlic, minced
- 3-4 fresh basil leaves, chopped

Directions:
1. Put all of the ingredients into the Instant Pot. With a spatula, break the meat up and mix to combine.
2. Cover and lock the lid. Press the MANUAL key, set the pressure to HIGH, and set the timer for 8 minutes.
3. When the Instant Pot timer beeps, press the CANCEL key and unplug the Instant Pot. Turn the steam valve to quick release the pressure.
4. Unlock and carefully open the lid.

Nutritional Info (per serving): Calories - 363; Fat – 11.7; Fiber – 4.6; Carbs – 24.4; Protein – 37.7

BBQ Sauce

(Prep + Cook Time: 25 minutes |Cups: 2)

Ingredients:
- ¾ cup seedless dried plums (or prunes), tightly packed into the measuring cup
- 1/8 tsp ground clove powder
- 1/8 tsp cumin powder
- ½ tsp granulated garlic
- ½ cup water
- ½ cup tomato puree OR passata
- 1 tsp sea salt
- 1 tsp liquid smoke
- 1 tsp hot sauce, OR home-made Tabasco
- 1 tbsp sesame seed oil OR avocado, peanut, or grapeseed oil or any high smoke-pint oil
- 1 onion, medium-sized, roughly chopped
- 4 tbsp honey
- 4 tbsp white vinegar OR apple cider vinegar

Directions:

1. Press the SAUTE key of the Instant Pot and wait until hot.
2. Add the sesame oil and the onion; sauté, stirring occasionally, until the edges of the onion start to brown.
3. In a 2-cup measuring cup or a small-sized mixing bowl, add the tomato puree, honey, water, and vinegar.
4. Add the salt, hot sauce, garlic, cumin powder, liquid smoke, and clove.
5. Mix well until the contents are combined and the honey is evenly dissolved in the liquid.
6. Pour the mixture into the Instant Pot, scraping the bottom of the pot using a spatula to remove any browned bits.
7. Add the plums. Press the CANCEL key to stop the sauté function. Cover and lock the lid.
8. Press the MANUAL key, set the pressure to HIGH, and set the timer for 10 minutes.
9. When the Instant Pot timer beeps, press the CANCEL key and unplug the Instant Pot.
10. Using an oven mitt or a long handled spoon, slowly turn the steam valve to release the pressure slowly. Unlock and carefully open the lid.
11. With an immersion blender, puree the contents in the Instant Pot. You may need to tilt the pot to immerse the blender in the liquid. Serve

Notes: Use 2.5 liter or larger Instant Pot.

Nutritional Info (per serving): Calories - 20; Fat – 0.5; Fiber – 0; Carbs – 4.2; Protein – 0.2

Chipotle Honey BBQ Sauce

(Prep + Cook Time: 25 minutes | Cups: 2)

Ingredients:

- 1 tsp olive oil
- 1 onion, medium-sized, chopped
- ½ tsp cumin
- ¼ cup honey
- 2 chipotles in adobo sauce
- 1 tbsp adobo sauce
- 2 tsp apple cider vinegar
- 1 cup ketchup
- 1 tsp chili powder
- 1 tsp paprika
- 1 tsp salt
- ½ tsp pepper
- ¼ cup orange juice
- 2 cloves garlic, chopped

Directions:

1. Press the SAUTE key of the Instant Pot. Put the olive oil in the pot and heat until shimmering.
2. Add the garlic and onion; sauté for about 3 minutes or until soft. While the veggies are sautéing, whisk the ketchup with the orange juice, honey, and apple cider vinegar.
3. Pour the ketchup mix over the veggies.
4. Add the adobo sauce, chipotles, seasoning, and spices. Press the CANCEL key to stop the sauté function. Cover and lock the lid.
5. Turn the steam valve to SEALING. Press the MANUAL key, set the pressure to HIGH, and set the timer for 8 minutes.
6. When the Instant Pot timer beeps, press the CANCEL key and unplug the Instant Pot.
7. Using an oven mitt or a long handled spoon, turn the steam valve to VENTING to quick release the pressure. Unlock and carefully open the lid.
8. Pour the sauce carefully into a blender and puree.
9. Pour the sauce in a glass jar and store in the refrigerator for up to 1 week.

Nutritional Info (per serving): Calories - 173; Fat – 1.7; Fiber – 1.7; Carbs – 41.6; Protein – 2.3

Fish Stock

(Prep + Cook Time: 65 minutes | Quarts: 3)

Ingredients:

- 2 salmon heads, large-sized, cut into quarters
- 2 lemongrass stalks, roughly chopped
- 1 cup carrots, roughly chopped
- 1 cup celery, roughly chopped
- 2 cloves garlic
- Water, filtered
- Handful fresh thyme, including stems
- Oil, for frying the fish heads

Directions:

1. Wash the fish heads with cold water – make sure there is no blood – and then pat them dry.
2. Put the oil in a pan and lightly sear the fish heads – this will minimize the fish meat from falling apart.
3. Slice the vegetables and put them in the Instant Pot.
4. Add the fish and thyme. Pour water in the pot until the level reaches 3 quarts or just cover the fish. Cover and lock the lid.
5. Press the SOUP key, set the pressure to HIGH, and set the timer for 45 minutes.
6. When the Instant Pot timer beeps, press the CANCEL key and unplug the Instant Pot. Let the pressure release naturally for 10-15 minutes or until the valve drops. Using an oven mitt or a long handled spoon, turn the steam valve to release remaining pressure. Unlock and carefully open the lid.
7. Strain the fish and vegetable and store the stock.

Nutritional Info (per serving): Calories - 42; Fat – 2; Fiber – 0; Carbs – 0; Protein – 5.6

Basil Fresh Tomato Sauce (veg)

(Prep + Cook Time: 40 minutes | Cups: 8)

Ingredients:

- 4 ½ -5 pounds Roma tomatoes, diced
- ½ cup fresh basil, chopped
- 2 tbsp olive oil
- ¼ tsp crushed peppers
- ½ tbsp pepper
- ½ tbsp garlic powder
- 1 tbsp salt
- 1 onion, diced
- 1 bay leaf
- 1 ½ tbsp Italian seasoning
- 6 cloves garlic, minced

Directions:

1. Press the SAUTE key of the Instant Pot and select the MORE option. Put the olive in the pot.
2. Add the onions and garlic. Sauté for about 5 minutes or until the onions are soft.
3. Add the tomatoes, crushed pepper, Italian seasoning, garlic powder, pepper, salt, and bay leaf in the pot. Stir to combine.
4. Cover and lock the lid. Press the MANUAL key, set the pressure to HIGH, and set the timer for 10 minutes.
5. When the Instant Pot timer beeps, press the CANCEL key and unplug the Instant Pot. Using an oven mitt or a long handled spoon, turn the steam valve to quick release the pressure.
6. Unlock and carefully open the lid. Add the basil in the pot and stir.
7. Press the SAUTE key and select the MORE option. Simmer for 5 minutes.
8. Remove the bay leaf and serve or use in a different recipe.
9. This sauce can be kept for up to 5 days in the fridge or you can freezer for a much later use.

Nutritional Info (per serving): Calories - 77; Fat – 0; Fiber – 2.9; Carbs – 10.4; Protein – 2.2

Sneaky Marinara Sauce (veg)

(Prep + Cook Time: 25 minutes | Cups: 8)

Ingredients:

- 2 cans (28 oz) crushed tomatoes
- 1 sweet potato, large-sized, diced (about 2 cups)
- ½ cup red lentils
- 1 tsp salt
- 1 ½ cups water
- 2-3 cloves garlic, minced

Directions:

1. Pick over the lentils. Remove any shriveled lentils or any stones. Put in a fine mesh sieve and rinse to clean.
2. Press the SAUTE key of the Instant Pot. Add the sweet potatoes, lentils, and garlic. Sprinkle with the salt and sauté for about 1-2 minutes to bring the garlic flavor out and warm the pot.
3. Add the crushed tomatoes and pour in the water. Stir very well to combine, making sure that the lentils are not stuck on the bottom of the pot.
4. Press the CANCEL key to stop the sauté function. Cover and lock the lid. Press the MANUAL key, set the pressure to HIGH, and set the timer for 13 minutes.
5. When the Instant Pot timer beeps, press the CANCEL key and unplug the Instant Pot. Let the pressure release naturally for 10-15 minutes or until the valve drops.
6. Using an oven mitt or a long handled spoon, turn the steam to release remaining pressure. Unlock and carefully open the lid.
7. Stir the marinara to combine. If desired, puree using an immersion blender.
8. Serve.

Note: You can double this recipe in the Instant Pot without going over the maximum volume limit. It makes 4 quarts with some left over.

Nutritional Info (per serving): Calories - 136; Fat – 0.1; Fiber – 10.5; Carbs – 26.3; Protein – 8.2

Mushroom Sauce (veg)

(Prep + Cook Time: 15 minutes | Cups: 2)

Ingredients:

- 10 mushrooms, chopped
- 1 yellow onion, chopped
- 2 garlic cloves, minced
- 1 tsp thyme, dried
- 2 cups veggie stock
- ½ tsp rosemary, dried
- ½ tsp sage
- 1 tsp sherry
- 1 tbsp water
- 1 tbsp nutritional yeast
- 1 tbsp coconut aminos
- Salt and black pepper to the taste
- ¼ cup almond milk
- 2 tbsp rice flour

Directions:

1. Set your Instant Pot on SAUTE mode, add onion and brown for 5 minutes.
2. Add mushrooms and the water, stir and cook for 3 minutes.
3. Add garlic, stir again and cook for 1 minute.
4. Add stock, yeast, sherry, soy sauce, salt, pepper, sage, thyme and rosemary, coconut aminos, stir, cover and cook on HIGH pressure for 4 minutes.
5. Meanwhile, in a bowl, mix milk with rice flour and stir well.
6. Release pressure from the pot, add milk mix, stir well, cover and cook on HIGH for 6 more minutes.
7. Relies pressure again and serve sauce.

Cranberry Apple Sauce (veg)

(Prep + Cook Time: 20 minutes | Cups: 2)

Ingredients:

- 1-2 apples, medium-sized, peeled, cored, and then cut into chunks
- 10 oz cranberries, frozen or fresh, preferably organic
- ¼ tsp sea salt
- ¼ cup lemon juice
- ½ cup maple syrup OR honey
- 1 tsp cinnamon

Directions:

1. Put all of the ingredients in the Instant Pot and combine.
2. Cover and lock the lid. Press the MANUAL key, set the pressure to HIGH, and set the timer for1 minute.
3. When the Instant Pot timer beeps, let the pressure release naturally for 10-15 minutes or until the valve drops. Press the CANCEL key and unplug the Instant Pot.
4. Unlock and carefully open the lid. Using a wooden spoon, mash the fruit a bit.
5. Press the SAUTE key and simmer for 1-2 minutes to allow some of the water to evaporate and the mix to thicken.
6. Press the CANCEL key. If you omitted the maple syrup/honey and want to sweeten with stevia, then add to taste.
7. Stir to combine. Transfer into a pint jar and refrigerate.

Nutritional Info (per serving): Calories - 176; Fat – 0.3; Fiber – 4.3; Carbs – 41.4; Protein – 0.3

Apple Sauce (veg)
(Prep + Cook Time: 30 minutes | Cups: 3)

Ingredients:
- 12 apples, organic, peeled if preferred and then quartered
- ¼ tsp sea salt
- ½ lemon, organic, fresh juiced
- 1 tbsp raw honey, light colored
- 1 tbsp ground cinnamon
- 1 cup water, filtered
- 2 tbsp ghee (optional)

Directions:
1. Wash and prepare all the apples. If you don't like apple skin, you can peel them off. If you don't mind the skin, you can leave them on. Cut the apples into quarters and put them in the Instant Pot.
2. Add ghee, honey, cinnamon, water, and sea salt in the pot.
3. Cover and lock the lid. Press the MANUAL key, set the pressure to HIGH, and set the timer for 3 minutes.
4. When the Instant Pot timer beeps, press the CANCEL key and unplug the Instant Pot. Let the pressure release naturally for 10-15 minutes or until the valve drops. Turn the steam valve to release remaining pressure. Unlock and carefully open the lid.
5. Ladle the apple mix in a high-powered blender or a food processor.
6. If there is a lot of excess liquid left in the Instant Pot, use only about 1/2 of the cooking liquid.
7. Pulse until the apples and cooking liquid are completely combines and the mixture is smooth.
8. If needed, add remaining liquid in the blender/ food processor to achieve desired consistency.
9. Alternatively, you can use a hand-held immersion blender to puree the sauce.

Notes: Store in an airtight container and keep for 3 days in the refrigerator.

Nutritional Info (per serving): Calories - 280; Fat – 4.7; Fiber – 11.4; Carbs – 65.4; Protein – 1.3

Tabasco Sauce (veg)

(Prep + Cook Time: 25 minutes | Cups: 2)

Ingredients:

- 12 oz fresh hot peppers OR any kind, stems removed
- 2 tsp smoked or plain salt
- 1 ¼ cup apple vinegar

Directions:

1. Press the SAUTE key of the Instant Pot.
2. Roughly chop the hot peppers and put into the Instant Pot. Pour in just enough vinegar to cover the peppers. Add the salt.
3. Press the CANCEL key to stop the sauté function. Cover and lock the lid. Press the MANUAL key, set the pressure to HIGH, and set the timer for 1 minute.
4. When the Instant Pot timer beeps, press the CANCEL key and unplug the Instant Pot. Let the pressure release naturally for 10-15 minutes or until the valve drops.
5. Using an oven mitt or a long handled spoon, turn the steam valve to release remaining pressure. Unlock and carefully open the lid.
6. Using an immersion blender, puree the contents and strain into a fresh dished-washed or sterilized bottle.
7. Refrigerate for up to 3 months or transfer into a suitable container and freeze for up to 1 year.

Nutritional Info (per serving): Calories - 14; Fat – 0.1; Fiber – 0; Carbs – 3.3; Protein – 0.3

Mixed-Veggie Sauce (veg)

(Prep + Cook Time: 30 minutes | Cups: 2)

Ingredients:

- 4 chopped tomatoes
- 4-5 cubes of pumpkin
- 4 minced garlic cloves
- 2 chopped green chilies
- 2 chopped celery stalks
- 1 sliced leek
- 1 chopped onion
- 1 chopped red bell pepper
- 1 chopped carrot
- 1 tbsp sugar
- 2 tsp olive oil
- 1 tsp red chili flakes
- Splash of vinegar
- Salt to taste

Directions:

1. Prep your veggies.
2. Heat your oil in the Instant Pot.
3. Add onion and garlic, and cook until the onion is clear.
4. Add pumpkin, carrots, green chilies, and bell pepper. Stir before adding the leek, celery, and tomatoes.
5. After a minute or so, toss in salt and red chili flakes.
6. Close and seal the pressure cooker. Adjust time to 6 minutes on the MANUAL setting.
7. When time is up, hit CANCEL and let the pressure come down on its own.
8. The veggies should be very soft. Let the mixture cool a little before moving to a blender.
9. Puree until smooth. Pour back into the pot and add vinegar and sugar.
10. Simmer on the lowest SAUTE setting for a few minutes before serving.

Nutritional Info (per serving): Calories - 126; Fiber – 4; Carbs – 22; Protein – 3

Salted Caramel Sauce

(Prep + Cook Time: 20 minutes | Cups: 1)

Ingredients:
- ½ tsp sea salt
- 1/3 cup heavy cream
- 3 tbsp butter, cut into
- ½ inch pieces
- 1 cup sugar
- ½ tsp vanilla
- 1/3 cup water

Directions:
1. Press the SAUTE key of the Instant Pot.
2. Add the water and the sugar. Stir to combine and let cook for 13 minutes without touching the pot.
3. When 13 minutes are up, immediately whisk the butter in the pot, followed by the cream. Whisk until smooth.
4. Add the vanilla and the salt. Immediately remove press the CANCEL key and with an oven mitt gloved hand, remove the inner pot from the housing to remove from heat.
5. Pour the salted caramel into a heat-safe glass and let cool. Store in the fridge for up to 5 days.

Nutritional Info (per serving): Calories - 150; Fat – 6.2; Fiber – 0; Carbs – 25.2; Protein – 0.2

Pasta And Spaghetti Sauce

(Prep + Cook Time: 25 minutes | Servings: 6)

Ingredients:

- 2 pounds Italian sausage, casings removed (hot or mild), optional
- 1 can (28 ounces) diced tomatoes
- 1 onion, small-sized, chopped, optional
- 1 tbsp olive oil
- ½ cup red wine (use a cabernet)
- ½ cup water
- ¼ tsp coarse black pepper, fresh ground
- ¼ - ½ tsp crushed red pepper flakes
- 2 cans (15 ounces) tomato sauce
- 2 tsp brown sugar
- 2 tsp dried parsley flakes
- 2 tsp fennel seed, crushed
- 2 tsp salt
- 3 tsp basil
- 3-4 cloves garlic, minced
- 6 ounces tomato paste
- Parmesan cheese OR a piece of rind, optional

Directions:

1. Press the SAUTE key of the Instant Pot and wait until hot. Put 1 tablespoon olive oil in the pot and add the sausage.
2. Cook until browned, breaking the sausages in the process as you stir.
3. Add the rest of the ingredients in the pot. If you are not using any meat, then start at this step.
4. Press the CANCEL key to stop the sauté function. Cover and lock the lid.
5. Press the MANUAL key, set the pressure to HIGH, and set the timer for 10 minutes.
6. When the Instant Pot timer beeps, press the CANCEL key and unplug the Instant Pot. Let the pressure release naturally for 10-15 minutes or until the valve drops. Turn the steam valve to release remaining pressure.
7. Unlock and carefully open the lid.
8. Serve with your spaghetti or your favorite pasta.

Nutritional Info (per serving): Calories - 646; Fat – 46; Fiber – 5.6; Carbs – 22.4; Protein – 34.1

Bolognese Eggolant Sauce

(Prep + Cook Time: 45 minutes | Servings: 8)

Ingredients:

- 1 pound ground meat, your choice (I used ground pork)
- 1 can (28 ounces) tomatoes, drained, and then gently pureed
- 1 can (5.5 ounces) tomato paste
- 5 cloves garlic, smashed
- ½ sweet onion, large-sized, chopped
- 1 eggplant, sliced into halves and then diced
- ½ cup olive oil
- 1 cup bone broth OR filtered water
- ½ tsp turmeric
- ½ tsp dried dill
- 1 tbsp apple cider vinegar
- ¼ cup fresh parsley, chopped
- 1 tsp Himalayan pink salt
- Salt and pepper to taste
- Fresh lemon, to serve

Directions:

1. Plug the Instant Pot and press the SAUTE key.
2. Add the ground meat of your choice in the pot and cook until no longer pink.
3. Remove the meat and cooking liquid and transfer into a plate. Set aside. Add the olive oil into the pot.
4. Add the onion and sauté until starting to turn translucent and soft. Sprinkle with a pinch of salt to release the juices and bring out the flavors.
5. Add the garlic and cook for 1 minute or until the garlic is fragrant.
6. Add the apple cider vinegar and stir well to combine. Continuously stirring the mix, cook for about 1-2 minutes.

7. Scrape up any browned bits off from the bottom of the pot. If it starts to brown quickly, add a little more olive oil or water to prevent from burning.
8. Add the can of tomato paste into the pot. Stir well and cook for about 1-2 minutes to soften the flavor of the tomato paste.
9. Add the can of pureed tomatoes, 1 teaspoon salt, spices, ground meat with any juices accumulated on the plate, and fresh parsley.
10. Stir to combine and pour in 1 cup of water or bone broth. Stir to mix. Press the CANCEL key to stop the sauté function. Cover and lock the lid.
11. Press the MANUAL key, set the pressure to HIGH, and set the timer for 15 minutes. When the Instant Pot timer beeps, keep the pot in KEEP WARM mode for 10 minutes. Press the CANCEL key. Using an oven mitt or a long handled spoon, turn the steam valve to quick release the pressure. Unlock and carefully open the lid.
12. Taste for seasoning. Add more fresh cracked pepper, pink salt, and freshly squeezed lemon to taste.
13. Enjoy with fresh cracked pepper, avocado chunks, and lemon wedges.
14. You can also serve over spiralized veggies, rice, or pasta.

Nutritional Info (per serving): Calories - 246; Fat – 15.1; Fiber – 4.3; Carbs – 12.5; Protein – 17.5

Cheesy Sauce

(Prep + Cook Time: 25 minutes | Servings: 8)

Ingredients:

- 1 cup carrot, chopped
- 1 tbsp turmeric, chopped OR
- 1 tsp turmeric powder
- 1 tsp salt
- ½ cup nutritional yeast
- ½ cup onion, chopped
- ½ cup raw cashews
- 2 cups potato, peeled and then chopped
- 2 cups water
- 3 cloves garlic, peeled and left whole

Directions:

1. Put all of the ingredients in the Instant Pot. Cover and lock the lid.
2. Press the MANUAL key, set the pressure to HIGH, and set the timer for 5 minutes.
3. When the Instant Pot timer beeps, press the CANCEL key and unplug the Instant Pot. Using an oven mitt or a long handled spoon, turn the steam valve to quick release the pressure. Unlock and carefully open the lid. Let cool for about 10-15 minutes.
4. Transfer into a blender and blend for about 2 minutes or until super smooth and creamy.

Nutritional Info (per serving): Calories - 220; Fat – 9.1; Fiber – 7.5; Carbs – 26.5; Protein – 13.1

Bean And Sausage Pasta Sauce

(Prep + Cook Time: 30 minutes | Servings: 10)

Ingredients:

- 1 can cannellini beans
- 1 can diced tomatoes
- 1 punnet homshimeiji mushrooms, trimmed
- 1 tbsp fish sauce (optional)
- 1 tsp dried herbs (I used a Provençal herb mix, but can be a combination of thyme and oregano)
- 1 tsp sea salt
- ½ cup chicken stock
- ½ onion, finely chopped
- ½ tsp ground black pepper
- ¼ cup red wine
- 1-2 tbsp olive oil
- 2 carrots, finely chopped
- 2 tbsp balsamic vinegar
- 2 tbsp tomato paste
- 3 chorizo sausages, sliced into inch-long pieces
- 4 ribs celery, finely chopped
- 5 cloves garlic, finely chopped
- 5 slices ham, sliced into thin strips

Directions:

1. Press the SAUTE key of the Instant Pot. Add the olive oil.
2. Add the onions, garlic, celery, and carrots; sauté until caramelized and soft.
3. Add the ham and the sausages; sauté for a few minutes. Add the balsamic vinegar; sauté until the vinegar is mostly evaporated.
4. Add the red wine, fish sauce, chicken stock, beans, tomato paste, diced tomatoes, pepper, salt, and herbs.
5. Press the CANCEL key to stop the sauté function. Cover and lock the lid.
6. Press the MANUAL key, set the pressure to HIGH, and set the timer for 7 minutes.
7. When the Instant Pot timer beeps, using an oven mitt or a long handled spoon, turn the steam valve to VENTING to quick release the pressure. Unlock and carefully open the lid.
8. Press the SAUTE key and add the honshimeiji mushrooms.
9. Stir and cook for 1 minute or until the mushrooms are slightly soft. Serve over pasta.

Chili Dog Sauce

(Prep + Cook Time: 35 minutes | Cups: 3)

Ingredients:

- 8 ounces ground beef
- 2 tsp chili powder
- 2 tsp prepared yellow mustard
- 2 cups pinto beans, cooked
- ¼ cup tomato paste
- ½ cup onion, minced
- 1 tsp white vinegar
- 1 tsp garlic powder
- 1 tsp cumin powder
- 1 tbsp Worcestershire sauce
- 1 cup beef stock
- Kosher salt, to taste
- 2 tsp hot sauce, optional

Directions:

1. Put the ground beef, beans, and beef stock into the Instant Pot. Stir to combine.
2. With a potato masher, mash the ground beef and the beans until very fine.
3. Add the Worcestershire sauce, vinegar, garlic, cumin, chili powder, onion, mustard, and tomato paste into the pot. Cover and lock the lid.
4. Press the MANUAL key, set the pressure to HIGH, and set the timer for 5 minutes.
5. When the Instant Pot timer beeps, press the CANCEL key and unplug the Instant Pot. Using an oven mitt or a long handled spoon, turn the steam valve to quick release the pressure. Unlock and carefully open the lid. Stir and taste the sauce.
6. Adjust seasoning as needed.

Notes: You can use canned beans for this recipe. If using dry beans, pressure cook 2 cups of pinto beans with 6 cups water for 40 minutes on HIGH pressure. When cooking time is up, release the pressure naturally. Rinse and strain the beans, whether pressure-cooked or canned, before using in this recipe.

Nutritional Info (per serving): Calories - 637; Fat – 7.2; Fiber – 22.1; Carbs – 89.6; Protein – 53.2

Vegan Alfredo Sauce (veg)

(Prep + Cook Time: 20 minutes | Servings: 4)

Ingredients:

- 12-ounces cauliflower florets
- ½ cup water
- Almond milk if needed
- Garlic salt to taste
- Black pepper to taste

Directions:

1. Pour water into your Instant Pot.
2. Put cauliflower florets into your steamer basket and lower into cooker. Seal the lid.
3. Hit MANUAL and cook for 3 minutes.
4. When the timer beeps, hit CANCEL and wait for a natural pressure release.
5. Remove steamer basket and cool cauliflower for a few minutes.
6. Pulse cauliflower with pot liquid in a blender until very smooth. If it isn't quite creamy enough, add a splash of almond milk.
7. Season with garlic salt and black pepper.

Nutritional Info (per serving): Calories - 39; Fat – 0; Fiber – 1.7; Carbs – 5; Protein – 3

Apple Crisp (veg)
(Prep + Cook Time: 15 minutes | Servings: 4)

Ingredients:
- 5 medium sized apples, peeled and then chopped into chunks
- 4 tbsp butter
- ¾ cup old fashioned rolled oats
- 2 tsp cinnamon
- ¼ cup flour
- ¼ cup brown sugar
- ½ tsp salt
- ½ tsp nutmeg
- ½ cup water
- 1 tbsp maple syrup

Directions:
1. Put the apples into the bottom of the Instant Pot container. Sprinkle with nutmeg and cinnamon.
2. Pour in the water and drizzle with the maple syrup.
3. Melt the butter. In a small-sized bowl, mix the butter with the flour, oats, brown sugar, and salt.
4. By spoonful, drop the mix on top of the apples.
5. Close the lid of the pot and make sure the valve is closed. Set to MANUAL, the pressure to HIGH, and the timer to 8 minutes.
6. When the timer beeps, let the pressure release naturally and let sit for a couple of minutes to allow the sauce to thicken.
7. Serve as a warm breakfast.

Notes: You can also top this dish with vanilla ice cream and serve as a scrumptious dessert.

Nutritional Info (per serving): Calories - 359; Fat – 13.1; Fiber – 7.9; Carbs – 61.1; Protein – 3.6

Cranberry Apple Steel Cut Oats

(Prep + Cook Time: 50 minutes | Servings: 6)

Ingredients:

- 1 ½ cup fresh cranberries (dried cranberries or cherries)
- 1 cup yogurt (or 1 cup milk or part whey)
- 1 tsp fresh lemon juice
- ½ tsp nutmeg
- ½ tsp salt
- ¼ cup maple syrup
- 1-2 tsp cinnamon
- 2 cups steel cut oats
- 2-4 tbsp butter and/ or virgin coconut oil
- 3 cups water
- 4 apples, diced (or 1-2 cups applesauce)
- 2 cups milk
- 2 tsp vanilla (optional)

Directions:

1. Grease the bottom of the Instant Pot container with butter/ oil.
2. Except for the salt, maple syrup, and vanilla, put the rest of the ingredients into the pot; let soak overnight.
3. In the morning, add the salt, maple syrup, and, if using, vanilla; cook on PORRIDGE for about 35-40 minutes. Be sure to close the valve.
4. When the timer beeps, turn the steam valve to quick release the pressure.
5. Serve with your favorite milk.

Notes: The Instant Pot will automatically switch to warm and naturally release the pressure when the timer beeps.

Nutritional Info (per serving): Calories - 321; Fat – 8.1; Fiber – 6.9; Carbs – 53.8; Protein – 9

Baked Apples (veg)

(Prep + Cook Time: 40 minutes | Servings: 6)

Ingredients:

- 6 apples
- 4 oz white sugar
- 1 tsp cinnamon powder
- 1 oz raisins
- 8 oz red wine

Directions:

1. Rinse and core apple and place in a 6-quarts Instant Pot. Sprinkle with sugar, cinnamon, and add raisins and red wine.
2. Secure pot with lid, then position pressure indicator, select MANUAL option and adjust cooking time on timer pad to 10 minutes and let cook.
3. When the timer beeps, switch off the Instant Pot and let pressure release naturally for 10 minutes and then do quick pressure release.
4. Then uncover the pot and scoop out apples.
5. Serve apples with the cooking liquid.

Nutritional Info (per serving): Calories - 188; Fat – 0.3; Fiber – 3.8; Carbs – 34.7; Protein – 0.6

Carrot Cake Breakfast Oatmeal (veg)

(Prep + Cook Time: 25 minutes | Servings: 6)

Ingredients:

- 1 cup grated carrots
- 1 cup steel cut oats
- 1 tbsp butter
- 1 tsp pumpkin pie spice
- ¼ cup chia seeds
- ¼ tsp salt
- 2 tsp cinnamon
- 3 tbsp maple syrup
- ¾ cup raisins
- 4 cups water

Directions:

1. Put the butter into the Instant Pot; select SAUTE.
2. When the butter is melted, add the oats; toast, constantly stirring for about 3 minutes or until the oats are nutty.
3. Add the water, carrots, cinnamon, maple syrup, salt, and pumpkin pie spice. Close the lid of the pot. Set the pressure to HIGH and the timer to 10 minutes.
4. When the timer beeps, turn off the pot, let the pressure release naturally for 10 minutes, then turn the steam valve to release remaining pressure.
5. When the valve drops, carefully open the lid. Stir in the oats, chia seeds, and raisins.
6. Close the lid and let sit for about 5-10 minutes or until the oats are cooked in the heat to desired thickness.
7. Serve topped with milk, chopped nuts, and additional raisins and maple syrup.

Notes: You can cook a batch ahead of time; just freeze individual portions. When ready to serve, add a bit of milk and serve cold or microwave until heated.

Nutritional Info (per serving): Calories - 159; Fat – 3; Fiber – 2.9; Carbs – 32.9; Protein – 2.6

Soy Yogurt (veg)

(Prep + Cook Time: 12 hours | Servings: 4)

Ingredients:

- 1 quart soy milk (use only made soybeans and water, no vitamins or sugar added)
- 1 packet vegan yogurt culture
- Sweetener, if desired

Directions:

1. Pour the soymilk into a wide mouth, 1-quart Mason jar with lid or into multiple heatproof containers with a lids.
2. Add the vegan yogurt culture. Close the lid and shake to mix. Remove the lid from the jar; you don't need it at this point.
3. Put the Mason jar directly into the Instant Pot container. Close and lock the Instant Pot lid. You can leave the steam valve to SEALING or RELEASING; it won't affect the cooking. Press the YOGURT button and the timer to 12 hours.
4. When the timer beeps at the end of the cooking cycle, carefully remove the Mason jar from the pot, cover with its lid and refrigerate for at least 6 hours.
5. Sweeten and/ or flavor, if desired. This will keep for up to 6 days in the refrigerator.

Notes: This thick, creamy, unsweetened, tart soy yogurt can be used as a sour cream substitute or in recipes. You can enjoy it topped with pears and cinnamons, with bananas, shredded coconut, and pecans, with jam, or sweetened with coconut sugar. You can also strain it overnight to make yogurt cheese.

Nutritional Info (per serving): Calories - 133; Fat – 4.3; Fiber – 1.5; Carbs – 15.5; Protein – 8.1

Fruity Yogurt

(Prep + Cook Time: 12 hours | Servings: 4)

Ingredients:

- 5 2/3 cups milk, organic, reduced fat or whole
- 4 tbsp sugar, all natural, divided
- 4 tbsp dry milk powder, non-fat, divided
- 2 cups fresh fruit, chopped
- 1 ½ cup water, for the pot
- 4 tbsp yogurt culture, plain, divided

Equipment:

- 4 wide mouth pint jars

Directions:

1. Pour the water into the Instant Pot and then put a rack or a grate in the pot.
2. Pour 1 1/3 cup into each jars and the cover the jar loosely with their lids. Put the jars onto the rack/ grate.
3. Set the Instant Pot to Pressure Cycle and set the timer to 2 minutes; this will heat the milk and kill any pathogens that might be in the milk.
4. When the cycle is done, turn the steam valve to quick release the pressure.
5. Open the pot lid and with a jar lifter, remove the jars from the pot. Put the jars into cool water and carefully remove the jar lids.
6. Once the milk is below 100F, add 1 tablespoon yogurt culture, 1 tablespoon dry milk powder, and 1 tablespoon sugar into each jar; stir until well mixed.
7. Carefully add about 1/2 cup of fresh fruits into each jar; do not over fill them and leave at least 1/ 8-inch clear from the top each jar. Return the jar lids back.
8. Check and make sure that there is still 1 1/2 cup of water in the bottom of the Instant Pot.
9. Put the jars back onto the rack/ grate. Press the yogurt cycle and set the timer for 8-12 hours.

10. When the cycle is complete, put the jars in the refrigerator; this will cool them down and stop the cooking process.

Notes: Making the yogurt in jars enables you to make plain or different flavored yogurt at the same time.

Nutritional Info (per serving): Calories - 270; Fat – 7.6; Fiber – 1.6; Carbs – 41.5; Protein – 10.6

Tapioca with Fresh Berries (veg)

(Prep + Cook Time: 20 minutes | Servings: 4)

Ingredients:

- 2 cups almond milk
- 2 cups fresh berries
- ½ cup small pearl tapioca
- ¼ cup organic sugar
- 1 tsp pure vanilla

Directions:

1. Rinse tapioca under cold water for half a minute.
2. Pour milk into the Instant Pot, and then add the tapioca.
3. Stir and seal the lid. Hit MANUAL and cook for 4 minutes.
4. When time is up, hit CANCEL and wait 10 minutes before quick-releasing leftover pressure.
5. Mix in sugar and vanilla. To make it a parfait, spoon 2 tablespoons of berries in a glass, followed by tapioca, and then berries, and so on.
6. Serve.

Nutritional Info (per serving): Calories - 180; Fat – 2; Fiber – 1; Carbs – 39; Protein – 2

Tapioca Pudding (veg)

(Prep + Cook Time: 30 minutes | Servings: 4)

Ingredients:

- 1 ¼ cups almond milk
- ½ cup water
- ⅓ cup sugar
- ½ split vanilla bean
- ⅓ cup seed tapioca pearls

Directions:

1. Pour 1 cup of water into your Instant Pot. Rinse tapioca pearls.
2. In a 4-bowl bowl (safe for pressure cooker), add tapioca, water, milk, sugar, and vanilla and mix.
3. When the sugar has dissolved, lower into steamer basket and then into cooker.
4. Select MANUAL and cook on HIGH pressure for 8 minutes.
5. When time is up, hit CANCEL and wait for the pressure to come down on its own.
6. When pressure is released, wait 5 minutes before opening the lid. Stir.
7. Serve warm or cool in a fridge (covered with cling wrap) for at least 3 hours.

Notes: If you want a more porridge-like consistency, add ½ cup more of milk.

Nutritional Info (per serving): Calories - 187; Fat – 2.5; Fiber – 1; Carbs – 39.6; Protein – 2.5

Rice Pudding

(Prep + Cook Time: 30 minutes | Servings: 6)

Ingredients:
- 1 cup basmati rice
- ¾ cup heavy cream OR coconut cream
- 2 cups milk, your choice (soaked nut milk OR raw milk)
- 1/8 tsp sea salt
- ¼ cup maple syrup
- 1 vanilla bean scrapings OR
- 1 tsp vanilla extract
- 1 ¼ cups water

Directions:
1. Put the rice in a fine mesh colander.
2. Rinse well with several changes of water. Transfer into the Instant Pot.
3. Add the milk, water, sea salt, and maple syrup in the pot. Briefly stir. Cover and lock the lid.
4. Press the PORRIDGE key and let cook on preset time of 20 minutes.
5. When the Instant Pot timer beeps, press the CANCEL key and unplug the Instant Pot. Let the pressure release naturally for 10-15 minutes or until the valve drops. Using an oven mitt or a long handled spoon, turn the steam valve to release remaining pressure. Unlock and carefully open the lid.
6. Add the cream and the vanilla.
7. Stir well until mixed. Serve with optional toppings.

Notes: You can top this rice pudding with berry jam, cream, dates, raisins, nuts, cinnamon, maple syrup, chocolate chips, and butter. This dessert is best served while still warm, but you can pour it into individual mason jars, top with choice of topping, and pack into lunch boxes.

Nutritional Info (per serving): Calories - 241; Fat – 7.5; Fiber – 0; Carbs – 38; Protein – 5.2

Bread Pudding

(Prep + Cook Time: 50 minutes | Servings: 8)

Ingredients:
- 6 slices cinnamon or raisin bread, dried out, cut-up
- 1 tbsp butter
- 2 cups water

For the custard:
- 3 large eggs
- 3 cups milk
- 1 tsp vanilla
- ½ tsp salt
- ½ - ¾ cup sugar, or to taste
- Cinnamon, to taste (or nutmeg or raisins)

Directions:
1. Combine all of the custard ingredients in a mixing bowl. Butter a 5-cup stainless steel bowl that can fit in the Instant Pot.
2. Put the cut up bread pieces into the bowl.
3. Pour the custard mix over the bread pieces and let stand for 15 minutes to allow the bread to absorb the custard mix.
4. Dot the top with 1 tablespoon of butter. Butter an aluminum foil. With the buttered side faced down, tightly cover the aluminum foil on the bowl.
5. Pour the water into the Instant Pot and then put the steamer rack in the pot.
6. Put the bowl on the rack. Lock the lid, press MANUAL, set the pressure on HIGH, and set the timer for 25 minutes.
7. When the timer beeps, let the pressure release for 15 minutes naturally and then turn the valve VENTING to release remaining pressure.
8. Lift the bowl out of the Instant Pot. If there is some water in the foil, just wipe with a clean towel.
9. With a fork, puncture the foil a few times to let the pudding cool.
10. Enjoy warm or you can refrigerate the pudding if you want enjoy them cold.
11. The pudding will thicken as it cools.

Nutritional Info (per serving): Calories - 152; Fat – 5.4; Fiber – 0; Carbs – 21; Protein – 5.9

Pumpking Pudding

(Prep + Cook Time: 50 minutes | Servings: 6)

Ingredients:

For the pumpkin pudding:
- ¾ cup pumpkin, packed OR pumpkin puree, homemade, well-drained
- 2 tsp gelatin, sustainably-sourced
- ¼ tsp ground cloves
- ½ tsp sea salt
- ½ tsp ground nutmeg
- ½ tsp ground ginger
- ½ tsp allspice
- ½ cup coconut sugar
- ½ cup coconut milk OR raw milk
- 1 tsp ground cinnamon
- 1 egg, pastured
- 1 cup water

For the coconut-ginger glaze:
- ¾ cup coconut cream, at room temperature
- 1/16 tsp stevia
- 1 tsp ground ginger

Directions:

1. Pour the milk into a saucepan. Sprinkle with the gelatin. Turn on the heat to medium-low to gently heat.
2. Whisk to dissolve the gelatin and then remove from heat. In a medium-sized mixing bowl, combine the milk-gelatin, coconut sugar, pumpkin, egg, salt, and spices.
3. Whisk until smooth. Pour the milk-gelatin mix into a well-greased 3-cup jello mold, soufflé dish, mini bundt pan, or bowl.
4. Place a trivet in the Instant Pot and pour in 1 cup of water. Put the mold/ pan/ dish/ bowl on the trivet. Cover and lock the lid.
5. Press the MANUAL key, set the pressure to HIGH, and set the timer for 30 minutes.
6. When the Instant Pot timer beeps, press the CANCEL key and unplug the Instant Pot.
7. Turn the steam valve to quick release the pressure.
8. Unlock and carefully open the lid. Carefully remove the mold/ pan/ dish/ bowl from the pot and let cool to room temperature – do not disturb while it cools.

9. When cool, put the mold/ dish/ bowl in the fridge and chill for about 4-6 hours or until completely set.
10. When chilled, run a butter knife around the edge of the pudding and turn over onto a cake stand or a plate.
11. In a small-sized bowl, combine the glaze ingredients until smooth.
12. Drizzle over the pudding. If desired, garnish with crispy walnuts. Enjoy!

Nutritional Info (per serving): Calories - 181; Fat – 15.4; Fiber – 5.3; Carbs – 13.8; Protein – 4.7

White-Chocolate Lemon Pudding
(Prep + Cook Time: 40 minutes | Servings: 6)

Ingredients:
- 6-ounces of chopped white chocolate
- 4 whisked egg yolks
- 1 cup heavy cream
- 1 cup half-and-half
- 1 tbsp white sugar
- 1 tbsp finely-grated lemon zest
- ¼ tsp lemon extract
- 2 cups water

Directions:
1. Pour half-and-half and cream into a stovetop saucepan and heat until tiny bubbles appear on the edges.
2. Quickly pour over white chocolate in a bowl, and whisk until smooth.
3. Add in whisked egg yolks, lemon extract, lemon zest, and sugar.
4. Pour liquid pudding into six, ½-cup ramekins that are pressure-cooker safe, and wrap tightly in foil.
5. Pour 2 cups of water into the Instant Pot and lower in the steamer basket, with the ramekins inside it, and not stacked right on top of each other. Close and seal the cooker lid.
6. Select MANUAL and adjust time to 15 minutes on HIGH pressure.
7. When the timer beeps, hit CANCEL and wait for a natural pressure release.
8. Unwrap the ramekins and let them rest on a cooling rack before eating.
9. For a chilled pudding, store in the fridge for no longer than 3 days.

Nutritional Info (per serving): Calories - 369; Fat – 19; Fiber – 1; Carbs – 19; Protein – 6

Sticky Toffee

(Prep + Cook Time: 45 minutes | Servings: 8)

Ingredients:
- 1 ¼ cups finely-chopped dates
- 1 ¼ cups flour
- 1 egg
- ¾ cup brown sugar
- ¾ cup boiling water
- ⅓ cup room temperature butter
- ¼ cup blackstrap molasses
- 1 tsp baking powder
- 1 tsp vanilla extract
- ¼ tsp salt
- 2 cups water

Caramel Sauce:
- ⅔ cup packed dark brown sugar
- ⅓ cup whipping cream
- ¼ cup butter
- 1 tsp vanilla extract

Directions:
1. Grease 8 ramekins. In a bowl, mix boiling water, molasses, and dates, and wait to cool.
2. In a separate bowl, mix baking powder, flour, and salt.
3. Cream brown sugar and butter with a mixer till fluffy. Add eggs and vanilla, and mix.
4. Alternate with the date and flour bowls, blending into the creamed eggs and mixing after each add.
5. Divide batter into ramekins. Wrap ramekins tightly with buttered foil.
6. Pour 2 cups of water into your Instant Pot and lower in the rack. Put the ramekins on the rack.
7. They can stack on top of each other, but not directly on top. Close and seal lid.
8. Hit MANUAL and adjust time to 25 minutes.
9. While the pudding cooks, make caramel sauce by mixing brown sugar, butter, cream, and vanilla in a saucepan.
10. Bring to a boil, stirring, so the sugar dissolves. Reduce heat and simmer for 5 minutes.
11. Remove from heat when thickened.
12. When the pudding is done, hit CANCEL and quick-release.

13. Unwrap the ramekins and let the pudding cool a little before serving with the caramel sauce on top.

Nutritional Info (per serving): Calories - 512; Fat – 26; Fiber – 1.7; Carbs – 66; Protein – 4.5

Lemon-Ruby Pears (veg)
(Prep + Cook Time: 40 minutes | Servings: 4)

Ingredients:
- 4 ripe Bosc pears
- 3 cups grape juice
- 1 cup currant jelly
- 1 lemon
- ½ split vanilla bean

Directions:
1. Remove the core from the pears, but leave the top of the pear and stem intact.
2. Pour grape juice and jelly into the Instant Pot.
3. Hit SAUTE and heat until jelly melts.
4. Grate the lemon into the pot, and then squeeze in the juice, as well. Toss in vanilla bean.
5. Cut out four squares of foil, to wrap your pears in. Before wrapping, turn the pears in the cooker sauce.
6. Wrap pears in foil tightly and put in your steamer basket. Insert basket into cooker.
7. Seal the lid. Hit MANUAL and adjust to 11 minutes.
8. When the timer beeps, hit CANCEL and quick-release the pressure.
9. Unwrap the pears, put in a baking dish, and pour over sauce.
10. Wait till pears are room temperature before storing them in the fridge overnight and then serve!

Nutritional Info (per serving): Calories - 414; Fat – 0; Fiber – 5.5; Carbs – 109; Protein – 1

Chocolate Cheesecake (veg)

(Prep + Cook Time: 2 hours 10 minutes | Servings: 6)

Ingredients:

- 12 cups cashews, soaked
- 5 oz almond flour
- 2 tbsp coconut flour
- 2 oz melted coconut oil
- ½ tsp salt
- 2/3 cup brown sugar
- 1 tbsp cocoa powder
- 3 tsp vanilla extract, divided
- 2 tbsp honey
- 4 oz maple syrup
- 8 fluid ounce almond milk
- 16 fluid ounce water
- 2 oz vegan chocolate chips

Directions:

1. Add almond flour, maple syrup and coconut oil in a food processor and pulse until mixture comes together. Blend in 1-2 tablespoons water if the mixture is too dry.
2. Take a 7-inch spring form pan, then spoon oats mixture into it and press into the bottom and a little on the sides.
3. Place pan in a refrigerator until filling is prepared.
4. Drain cashews and reserve their soaking liquid.
5. Add cashew and half of the soaking liquid and pulse until smooth.
6. Then blend in salt, sugar, vanilla and milk and pulse until combined well and pour this mixture into a bowl and then stir in coconut flour and chocolate chip until just mixed.
7. Spoon filling into prepared spring form pan and smooth the top. Pour water in the Instant Pot and insert a trivet.
8. Place prepared spring form pan on the trivet and secure pot with lid.
9. Then position pressure indicator, select MANUAL option and adjust cooking time on timer pad to 55 minutes and let cook.

10. When the timer beeps, switch off the Instant Pot and let pressure release naturally for 10 minutes and then do quick pressure release.
11. Then uncover the pot, carefully remove pan and let the pan cool completely on a wire rack.
12. Chill cake in the refrigerator for 2 hours. Remove outer part of the spring form pan before slicing the cake to serve.

Nutritional Info (per serving): Calories - 321; Fat – 19.5; Fiber – 7; Carbs – 43; Protein – 14

Chocolate Fondue with Coconut Cream (veg)
(Prep + Cook Time: 5 minutes | Servings: 4)

Ingredients:
- 2 cups water
- 3.5 oz
- 70% dark bittersweet chocolate
- 3.5 oz coconut cream
- 1 tsp sugar

Directions:
- Pour 2 cups of water into your Instant Pot and lower in trivet.
- In a heatproof bowl, add chocolate chunks.
- Add coconut cream and sugar.
- Put the bowl on top of the trivet. Close and seal the lid.
- Hit MANUAL and cook on high pressure for 2 minutes.
- When time is up, hit CANCEL and quick-release.
- Carefully remove bowl and whisk with a fork until it becomes smooth. Serve!

Nutritional Info (per serving): Calories - 216; Fat – 20.3; Fiber – 2.6; Carbs – 11.7; Protein – 1.8

Chocolate Zucchini Muffins

(Prep + Cook Time: 35 minutes | Servings: 24)

Ingredients:

- 1 cup water
- 1 cup flour
- 1 cup grated zucchini
- 2 eggs
- ¾-1 cup cane juice
- ½ cup coconut oil
- ⅓ cup chocolate chips
- 3 tbsp cocoa powder
- 1 tbsp melted butter
- 2 tsp pure vanilla extract
- ¾ tsp cinnamon
- ½ tsp baking soda
- ¼ tsp salt

Directions:

1. Mix cane juice, eggs, coconut oil, and vanilla. In a separate bowl, mix melted butter with cocoa powder.
2. Add to the egg mixture and mix. Add in dry ingredients (flour, baking soda, cinnamon, and salt).
3. Fold in the chocolate chips and zucchini. Pour 1 cup of water into your Instant Pot and lower in the trivet.
4. Turn the pot to SAUTE so it preheats.
5. Fill silicone muffin cups ⅔ of the way full with muffin batter. Put cups in the pressure cooker.
6. For the second layer, separate with a piece of parchment paper, foil, and another trivet.
7. Finish layering muffins, and cover again with parchment paper, foil, and then a plate. Close and seal the lid.
8. Cook on HIGH pressure for 8 minutes.
9. When time is up, unplug the cooker (or hit CANCEL and wait 15 minutes. Quick-release any leftover pressure.
10. If a toothpick comes out clean from the muffins, they're ready!

Nutritional Info (per serving): Calories - 109; Fat – 13; Fiber – 1.4; Carbs – 13; Protein – 1

Chocolate Custard

(Prep + Cook Time: 55 minutes | Servings: 6)

Ingredients:

- 13-ounces chopped dark chocolate
- 6 whisked egg yolks Just over
- 1 cup cream (1.2 cups)
- 1 cup whole milk
- ½ cup sugar
- 1 tsp vanilla extract

Directions:

1. In a saucepan, simmer milk, cream, vanilla, and sugar until sugar has dissolved.
2. Take the pan off the heat and add chocolate.
3. When melted, slowly add whisked egg yolks, being careful that they don't cook.
4. Pour into an 18-20cm baking dish.
5. Pour 4 cups of water into your Instant Pot and insert trivet. Put the custard pan on the trivet and seal the lid.
6. Select MANUAL and cook on HIGH pressure for 30 minutes.
7. When time is up, hit CANCEL and let the pressure come down naturally for 10 minutes before quick-releasing.
8. The custard will have a wobbly center, like a jello. Serve hot or cold.

Nutritional Info (per serving): Calories - 549; Fat – 38; Fiber – 0; Carbs – 55; Protein – 9

Cashew-Lemon Cheesecake (veg)

(Prep + Cook Time: 4 hours | Servings: 8)

Ingredients:

- 1 cup oats
- ½ cup chopped dates (soaked in ¼ cup water for 15-30 minutes)
- ½ cup walnuts
- 1 cup soaked cashews (2-4 hours of soak time)
- ½ cup coconut flour
- ½ cup sugar
- ½ cup vanilla almond milk
- ½ cup fresh raspberries
- 2 tbsp lemon juice
- 1 tbsp arrowroot powder
- 1 tsp vanilla extract
- 1-2 tsp lemon zest

Directions:

1. Drain your dates, but keep the liquid.
2. Pour 1 ½ cups of fresh water into your Instant Pot and add steamer basket.
3. To make the crust, mix ingredients in the first list in a food processor.
4. If it is too dry and crumbly, add 1 tablespoon of date-liquid until it's right.
5. Your dough should be firm, but not too moist so it's gooey.
6. Press down into a springform pan on the bottom and about an inch up the sides.
7. For the filling, drain the cashews, and keep the water. Add half of this water and cashews into a food processor and pulse until smooth.
8. Add flour, sugar, zest, lemon juice, vanilla, and milk. Blend, add arrowroot, and then blend for one last time.
9. Pour into the pan, using a spatula to smooth the top.
10. Wrap the pan with foil, so the top is covered. Lower into the steamer basket. Close and seal lid.
11. Hit MANUAL and adjust time to 20 minutes on HIGH pressure.

12. When time is up, hit CANCEL and wait for the pressure to come down naturally.
13. Carefully remove pan and cool for a little while.
14. Arrange raspberries on the cheesecake and then cool for at least 30 minutes before chilling in the fridge for at least 1 hour.

Nutritional Info (per serving): Calories - 346; Fat – 14; Fiber – 2.6; Carbs – 48; Protein – 10

New York Cheesecake

(Prep + Cook Time: 55 minutes | Servings:12)

Ingredients:
- 16 ounces cream cheese
- 15 Oreo cookies
- 1 tbsp vanilla
- 1 cup sugar
- 2 eggs
- 2 tbsp butter, melted
- 1 cup water

Equipment: 7-inch spring-form pan

Directions:
1. Put the Oreo cookies into a food processor and process until crumbled. Stir in the melted butter.
2. Transfer the Oreo cookie mix into the spring-form pan and press into an even layer.
3. In a medium-sized to large-sized bowl, put the eggs, cream cheese, vanilla, and sugar; mix until creamy and smooth.
4. Transfer in the spring-form pan and spread into an even layer. Put a trivet in the Instant Pot and pour in 1 cup water.
5. Take a long piece of foil and fold it lengthwise to create a strip long enough to allow you to lower the cheesecake onto the trivet and retrieve it later when the cooking time is done. Using the foil sling, lower the pan onto the trivet. Cover and lock the lid.
6. Press the MANUAL key, set the pressure to HIGH, and set the timer for 40 minutes.

7. When the Instant Pot timer beeps, press the CANCEL key and unplug the Instant Pot. Using an oven mitt or a long handled spoon, turn the steam valve to VENTING to quick release the pressure. Unlock and carefully open the lid.
8. Using the foil sling, carefully remove the cheesecake from the pot. Chill for about 1 hour. Top with your favorite topping or fruits.

Nutritional Info (per serving): Calories - 283; Fat – 18.2; Fiber – 0; Carbs – 26.8; Protein – 4.5

Simple Egg Custard
(Prep + Cook Time: 25 minutes | Servings: 6)

Ingredients:
- 6 big eggs
- 4 cups milk
- ¾ cup sugar
- 1 tsp vanilla extract
- ¼ tsp cinnamon
- Pinch of salt

Directions:
1. Mix the eggs in a bowl.
2. Add the salt, sugar, vanilla, and milk until just mixed. Pour into six ramekins and wrap in foil.
3. Poke a few holes in the foil. Pour 1 ½ cups of water into your Instant
4. Pot and lower in trivet. Put the ramekins on top of the trivet. Seal the lid.
5. Select MANUAL and cook for 7 minutes on high pressure.
6. When time is up, hit CANCEL and wait 10 minutes for the pressure to descend.
7. Release any leftover pressure and let the custard cool for 2 minutes, unwrapped.
8. Dust with cinnamon before serving.

Nutritional Info (per serving): Calories - 148; Fat – 6; Fiber – 0; Carbs – 16; Protein – 7

Classic Cheesecake

(Prep + Cook Time: 45 minutes | Servings: 8)

Ingredients:
- 1 pound cream cheese, brick-style, softened
- ¼ cup cottage cheese, preferably small-curd
- ½ tsp vanilla extract
- ½ lemon, zest and juice
- ½ cup granulated sugar
- 1 ¼ cups graham cracker crumbs
- 1 ½ tbsp all-purpose flour
- ¼ cup unsalted butter, melted
- 2 eggs, large-sized, at room temperature
- 2 cups water

Equipment: 6-inch spring-form pan

Directions:
1. Generously butter the spring-form pan. In a small-sized bowl, combine the graham cracker crumbs with the butter until evenly moist.
2. Press the mixture onto the bottom and halfway up the sides of the spring-form pan.
3. Put the cream cheese and sugar into a food processor; process until smooth, scraping down the sides of the bowl as needed.
4. With the food processor motor running, add the eggs through the feed tube; process until smooth.
5. Add the cottage cheese, flour, lemon juice, lemon zest, vanilla, and process for 2 minutes or until creamy and smooth.
6. Pour the batter into the pan and spread into an even layer. Cover the spring-form pan with unbleached parchment paper, top it with foil, and secure around the edges.
7. Put a trivet in the Instant Pot and pour in 2 cups water. Take a long piece of foil and fold it lengthwise to create a strip long

enough to allow you to lower the cheesecake onto the trivet and retrieve it later when the cooking time is done.

8. Using the foil sling, lower the pan onto the trivet. You don't need a foil sling if your trivet has a handle Cover and lock the lid.

9. Press the MANUAL key, set the pressure to HIGH, and set the timer for 25 minutes.

10. When the Instant Pot timer beeps, press the CANCEL key and unplug the Instant Pot. Let the pressure release naturally for 10-15 minutes or until the valve drops.

11. Using an oven mitt or a long handled spoon, turn the steam valve to release remaining pressure. Unlock and carefully open the lid.

12. Test the cake by inserting a toothpick in the center – it's cooked when the toothpick comes out clean.

13. If the cake needs more cooking, cover and lock the lid. Turn the steam valve to SEALING.

14. Press the MANUAL key, set the pressure to HIGH, and set the timer for 5 minutes.

15. Using the foil sling or the handle of the trivet, carefully remove the cheesecake from the pot.

16. Transfer the pot into a rack and let cool for 1 hour. Unmold the cake and chill in the fridge for at least 6 hours.

17. You can keep this cake in the fridge for up to 2 days.

Nutritional Info (per serving): Calories - 383; Fat – 28; Fiber – 1; Carbs – 26.7; Protein – 7.7

Mango Cake

(Prep + Cook Time: 50 minutes | Servings: 8)

Ingredients:

- 1 ¼ cups flour
- ¾ cup milk
- 1 cup water
- ½ cup sugar
- ¼ cup coconut oil
- 1 tbsp lemon juice
- 1 tsp mango syrup
- 1 tsp baking powder
- ¼ tsp baking soda
- ⅛ tsp salt

Directions:

1. Grease a baking pan that will fit in your Instant Pot.
2. Mix the sugar, oil, and milk in a bowl until the sugar has melted.
3. Pour in mango syrup and mix again.
4. Pour all the dry ingredients through a sieve into the wet.
5. Add lemon juice and mix well.
6. Pour into the baking pan.
7. Pour 1 cup of water into the Instant Pot and lower in a trivet.
8. Lower the baking pan into the cooker and close the lid.
9. Select MANUAL, and cook on high pressure for 35 minutes.
10. When time is up, press CANCEL and wait for the pressure to come down naturally.
11. Check the cake for doneness before cooling for 10 minutes.
12. Serve!

Nutritional Info (per serving): Calories - 230; Fat – 7; Fiber – 0; Carbs – 39; Protein – 2

Chocolate-Chip Banana Cake

(Prep + Cook Time: 75 minutes | Servings: 6)

Ingredients:

- 1 ½ cups flour
- 2 eggs
- 2 ripe bananas
- ½ cup milk + 1 tbsp
- 2/3 cup water
- ⅓ cup dark chocolate chips
- ¼ cup honey
- 3 tbsp coconut oil
- 1 tbsp vinegar
- 1 tsp baking soda
- ½ tsp cinnamon
- ⅛ tsp ground nutmeg

Directions:

1. Grease the 3-cup Bundt Pan.
2. Pour vinegar into milk and let the bowl sit until the milk curdles and turns to buttermilk.
3. In a separate bowl, mix bananas, honey, vanilla, eggs, coconut oil, and nutmeg.
4. Add buttermilk. When combined, stir in the cinnamon, baking soda, and flour.
5. With a spatula, fold in the chocolate chips. Pour batter into your Bundt Pan.
6. Pour ⅔ cup of water into the Instant Pot and lower in the trivet. Put the Bundt Pan on top of the trivet. Close and seal the lid.
7. Select MANUAL and adjust time to 25 minutes on HIGH pressure.
8. When time is up, hit CANCEL and quick-release. Take out the Bundt Pan and cool for 10 minutes.
9. Invert the cake and wait until fully cooled before serving.

Nutritional Info (per serving): Calories - 232; Fat – 13; Fiber – 1; Carbs – 30; Protein – 3

Cranberry-Pear Cake (veg)

(Prep + Cook Time: 55 minutes | Servings: 6)

Ingredients:

- 1 ½ cups water
- 1 cup chopped pears
- ½ cup fresh, chopped cranberries
- 1 ¼ cup whole-wheat flour
- ½ tsp baking soda
- ½ tsp baking powder
- ½ tsp ground cardamom
- ⅛ tsp salt
- ½ cup unsweetened almond milk
- ¼ cup agave syrup
- 2 tbsp applesauce
- 2 tbsp ground flax seeds

Directions:

1. Grease a 7-inch bundt pan.
2. Mix dry ingredients in a bowl. Mix wet ingredients in a separate bowl. Mix wet into dry before folding in pears and cranberries.
3. Pour batter into pan and wrap in foil. Pour water into your Instant Pot and lower in trivet or steamer basket. Lower the pan in.
4. Close and seal lid. Select MANUAL and cook on HIGH pressure for 35 minutes.
5. When time is up, hit CANCEL and let the pressure come down on its own.
6. Take out the pan and throw away the foil.
7. Cool before serving.

Nutritional Info (per serving): Calories - 163; Fat – 2; Fiber – 2; Carbs – 35; Protein – 4

Apple Crumb Cake

(Prep + Cook Time: 55 minutes | Servings: 6)

Ingredients:

- 6 small red apples
- ¾ cup melted butter
- ½ cup sugar
- ⅔ cup dry bread crumbs
- Juice and zest from
- ½ lemon
- 2 tbsp flour
- 1 tsp cinnamon
- 1 tsp ginger
- 1 ½ cups water

Directions:

1. To make the filling, mix bread crumbs, sugar, cinnamon, melted butter, ginger, lemon juice, and lemon zest.
2. Core the apples, leaving the peels on, and slice very thin.
3. Grease your baking dish with butter and coat with dusting flour. Lay down the apple slices in fan shapes.
4. Add a layer of the crumb filling, followed by apples, and keep going until everything is used up.
5. Wrap the dish tightly in foil. Pour 1 ½ cups of water into your Instant Pot and lower in the trivet.
6. Put the wrapped dish on top and seal the lid.
7. Select MANUAL and cook on HIGH pressure for 23 minutes.
8. When time is up, hit CANCEL and wait 10 minutes before quick-releasing.
9. Take out the cake and remove the foil.
10. Flip the cake on a dish. To finish, sprinkle raw sugar on top and broil for just 3 minutes, or until the sugar caramelizes. Serve!

Nutritional Info (per serving): Calories - 518; Fat – 28; Fiber – 1; Carbs – 69; Protein – 3

Apple-Ricotta Cake

(Prep + Cook Time: 45 minutes | Servings: 6)

Ingredients:

- 2 cups water
- 1 cup ricotta cheese
- 1 cup flour
- 1 egg
- ¼ cup raw sugar
- ⅓ cup sugar
- 1 sliced apple
- 1 diced apple
- 3 tbsp olive oil
- 1 tbsp lemon juice
- 2 tsp baking powder
- 1 tsp baking soda
- 1 tsp vanilla extract
- ⅛ tsp cinnamon

Directions:
1. Pour water into your Instant Pot and lower in steamer basket or trivet.
2. Mix your diced and sliced apple in lemon juice.
3. Put a piece of wax paper on the bottom of a 4-cup baking dish (shallow and wide), and oil it, and then dust it with flour.
4. Sprinkle in raw sugar before laying down the apple slices. In a bowl, whisk ricotta, sugar, olive oil, vanilla, and egg.
5. Sift in the cinnamon, flour, baking soda, and baking powder. Stir in the diced apples and then pour into your baking dish. Seal the lid.
6. Select MANUAL and cook for 20 minutes on HIGH pressure.
7. When time is up, hit CANCEL and wait 10 minutes before quick-releasing any leftover pressure.
8. To test for doneness, poke a toothpick in the middle.
9. If batter sticks to it, put back in the cooker and bake another 2 minutes under pressure.
10. To serve, chill or eat warm.

Nutritional Info (per serving): Calories - 463; Fat – 21; Fiber – 2; Carbs – 62; Protein – 13

Raspberry Jam

(Prep + Cook Time: 30 minutes | Servings: 2 pints)

Ingredients:
- 2 pounds fresh raspberries
- 1 ½ pounds light honey.

Directions:
1. Pour raspberries and honey into your Instant Pot. Turn the cooker to the KEEP WARP setting and stir for 3 minutes until the honey has become liquid.
2. Turn to SAUTE and stir until the pot begins to boil. Close and seal the lid immediately. Adjust time to 2 minutes after pressing MANUAL.
3. When the timer beeps, hit CANCEL and wait for the pressure to release on its own.
4. Take the lid off and on sauté, bring the jam to a boil again until it reaches 220-degrees F.
5. Pour jam into clean half-pint jars and screw on the lids. Jam will keep in the fridge for 4-6 weeks.

Nutritional Info (1 tablespoon recipe per serving): Calories - 181; Fat – 0; Fiber – 0; Carbs – 44; Protein – 1

Apple Dumplings

(Prep + Cook Time: 35 minutes | Servings: 6)

Ingredients:

- 8-ounces crescent rolls
- 1 big peeled and cored green apple cut into 8 wedges
- 4 tbsp butter
- ¾ cup apple cider
- ½ cup brown sugar
- 1 tsp ground cinnamon
- ½ tsp vanilla extract
- Pinch of ground nutmeg

Directions:

1. Turn your cooker to SAUTE.
2. Roll the crescent dough out flat, and wrap around the apple wedges, so one wedge gets one roll. Add butter to your cooker and hit CANCEL.
3. Mix in vanilla, brown sugar, cinnamon, and nutmeg, and stir until the remaining heat melts everything together.
4. Put the dumplings in the cooker and pour over the cider. Close and seal the lid.
5. Select MANUAL and adjust time to 10 minutes on HIGH pressure.
6. When time is up, hit CANCEL and wait for a natural pressure release.
7. Remove the dumplings and let them cool for a few minutes.
8. Serve with the cider syrup from the pot poured on top.

Nutritional Info (per serving): Calories - 267; Fat – 5; Fiber – 2; Carbs – 41; Protein – 4

Pumpkin-Spice Brown Rice Pudding with Dates (veg)

(Prep + Cook Time: 65 minutes | Servings: 6)

Ingredients:
- 3 cups almond milk
- 1 cup pumpkin puree
- 1 cup brown rice
- 1 stick cinnamon
- ½ cup maple syrup
- ½ cup water
- ½ cup chopped pitted dates
- 1 tsp vanilla extract
- 1 tsp pumpkin spice
- ⅛ tsp salt

Directions:
1. Pour boiling water over your rice and wait at least 10 minutes.
2. Rinse. Pour milk and water in your Instant Pot.
3. Turn on cooker to SAUTE and when boiling, add rice, cinnamon, salt, and dates.
4. Close and seal lid. Hit MANUAL and cook on HIGH pressure for 10 minutes.
5. Hit CANCEL when the timer goes off and wait for the pressure to descend naturally.
6. Add pumpkin puree, maple syrup, and pumpkin spice.
7. Turn SAUTE back on and stir for 3-5 minutes until thick. Turn off cooker.
8. Pick out cinnamon stick and add vanilla. Move pudding to a bowl and cover in plastic wrap, so the plastic touches the top.
9. Wait 30 minutes to cool. Serve warm or chilled.

Nutritional Info (per serving): Calories - 193; Fat – 3; Fiber – 4; Carbs – 38; Protein – 1

Stewed Pears (veg)

(Prep + Cook Time: 40 minutes | Servings: 6)

Ingredients:
- 6 pears, peeled
- 16 oz brown sugar
- 1 tsp ground cinnamon
- 1 tsp ginger powder
- 4 whole cloves
- 1 bay leaf
- ½ cup basil leaves
- 26 oz red wine

Directions:
1. In the Instant Pot, pour in red wine, then stir in cinnamon, ginger and add cloves and bay leaf. Add pears and secure pot with lid.
2. Then position pressure indicator, select MANUAL option and adjust cooking time on timer pad to 4 minutes and let cook.
3. When the timer beeps, switch off the Instant Pot and let pressure release naturally for 10 minutes and then do quick pressure release.
4. Then uncover the pot and pull out pears and set aside. Turn on the pot, select SAUTE option and simmer cooking liquid or until reduced to one-third of the actual amount.
5. Drizzle pears with its cooking liquid, sprinkle with basil and serve.

Nutritional Info (per serving): Calories - 197; Fat – 0.35; Fiber – 4.3; Carbs – 51; Protein – 0.53

Blueberry Pudding

(Prep + Cook Time: 55 minutes | Servings: 4)

Ingredients:

- ½ pound blueberries
- 1 cup flour
- 1 beaten egg
- 5 ounces milk
- ½ cup white sugar
- ½ cup cubed butter
- 2 ½ tbsp breadcrumbs
- 1 ½ tsp baking powder
- ½ tsp salt

Directions:

1. Grease a 4-6 cup pudding basin, or baking dish. In a large bowl, sift in the baking powder, salt, and flour.
2. Add the butter by "cutting" it in, which means using two knives until you get a crumbly, mixed texture.
3. Mix in the breadcrumbs and sugar.
4. Add milk and egg, blending together, before adding blueberries.
5. Pour into your baking dish ¾ of the way full.
6. Cover the top of the dish with a piece of buttered parchment paper, tying with some kitchen string so it stays secured.
7. The paper should have a little pleat in it, so when the pudding rises, it has room.
8. Pour 2-inches worth of hot water in your cooker and lower in the trivet.
9. Put the dish on top and close - not seal - the lid. You're going to just STEAM the pudding for 15 minutes.
10. When that time has passed, now seal the lid.
11. Select MANUAL and cook for 35 minutes on HIGH pressure.
12. When time is up, press CANCEL and quick-release.
13. Take out the pudding and cool for a few minutes before inverting on a plate.

Nutritional Info (per serving): Calories - 493; Fat – 2; Fiber – 0; Carbs – 60; Protein – 8

Triple-Berry Jam

(Prep + Cook Time: 1 hour 25 minutes | Servings: 2 cups)

Ingredients:

- 8-ounces raspberries
- 8-ounces halved strawberries
- 8-ounces blueberries
- 1 cup sugar
- ¼ cup honey (optional)
- 2 tsp lemon juice
- 1 tsp grated lemon zest

Directions:

1. Add sugar and raspberries to your Instant Pot.
2. Let the mixture marinate (called macerate) for at least 15 minutes, but no longer than 1 hour.
3. After that time, turn the Pot on to SAUTE and bring it to a boil for 3 minutes. Close and seal the lid.
4. Press MANUAL and adjust time to 8 minutes on HIGH pressure.
5. When time is up, hit CANCEL and wait 10 minutes for a natural pressure release.
6. Take off the lid and hit SAUTE again. Add lemon zest and juice.
7. Taste the jam (it's hot, so be careful) and add up to ¼ cup honey if you want the jam to be sweeter. Boil for 3-4 minutes, stirring, until the jam gets that gel-like consistency and reaches 220-degrees F.
8. Push CANCEL on your cooker. If you like smooth jam, mash it all together.
9. Transfer to clean Mason jars and screw on the lids.
10. When cool, move to the fridge for 3 weeks, or a freezer, for up to 6 months.

Nutritional Info (per serving): Calories - 134; Fat – 0; Fiber – 3; Carbs – 35; Protein – 1

Fruity Yogurt

(Prep + Cook Time: 9-12 hours | Servings: 4)

Ingredients:

- 5 2/3 cups milk, organic, reduced fat or whole
- 4 tbsp sugar, all natural, divided
- 4 tbsp dry milk powder, non-fat, divided
- 2 cups fresh fruit, chopped
- 1 ½ cup water, for the pot
- 4 tbsp yogurt culture, plain, divided

Equipment: wide mouth pint jars

Directions:

1. Pour the water into the Instant Pot and then put a rack or a grate in the pot. Pour 1 1/3 cup into each jars and the cover the jar loosely with their lids.
2. Put the jars onto the rack/ grate. Set the Instant Pot to Pressure Cycle and set the timer to 2 minutes; this will heat the milk and kill any pathogens that might be in the milk.
3. When the cycle is done, turn the steam valve to quick release the pressure.
4. Open the pot lid and with a jar lifter, remove the jars from the pot.
5. Put the jars into cool water and carefully remove the jar lids.
6. Once the milk is below 100F, add 1 tablespoon yogurt culture, 1 tablespoon dry milk powder, and 1 tablespoon sugar into each jar; stir until well mixed.
7. Carefully add about 1/ 2 cup of fresh fruits into each jar; do not over fill them and leave at least 1/ 8-inch clear from the top each jar.
8. Return the jar lids back. Check and make sure that there is still 1 1/ 2 cup of water in the bottom of the Instant Pot.
9. Put the jars back onto the rack/ grate. Press the yogurt cycle and set the timer for 8-12 hours.
10. When the cycle is complete, put the jars in the refrigerator; this will cool them down and stop the cooking process.

Notes: Making the yogurt in jars enables you to make plain or different flavored yogurt at the same time.

Nutritional Info (per serving): Calories - 270; Fat – 7.6; Fiber – 1.6; Carbs – 41.5; Protein – 10.6

Stuffed Peaches

(Prep + Cook Time: 35 minutes | Servings: 6)

Ingredients:

- 5 peaches, organic, medium-sized OR 6 - small-sized
- 2 tbsp butter, grass-fed
- ¼ tsp pure almond extract
- ¼ cup maple sugar, sucanat, mascobado
- ¼ cup cassava flour (I used Otto's)
- ½ tsp ground cinnamon
- Pinch Celtic sea salt

For the Instant Pot:

- ¼ tsp pure almond extract
- 1 cup water

Directions:

1. Slice 1/ 4-inch off from the top of the peaches; discard the cut off top.
2. With a sharp paring knife, cut around the pits and remove them so the peaches are hollowed out – leave at least 1/ 2-inch of flesh from the skin so they stay intact.
3. If the peaches are very firm, use a spoon to help loosen and scoop out the pit and the flesh around it. Set aside.
4. In a shallow dish or a mixing bowl, put the cassava flour, your choice of unrefined sweetener, cinnamon, butter, sea salt, and almond extract.
5. Using clean hands, mix until the mixture is crumbly. Fill the hollowed peaches with the crumble mix until full.
6. Put a trivet in the Instant Pot and pour in 1 cup water.
7. Add the almond extract. Carefully put the filled peaches onto the trivet. Cover and lock the lid.
8. Press the MANUAL key, set the pressure to HIGH, and set the timer for 3 minutes.
9. When the Instant Pot timer beeps, press the CANCEL key and unplug the Instant Pot. Turn the steam valve to quick release the pressure. Unlock and carefully open the lid.
10. With tongs and an oven mitt, carefully lift and remove the trivet and put in a dish.
11. Let the peaches rest and cool for about 10 minutes.
12. Serve with vanilla ice cream.

Nutritional Info (per serving): Calories - 143; Fat – 5.1; Fiber – 2.6; Carbs – 24.7; Protein – 1.6

2 Ingredients Blueberry Jam

(Prep + Cook Time: 25 minutes | Tbsp: 26)

Ingredients:
- 2 pounds blueberries, frozen or fresh
- 1 pound honey, preferably local

Directions:
1. Put the blueberries in the Instant Pot. Pour in the honey.
2. Press the KEEP WARM function to melt the honey, occasionally stirring. If you are using frozen berries, this may take a while, but this step is worth it.
3. When the honey is melted, press the SAUTÉ key and let the honey boil – there will be white-pink bubbles around the blueberries.
4. When the honey is boiling, quickly press the CANCEL key to stop the sauté function. Cover and lock the lid.
5. Press the MANUAL key, set the pressure to HIGH, and set the timer for 2 minutes.
6. When the Instant Pot timer beeps, press the CANCEL key and unplug the Instant Pot. Let the pressure release naturally for 10-15 minutes or until the valve drops.
7. Using an oven mitt or a long handled spoon, turn the steam valve to release remaining pressure. Unlock and carefully open the lid.
8. Press the SAUTÉ key and let boil until some of the water has evaporated off and the jam is nicely gelled when dripped off with a spoon.
9. Make sure to scrape the bottom of the pot frequently with a wooden spoon to ensure even gelling.
10. Pour the jam into clean half-pint jars. Store the jars in the fridge.

Notes: If you plan to use other fruits, seed, stem, peel, and cut them into smaller pieces. If using frozen or larger chunk fruits, set the timer for 3 minutes and then mash using a potato masher to get a smoother consistency. You can combine fruits for a unique jam flavor.

Nutritional Info (per serving): Calories - 41; Fat – 0.1; Fiber – 0.5; Carbs – 11; Protein – 0.2

Pears Stewed In Red Wine

(Prep + Cook Time: 15 minutes | Servings: 6)

Ingredients:

- 6 pears, firm ripe, peeled
- 4 cloves (the spice)
- 2 cups sugar, optional
- 1 stick cinnamon OR 1 tsp cinnamon
- 1 piece fresh ginger OR 1 tsp ginger
- 1 bunch herbs, for decoration - mint, sage, basil, or oregano
- 1 bottle red wine (something dry, tarty, and tannic, like Barbaresco or Sangiovese)
- 1 bay laurel leaf

Directions:

1. Peel the pears – leave the stem attached. Pour the bottle of wine into the Instant Pot.
2. Add the sugar, ginger, cinnamon, cloves, and bay.
3. Mix well until the sugar is dissolved.
4. Add the pears into the pot. Cover and lock the lid. Turn the steam valve to SEALING.
5. Press the MANUAL key, set the pressure to HIGH, and set the timer for 5-7 minutes.
6. When the Instant Pot timer beeps, press the CANCEL key. Let the pressure release naturally for 10 minutes.
7. Using an oven mitt or a long handled spoon, turn the steam valve to release remaining pressure. Unlock and carefully open the lid. Using 2 spoons or tongs, carefully pull out the pears from the pot.
8. Transfer them onto a plate and set aside.
9. Press the SAUTÉ key. Cook the cooking liquid until reduced to a third of its original amount.
10. Drizzle the syrup over the pears, decorate with some herbs, and serve at room temperature or chilled.

Notes: If you are making ahead of time, refrigerate the pears in the cooking liquid syrup.

Nutritional Info (per serving): Calories - 232; Fat – 0.6; Fiber – 7.4; Carbs – 36.8; Protein – 1

Two-Ingredient Chocolate Fondue

(Prep + Cook Time: 5 minutes | Servings: 4)

Ingredients:
- 3.5-ounces of dark chocolate (minimum 70% cocoa)
- 3.5-ounces of cream

Directions:
1. Pour two cups of water into the Instant Pot and lower in the trivet.
2. Put chocolate chunks in a ceramic, heat-proof container that fits into the pressure cooker, and pour over the cream.
3. Put into the Instant Pot, uncovered.
4. Close the lid and select MANUAL, then adjust time to 2 minutes on high pressure.
5. When time is up, hit CANCEL and carefully quick-release.
6. Open the lid and remove the container.
7. Whisk quickly until the chocolate becomes smooth.
8. Serve right away!

<u>Notes:</u> If you want to make your fondue unique, add 1 teaspoon of Amaretto liquor before closing up the pressure. Other flavor options include chili powder, peppermint extract, orange extract, or Bailey's.

Nutritional Info (per serving): Calories - 216; Fat – 20.3; Fiber – 2.6; Carbs – 11.7; Protein – 1.8

Fudge Brownie for Four

(Prep + Cook Time: 45 minutes | Servings: 4)

Ingredients:
- 2 cups water
- 2 eggs
- 1 cup sugar
- ¾ cup flour
- ½ cup melted butter
- ¼ cup unsweetened cocoa powder
- 1 tbsp honey
- ¾ tsp baking powder
- ¼ tsp salt

Directions:

1. Mix melted butter with the cocoa powder.
2. In another bowl, mix the flour, sugar, salt, and baking powder.
3. Add honey, eggs, and the melted butter/ cocoa mix, making sure it has cooled a little, so it doesn't cook the eggs.
4. When the batter is mixed well, pour into a greased 8-inch round pan that's pressure-cooker safe.
5. Wrap completely in foil. Pour 2 cups of water into your Instant Pot and lower in the trivet.
6. Put the wrapped brownie pan on top. Seal the lid.
7. Select MANUAL and cook on HIGH pressure for 35 minutes.
8. When time is up, hit CANCEL and carefully quick-release.
9. Serve warm or chilled.

Nutritional Info (per serving): Calories - 538; Fat – 27; Fiber – 0; Carbs – 74; Protein – 8

Molten Lava Cake
(Prep + Cook Time: 25 minutes | Servings: 2)

Ingredients:

- ½ cup semi-sweet chocolate chips
- ¼ cup powdered sugar
- 4 tbsp room temperature butter
- 2 tbsp flour
- 1 room temperature egg
- 1 tsp vanilla extract
- 2 cups water

Directions:

1. Prep your Instant Pot with 2 cups of water and put in the trivet.
2. Grease your cake mold/ ramekin with butter.
3. Melt the chocolate and mix in egg and vanilla, making sure the egg doesn't cook. Add in sugar and flour.
4. Fill your ramekin halfway-full and place on the trivet in the cooker. Close and seal the lid.
5. Select MANUAL and cook on high pressure for 7 minutes.
6. When time is up, hit CANCEL and wait for a natural pressure release. Serve and enjoy!

Nutritional Info (per serving): Calories - 525; Fat – 38; Fiber – 0; Carbs – 48; Protein – 66

Vanilla Sponge Cake

(Prep + Cook Time: 1 hour 10 minutes | Servings: 6)

Ingredients:

- 1 ½ cups powdered sugar
- 2 room temperature eggs
- 1 ¼ cups flour
- ½ cup milk
- ½ cup canola oil
- 1 ½ tsp baking powder
- ¾ tsp vanilla extract

Directions:

1. Grease a 6-inch square pan with butter and a dusting of flour.
2. In a mixing bowl, beat eggs and sugar until frothy. Sift in the flour.
3. Add milk and canola oil, and blend. Last, add the vanilla and baking powder.
4. Turn your cooker to SAUTE and wait 10 minutes for the pot to warm up.
5. Fill the square pan with batter to the ½-way mark and put in the Instant Pot on top of the trivet.
6. You are not bringing the cooker to pressure, so you don't add water.
7. Remove the gasket (the silicone) ring from your pot's lid before putting it on the cooker.
8. Let the heat from the cooker "bake" the cake for 40 minutes.
9. Check the cake when that time is up.
10. A few crumbs on the toothpick is perfect.
11. Wait 10 minutes before removing the cake and serving.

Nutritional Info (per serving): Calories - 405; Fat – 22; Fiber – 0; Carbs – 49; Protein – 6

Carrot-Raisin Bread with Walnuts

(Prep + Cook Time: 1 hour 50 minutes | Servings: 6)

Ingredients:

- 2 cups flour
- 1 ⅓ cups sugar
- 1 ½ cups cold water
- 2 grated carrots
- 1 cup chopped walnuts
- 1 cup raisins
- 2 tbsp butter
- 2 tsp baking soda
- 1 tsp cinnamon
- ½ tsp allspice
- ¼ tsp nutmeg
- ¼ tsp salt

Directions:

1. Boil the water, sugar, raisins, butter, and spices on the stove for 10 minutes.
2. Let it cool completely, storing in the fridge to speed up the process.
3. When cool, add the flour, salt, baking soda, carrots and nuts.
4. Stir to combine right away and then pour into a greased baking dish.
5. Pour 1 ½ cups of water into your Instant Pot and lower in trivet.
6. Put the dish on top and seal the lid.
7. Select MANUAL and cook for 1 hour, 10 minutes on high pressure.
8. When time is up, hit CANCEL and wait 10 minutes before quick-releasing. Test the cake with a toothpick.
9. Cool a little while before removing the cake to cool completely.

Nutritional Info (per serving): Calories - 566; Fat – 18; Fiber – 5; Carbs – 100; Protein – 10

Simple Egg Custard

(Prep + Cook Time: 25 minutes | Servings: 6)

Ingredients:

- 6 big eggs
- 4 cups milk
- ¾ cup sugar
- 1 tsp vanilla extract
- ¼ tsp cinnamon
- Pinch of salt

Directions:
1. Mix the eggs in a bowl.
2. Add the salt, sugar, vanilla, and milk until just mixed.
3. Pour into six ramekins and wrap in foil. Poke a few holes in the foil.
4. Pour 1 ½ cups of water into your Instant Pot and lower in trivet.
5. Put the ramekins on top of the trivet. Seal the lid. Select MANUAL and cook for 7 minutes on HIGH pressure.
6. When time is up, hit CANCEL and wait 10 minutes for the pressure to descend.
7. Release any leftover pressure and let the custard cool for 2 minutes, unwrapped.
8. Dust with cinnamon before serving.

Nutritional Info (per serving): Calories - 148; Fat – 6; Fiber – 0; Carbs – 16; Protein – 7

Almond Fudge Drop Candy

(Prep + Cook Time: 30 minutes | Servings: 30 pieces)

Ingredients:
- One 14-ounce can of sweetened condensed milk
- 12-ounces semi-sweet chocolate chips
- 2 cups water
- 1 cup chopped almonds
- 1 tsp vanilla

Directions:
1. Add milk and chocolate chips into a cooker-safe bowl and wrap in foil.
2. Pour water into your pressure cooker and add the trivet.
3. Put bowl on top of trivet and seal the lid.
4. Hit MANUAL and adjust time to 5 minutes.
5. When time is up, hit CANCEL and quick-release.
6. Unwrap the bowl and mix in nuts and vanilla.
7. With a teaspoon, drop candy pieces on a wax-paper lined cookie sheet.
8. Freeze for 20 minutes.

Nutritional Info (per serving): Calories - 122; Fat – 6; Fiber – 0; Carbs – 16; Protein – 3

Chai Rice Pudding

(Prep + Cook Time: 45 minutes | Servings: 8)

Ingredients:

- 5 cups 1% milk
- 1 ½ cups Arborio rice
- 1 cup raisins
- 1 cup half-and-half
- 2 eggs
- ¾ cup sugar
- 1 ½ tsp pure vanilla extract
- ¾ tsp ground cinnamon
- ½ tsp ground cardamom
- ½ tsp ground allspice
- ½ tsp salt

Directions:

1. Mix rice, sugar, milk, and salt in your Instant Pot.
2. Turn on to the SAUTE setting and stir until it comes to a boil and the sugar has dissolved. Once the liquid is boiling, immediately seal the lid.
3. Select MANUAL and cook for 16 minutes on LOW pressure. In the meantime, whisk vanilla, eggs, and half-and-half.
4. When time is up on the cooker, hit CANCEL and wait 10 minutes before quick-releasing.
5. Stir the rice before adding half-and-half mixture. Turn the cooker back to SAUTE and cook until it begins to boil again.
6. Turn off the cooker right away and stir in raisins and chai spices.
7. Serve right away or chill in the fridge until cold.

Nutritional Info (per serving): Calories - 399; Fat – 10; Fiber – 1; Carbs – 71; Protein – 10

78327928R00222

Made in the USA
Lexington, KY
07 January 2018